Polyamory

by Jaime M. Grant, PhD
Author of *Great Sex: Mapping Your Desire*

for
dummies®
A Wiley Brand

Polyamory For Dummies®

Published by: **John Wiley & Sons, Inc.**, 111 River Street, Hoboken, NJ 07030-5774, www.wiley.com

For general information on our other products and services, please contact our Customer Care Department within the U.S. at 877-762-2974, outside the U.S. at 317-572-3993, or fax 317-572-4002. For technical support, please visit https://hub.wiley.com/community/support/dummies.

Wiley publishes in a variety of print and electronic formats and by print-on-demand. Some material included with standard print versions of this book may not be included in e-books or in print-on-demand. For more information about Wiley products, visit www.wiley.com.

Library of Congress Control Number is available from the publisher.

ISBN: 978-1-394-28191-6 (pbk); ISBN 978-1-394-28193-0 (ebk); ISBN 978-1-394-28192-3 (ebk)

SKY10090211_110624

Contents at a Glance

Table of Contents

Introduction

Although monogamy is often championed as the *one and only true way* to have loving, successful relationships, polyamory has been around for thousands of years and is currently enjoying an explosion of popular interest.

Why the current rush toward multi-lover relationships? This book takes up this question and dozens more, including:

>> What do I say to dates or crushes about my interest in polyamory?

>> How can I tell my partner that I want to open our relationship?

>> How can I deal with my lover falling in love with someone else?

>> And most importantly, where are we going for the holidays, and with whom?

Even though much of the book addresses fears you might be holding as you consider polyamory, don't lose sight of the main point: For many, polyamory is a transformational, freeing, and joyful way to relate to their lovers and build family life.

In these pages, you can dig deep into the story of your relationship history, desires, and intimacy needs. Here, I hope you find all the tools and support you need to strike out on whatever love and relationship path is right for you.

Because you're the expert on you. And *anyone* telling you that they have the one and only true way for you is a danger.

About This Book

Polyamory For Dummies is for everyone on the journey to finding and building amazing relationships. Perhaps you've heard a lot about polyamory lately and wonder what the hype is about. Maybe you've left yet another monogamous relationship and are wondering why it doesn't work for you and what it is about you that is so wrong (spoiler alert: *nothing*). Maybe your friends are exploring polyamory, and they seem happy and vibrant in ways that make you want to know more.

Relationships are demanding. Commitments to anyone, over time, involve sacrifice, conflict, and hardship. This is true regardless of the relationship form you choose. *And* love and relationships bring so much meaning and verve to your life. They drive, nurture, and feed you, all at once. They're well worth the work.

This book takes up key relationship questions as they relate to polyamory:

>> How do people move beyond hypothetical or utopian ideas about polyamory to actually make it work?

>> What key social and emotional skills do you need to be a good poly partner?

>> How do you manage jealousy and the emotional demands of multi-partner relationships?

>> How do you deal with time constraints, housing, finances, parenting, the negative opinions of friends and family, and other high stakes issues?

>> What are some of the best practices for creating poly agreements and setting limits that take care of everyone?

>> How can you do polyamory when your trust has been broken?

>> How will you manage aging, illness, and other long-haul issues as a poly person?

>> How will you know if polyamory is right for you?

Although a lot of polyamorous literature and self-help books talk endlessly about processing in poly relationships, not anywhere near enough of them cover the joy of discovery and the astounding rewards of creating a life where new sexual partners and new intimate and emotional connections are presented over and over again. So prepare to be wowed.

Also prepare to have me talk about lovers and partners interchangeably, because some poly people have lovers, others have partners, and some have both. As long as everyone involved is cared for and supported, it's all good.

Foolish Assumptions

In writing this book, I make the following assumptions about you, dear reader:

>> You're curious enough to question the myth that monogamy is universal and the only true way to have caring, sustaining relationships.

>> You aren't naïve enough to believe that having more than one partner will solve all your relationship problems and eliminate sacrifices.

>> You reject the idea that you must have a particular sexuality, religious or spiritual belief, family background, gender, or political affiliation to be polyamorous or consider polyamory.

>> Just as you question whether monogamy works for everyone, you're skeptical about the idea that polyamory is better than monogamy or any other way of relating.

If there's one core idea you get from the book, I hope it's this: I'm thrilled to share my expertise on polyamory, and I offer it to support you in your quest to find the relationship path that's right *for you*. Whatever that is.

Icons Used in This Book

Throughout this book you'll see the following icons to draw your attention to important possibilities, concepts, and practices:

This icon highlights information that deserves special attention.

TIP

This icon gives you great ideas to consider and reinforces an important point.

REMEMBER

This icon cautions you about bad thinking and roadblocks on your journey to self-discovery.

WARNING

This icon introduces an interactive exercise that can help you figure out what your needs, values, desires, and next steps might be.

ACTIVITY

This icon introduces a personal story or example from one of the experienced poly contributors in my network of sex educators, activists, and poly enthusiasts.

POLYAMORY
STORY

Beyond This Book

This book is full of helpful information, analysis, self-reflection exercises, and resources about polyamory. But even more is available online! Just go to dummies. com and search for "Polyamory For Dummies Cheat Sheet" for additional support on your journey of learning about and considering polyamory.

Where to Go from Here

If you're completely new to all of this, as many *For Dummies* readers are, just start with the first segment of the book and find context, definitions, core ideas, and opening reflection exercises. If you get confused by any terms, go to Appendix A for help.

If you're already exploring polyamory, use the table of contents or index to find the topics you really want to know more about. Appendix B has some additional ideas and next places to go. Get help on the issues that matter the most to you right now.

Remember to breathe. Considering polyamory can go against a lot of foundational ideas in families and religious traditions. It can draw big reactions from your friends, lovers, or partners. Breathe some more. Give yourself a break.

You may want to keep a journal as you go through this book. I often ask my coaching clients to start a journal and have a dedicated space specifically for their desire explorations. Doing so can create some safety as you ask yourself big questions. It can also give your process a place of honor.

It's okay to question things — even *big*, fundamental things. It's okay to be curious and to seek information, supportive conversation, and resources as you figure out who and how to love as you create the family of your dreams.

1
The Basics of Polyamory

Understand what polyamory is, beyond all the myths and chatter, and how people manage it.

Sift through and explore common practices in modern polyamory.

Start to think more deeply about your own desires for intimacy, sex, relationship, and family, and consider what relationship forms might work for you.

Take in the many different ways that polyamorous people are creating partnership and family.

Chapter **1**

Finding More Love, More Pleasure

I n a time where your social, economic, and even geological security seems to be evaporating, polyamory holds out a tantalizing promise: *more love.*

Perhaps that's why the pushback against it is so strong: *Polyamory is just a fancy term for cheating.* Polyamorists can't commit. You use people. You spread disease and leave a trail of broken hearts in your wake.

Except, oops, you can name a dozen monogamous people you know who have acted in any of these ways, leaving their lovers and partners devastated.

This chapter serves as your jumping-off point into this book, where I take up a lot of your unanswered questions about this creative, expansive form of loving and making family. By day, I'm a sex and relationship coach with a doctorate in gender and sexuality. At home, I've practiced polyamory for more than 40 years. I'm also blessed to live in a vibrant community of people who have created all kinds of open, polyamorous relationships. Here, their stories bring all the theories and mysteries of polyamory to life.

What does it mean to be in love with more than one person? How do you do it without creating emotional train wrecks and hurting yourself and your beloveds? Buckle up. Here's how.

Encountering Polyamory

Polyamory literally means: *the love of many*. This expansive relationship form rests under a larger umbrella of a variety of non-monogamous ways of relating like hooking up, swinging, having threesomes, and participating in party or conference sex, but it's distinguished by the desire to create more significant bonds. People who are polyamorous often have a constellation or family of lovers, whose members may or may not be intimately, romantically, or sexually involved with each other. The following sections give you a brief overview of polyamory.

Recognizing what polyamory is

A hallmark of polyamory is the nurturing and maintenance of multiple, significant relationships, at the same time. And another core facet is that these relationships are all out in the open — everyone in them knows about everyone else. And all people involved are held with respect and care, even if their roles and functions differ greatly.

Although some poly people enjoy hooking up and have fleeting sexual encounters, people who describe themselves as polyamorous often inhabit a complex web of relationships that grow and shift and deepen over time. Chapter 2 discusses the historic practices of polyamory and what specific characteristics define this modern version.

Assessing whether polyamory is for you

How can you decide whether polyamory is something you can handle? Being in love with — or intimately connected to — more than one person sounds like a lot to deal with emotionally. And it is.

Chapter 3 helps you figure out why you picked up this book and what's going on with you, in your relationships, that makes you curious about polyamory. There, I offer a lot of reflection exercises so that you can start to dig around in your thinking and feelings about monogamy and polyamory.

Your reasons for considering polyamory are uniquely yours. And, in my practice as a coach, people generally arrive at my doorstep with a handful of pressing motivations, such as:

>> You don't know who you are. You've been living others' expectations for so long — your parents, friends, church, or partner — you don't even really know what your honest sexuality or relationships would look like. You've been covering over your true self for a long time.

>> You're a serial cheater, or a serial failed-monogamist. You're unhappy with or even ashamed of your relationship history. You don't know how to break out of repetitive, destructive patterns. You wonder whether monogamy is right for you.

>> You've lost a part of yourself along the way in your partnership. You don't know what your needs are anymore or how you got here. You feel trapped and may not have had sex or felt desirable for some time.

>> Your partner wants to open your relationship and you don't, or vice versa. Often, there has been a breach of trust — an actual affair or an emotional affair. This is a period of crisis and great hurt, and it takes some time to sort through whether healing is possible (see Chapter 13), and if polyamory makes sense for you as a couple (see Chapter 10).

>> Some kind of crisis or huge shift has happened in your life that makes you question many things that have just always been a given — and monogamy is one of those givens that needs reexamining.

Dreaming Your Polyamorous Dreams

Engaging in personal reflection activities can help you stretch out into your polyamorous dreams. These activities assist you in figuring out what you aren't telling even yourself about your desire and needs in your relationships and what you've always wanted to try but have held yourself back.

If nobody was looking or commenting, how would you conduct your intimate and sexual life and partnerships? Chapter 3 leads you through some activities to answer these questions for yourself. Chapter 4 gives you examples of how many others have already done so, creating joyful polyamorous practices and family life.

Focusing on Polyamory's Foundations

While the emotional and intimate rewards of polyamory are enormous, its demands are also significant. Communicating openly and honestly with multiple lovers — so that everyone has the same information, and you aren't hiding yourself, or manipulating partners through the omission of certain truths, or performing rather than relating to them — can be hard work! That's especially true when you're new to polyamory.

Developing your communication skills — by assessing what kind of communicator you are, developing new tools, and finding peers and poly community — can help you build the capacity for sustaining a polyamorous life. The following sections give you a quick overview.

Communicating with your partners

If you can start to identify and assess your core behaviors as a communicator, you can begin to appreciate your strengths. You also might be able to see where you've struggled with communication in your past relationships, so you can start to build a plan for getting more support and growing new skills. Chapter 5 looks at all kinds of foundational aspects of communication — introversion and extroversion, fight-or-flight responses, and neurodivergence among them.

WHEN I KNOW, YOU KNOW

One of my favorite polyamorous practices is: when I know, you know. When people are struggling in their relationships, they tend to mystify basic truths. A partner will say that they're confused or something is complex when the truth is, they aren't ready to say the hard thing that they already know. They're afraid of the consequences of their truth — whether a crush on a coworker, a realization that they don't want to be monogamous anymore, or an epiphany about how their sexual needs aren't getting met and they need a change. A common path from this kind of dodge is for a distressed or frightened partner to then make a series of bad decisions solo and then come to their partner with their often disastrous results — a breach of trust, an affair, or a series of lies.

Relationship coach Asha Leong, one of the many contributors whose stories you'll read in this book, notes that this poly practice is her most cherished. Everyone struggles to figure themselves out. But holding back what you know because you don't want to deal with a partner's feelings, or are worried their response won't align with what you want, isn't honest. In the end, it doesn't protect or help anyone and only reveals a kind of selfishness or disregard that is very hard to recover from. A foundational poly practice then: *When I know, you know.*

Becoming skilled at creating boundaries

Boundaries are to polyamorous relationships as breathing is to life. If you don't know where your edges are around what you can and can't handle emotionally and intimately — if you don't know how to ask for what you want and can't say no when you need to — then polyamory is going to be chaotic and painful for you.

TIP

In fact, many of my clients seek polyamory as a reprieve from painful communication patterns in their monogamous relationships. But polyamory isn't an escape from being unable to articulate and honor your needs. Chapter 6 offers exercises and tips to assess your skill at speaking your truth and setting and maintaining boundaries. You can also find activities and resources to help grow your capacity in this crucial arena.

Building trust with your partners

Attachment theory (a psychological theory that examines early experiences of attachment and abandonment and their impacts on adult relationships) offers a great window on why boundaries might be difficult for you to set in your relationships. And why it might be hard for you to trust yourself and your partners. In Chapter 7, you can discover what kind of attachment disruptions you might be carrying from your childhood that impact your day-to-day relationships. Then, you can consider how might they play out for you as you consider polyamory.

Living with trauma while poly

Today's culture is steeped in violence — emotional, social, physical, and sexual. Many people have experienced frightening, coercive, or controlling experiences in their youth, and many have survived physical and sexual abuse. Accordingly, as you figure out what kind of barriers you face as a communicator in intimate relationships, appreciating your history of exposure to coercion and violence can be very helpful. Past trauma can get reactivated in emotionally taxing situations and being in love with multiple partners who may have conflicting needs or very different ways of being is challenging. Chapter 8 can help you identify and affirm your needs as a trauma survivor and chart a path to developing the skills and relationships you want.

Loving Your Polyamorous Life

The foundation of your happy polyamorous life rests on a set of co-created agreements about how you and your partners are going to operate, to care for each other. For some, building these poly structures is a process of complex, detailed collaboration. For others, it involves a simple conversation with a clear, shared framework. Part 3 gets into some of the joyful and creative ways that people form their poly families. In this section, you can find many ideas about how to poly and also look at some of the big decisions you might make, like opening up your monogamous relationship or coming out to family members.

Establishing agreements and limits

Poly people love their relational maps. Chapter 4 includes several contributors' illustrations that describe their swirling poly formations. Some poly webs are deeply interconnected, and others aren't. Some polyamorists want to share everything with all their partners, and others want to keep their relationships separate, and the intimate activities they engage in with each partner private. Still others create a mix of privacy and integration among their partners and sexual practices. Only you know what you want and what kind of relating meets your needs and desires. In Chapter 9, you can consider what kind of agreements you want to make with your partners to support your desired constellation or web of relationships.

Going from monogamous to polyamorous

As a coach, a top reason people reach out to me is because they need help opening an existing monogamous relationship. Doing so can be tricky and tender work. Often one partner wants to do this more than the other. Sometimes promises have been broken by the time people make contact. And most often, a couple is on the precipice of monumental change — they're rethinking a fundamental agreement they made to be exclusive, and it can be shattering, even when everyone agrees to the way forward.

If you're considering opening an existing monogamous relationship and finding it difficult, you're in the right place. Chapter 10 moves through this often fraught territory with care and lots of resources.

Telling others that you're polyamorous

Coming out polyamorous is no small thing. Many people who are vocal and forthright about complex or controversial topics aren't out about being polyamorous, and for good reason. Poly people often experience social and economic consequences when coming out. In Chapter 11, you can assess your risks and vulnerabilities as you consider coming out and think about who your best supporters might be as you build your best polyamorous life. An important part of coming out is fortifying your support network, so Chapter 11 also provides an exercise where you can chart your pod of champions.

Dealing with Life's Many Changes

If you're like me and you choose to live a poly life over many decades, you'll run into a lot of challenges and changes. Change is a constant in any type of relationship, but in poly life, you must navigate these with multiple partners. Part 4 covers some of these challenges and changes, such as:

>> **Parenting while poly:** Chapter 14 addresses some important considerations, including aligning around core parenting values, deciding who has parenting responsibilities, and navigating whether or not to come out to the kids. Refer to the nearby sidebar as well.

>> **Breaking up while poly:** Chapter 15 explores breakups in interconnected poly constellations, helping you figure out when a relationship is really over and what to do if your other lover doesn't want to break up with the person you're breaking up with. This chapter also helps you think about how to navigate all this emotional complexity.

>> **Major life changes:** Chapter 16 examines all types of life changes, like aging, libido shifts, geographic moves, illness, and disability and walks you through managing big changes in poly relationships over time.

Life in any relationship form is full of change and unfolding obstacles. Polyamory offers many people a creative, freeing, and joyful way to relate to those challenges, and to build the life you want.

DANGER, WILL ROBINSON

You may be familiar with the sci-fi, *Lost in Space*, in which the family robot constantly alerts the young hero, Will Robinson, when danger is afoot.

If only you had a danger-discerning robot in your family! When you've invested deeply in a partner or lover, you might struggle with recognizing or tell yourself the truth when you've chosen someone who is a danger to your children. Emotional, physical, and sexual abuse of children is rampant in this country, partly fueled by authoritarian parenting mores that silence children and teach them to submit to various kinds of authorities — be they parents, clergy, teachers, or coaches.

For many years, a lot of abuse prevention in the United States centered around the risks presented by strangers. But thanks to women's and racial justice movement organizing and research over the past 40 years, the research shows that the most common perpetrators are people the children know.

(continued)

(continued)

Who you bring into your household matters so much. And the best way to prevent abuse of your children is to have a handle on your own abuse history — to fully understand the emotional, physical, or sexual abuse in your story, to take in the harm done, and to invest in your healing process. Only then can you be awake and aware enough to be able to interpret risks to your child's well-being.

As a survivor of childhood abuse myself, creating a household free from violence for my children has been an incredible joy. But I had to grow the capacity to listen to my intuition again, because it had been silenced by my abuse. And then I had to commit to staying awake, regardless of whatever new tantalizing crush crossed my path.

Over the years, I've stopped seeing a number of people who were attractive and interested in my family. People who were outwardly loving, but who also activated my intuition around my safety. Sometimes it was because I could see inconsistencies between the values they espoused and the ways they operated with other people, all while being very cherishing toward me. Sometimes it was because they seemed to need to improve me or control things as we were just getting to know one another.

These were red flags that people often miss in the early days of having great sex or a wonderful crush. And I'm grateful to have lived in a community of survivors invested in our healing over many years because I was able to recognize early on that these behaviors were problematic. That recognition helped me decide not to invest. The truly astonishing thing is that I now have my own, internal robot: *Danger, Jaime Grant.*

Chapter **2**

Laying Out What Polyamory Is

When I was growing up, I never heard the word "polyamory" because it didn't exist yet. As a teenage girl in Boston in the 1970s, what I did hear constantly was that sex was dirty and dangerous. That if I had sex before marriage, I'd destroy any possibility for a good life. That girls who had sex with anyone — *but especially more than one person* — were sluts: destined to be outcast. The only road to a good life was monogamous marriage after years of careful, chaste dating.

And here was an important detail: All I had to do to make that happen was to sit attractively still and wait for the right man to pick me out of the crowd.

What my Irish Catholic immigrant community didn't tell me — and likely didn't know — was that polyamory was common among our Irish ancestors. Colonization and Catholicism had suppressed these practices and covered over our history. And that this erasure had been common across cultures and nations around the world over the last 400 years.

COMPULSORY MONOGAMY

Like my Irish forbearers, First Nations people in North America practiced various kinds of non-monogamous and polyamorous family-making before colonization; English settlers deemed these practices savage and forced monogamous marriage onto the New World order. Peoples of the African continent were met with similar violence by their Dutch, Belgian, French, Portuguese, and English colonizers, suppressing multiple partner marriages and other non-monogamous familial arrangements.

My parents couldn't have anticipated that I would be growing up in the decade that ushered in an era of free love. They were unprepared for the explosion of social movements that pushed back on all kinds of authority. Throughout my childhood, the anti-war, civil rights, Black power, American Indian, LGBTQ+, and women's movements broke away from many long-held views of what was proper and acceptable.

It was out of these movements for peace and social change that a range of inter-racial, interfaith, cross-cultural, queer, binary-busting, and non-monogamous ways of relating emerged, including polyamory, a term coined within the West Coast Kerista commune in 1990.

This chapter looks at polyamory and examines the current explosion of interest — how did polyamory move from communes to your kitchen table? What does polyamory mean and look like at this moment in time and why is everyone talking about it?

Defining Polyamory: More Love

Polyamory literally means the love of many. A subcategory within the broader concept of non-monogamy, polyamory is distinguished by the desire to have more than one significant other, intimate, or lover as a core part of one's family.

You can think of non-monogamy as the big umbrella — under which a whole range of open-relationship arrangements and activities lie, including hook ups, swinging, don't-ask-don't-tell, extramarital sex on business trips, birthday free-passes, and threesomes.

REMEMBER

Although people in polyamorous relationships may choose to have hookups or other casual encounters in addition to their core partners, polyamory describes a relationship constructed by and for multiple, committed partners over time.

MODERN POLYAMORY'S PRECURSORS

Non-monogamy emerged in the United States well before the 1970s — one need only look back at the work of turn of the century free-love organizer Victoria Woodhull, the writings of the flapper era (*The Great Gatsby* anyone?), or the music of Black queer blues singers in the 1930s to find many versions of non-monogamous life in the United States in the early 20th century. But in the '60s and '70s, a perfect storm of movements for liberation lit a fire for reconsidering the family, women's rights, sexuality, gender, racism, and war. Within that storm, a vibrant group of communes took hold, including the Kerista commune, where member Morning Glory Zell-Ravenheart used the term *poly-amory* — the love of many — to describe their intentionally rotating relationships in 1990.

So, to boil it down to its core simplicity:

>> **Poly is:** An open, caring, relationship structure that equal partners co-create or consent to with respect, excitement, and aspiration.

>> **Poly isn't:** A secretive, confusing, coercive, ultimatum-driven, or dread-inducing relationship agreement that may or may not be grandfathered-in after a breach of trust.

The following sections focus on the pillars of modern polyamory as a relationship form.

TIP

Understanding the definitive characteristics of polyamory in the 21st century — *consent, full disclosure or transparency, and mutual respect* — is key to fully grasping how it's being practiced and reshaped. Here I explore how the growing emphasis on practices of full consent, honesty, and respect have created new possibilities for *more love* in the current era.

When you look at the non-monogamous experiments of the 1970s that led to the creation of the term polyamory, there's a lot to love there.

>> People were questioning authority of every kind and trying to create a new world.

>> The emergence of birth control meant that people could experiment with sex and new family forms without the fear of unwanted pregnancy.

>> Many people created extended families of lovers in this era that joyfully persisted against all odds and carried them through their lives.

And, like all starting places, there were big problems.

WHEN I LOOK AT MY FAMILY

Don't let people tell you polyamory doesn't exist, or that it's a made-up thing by a handful of people on the fringe. Polyamory has been around forever, and indeed, if you look hard enough, in many of your families. Here are three examples:

- **Aredvi:** My immigrant parents lost their families by moving away from their hometown. Then, I doubled down and moved away from my family. As valid as our reasons may be for moving far away, the cost of this loss remains significant. This is why for me polyamory is less a modern practice and more a reclamation of my ancestral and indigenous roots.

  During short visits to my parents' hometown, I watched small and large clumps of people come together in many formations to celebrate, grieve, eat, and play. I long for the expansiveness of showing up around other people and letting connections form organically.

- **Bishop:** I have an aunt who I grew up very close with and I always saw her date multiple men at the same time. I remember being young just thinking my aunt was a "ho" because she was unmarried and dating multiple men, and everything I saw in the media told me that that's what hoes do.

  But something that I observed watching my aunt was the amount of time she spent having very direct conversation with the men she was seeing. I remember asking once, "Auntie, when are you gonna get married?" and she laughed at me and said, "Probably never, I don't want to be married." I went on to ask if the men she dated would be mad if they knew she was dating them all, and she told me, "No man comes into my life without having a complete understanding of how I date . . . because I refuse to have someone knocking on my door trying to stick a 'Cheaters' camera in my face!" That conversation has stuck with me, and that style of very direct and clear boundary-setting sits at the core of my poly identity.

- **Mija:** I never heard polyamory as a word growing up, but I did have an elder who told me, "Nobody cared who or how you dated — you knew you weren't in the relationship anymore when your shoes were left outside."

While aiming for new, revolutionary ways of relating, many of the people practicing supposedly free love were stuck in very old ways of being. Most of the communes were shaped by World War II-era thinking about masculinity and the family. LGBTQ+ people were often closeted or ousted. While championing openness to all, these experiments were overwhelmingly white and middle class.

WARNING

Accordingly, some ideas that were promoted as free love in this era were actually forced-love as was the case of one commune that *required* that members rotate beds and lovers each night.

Often, when people — women, especially — in various experimental relationships expressed dissent or difficulty with these new free-love practices, they were pressured by the pronouncements of the leaders and the power they held in the group. This is where we can have a lot of gratitude for the current state of polyamory. So let me state, unequivocally:

There is no forced sharing of bodies, hearts, beds, or commitments in 21st century polyamory.

Consent among relative equals

The modern practice of polyamory involves consent among relative equals, full disclosure among all partners, and mutual respect — even if each lover has a different role, significance, or meaning in one's life. Consent is so central to polyamorous practice that it's also often referred to as *consensual non-monogamy (CNM)*.

Consent among relative equals is a complex idea. You can see the evidence of gains in the fight for equality all over polyamorous communities:

>> Women and LGBTQ+ people are writing the lion's share of books about polyamory, leading this conversation and the growth of equitable practices.

>> BIPOC polyamorous experts and communities are reclaiming pre-colonial poly practices and de-centering whiteness in the practicing and nurturing of modern poly ideas and community.

>> Women, BIPOC, and LGBTQ+ people historically disadvantaged under laws governing marriage, parenting, home ownership, and work have made legal, political, and economic gains over the past 35 years. They have the means to better define the terms of multiple partner relationships.

Four hundred years ago, when my Irish Ancestors were practicing multiple-lover relationships, families that consisted of multiple partners generally grew out of the choices made by the patriarch of the household.

In most cases, men held all the decision-making power. Women often had limited options and couldn't reject or leave these arrangements without dire social and economic consequences. Rather than polyamory, these families were practicing polygamy or *polygyny*, which is a family where one man defines and oversees a household consisting of multiple female partners.

In 1997, Dossie Easton and Janet Hardy published *The Ethical Slut*, which grew to become a Bible among modern polyamorists. In it, Easton and Hardy coined the term *ethical non-monogamy (ENM)* to describe a wide variety of non-monogamous practices that all shared the trio of the core aspects of modern polyamory discussed here: consent, transparency, and respect.

Despite many legal and social gains, *inequities persist*. The echoes of inequality in intimate and partnering spaces are tremendously distressing and can be found especially in lop-sided federal statistics on health access and outcomes, home ownership, disability, and intimate partner violence, where women, and BIPOC and LGBTQ+ people fare worse by many measures.

Those who historically have been on the vulnerable end of the equation in forming any kind of relationship remain there. And stepping into a polyamorous relationship may carry increased risks of abuse, ill-health, and impoverishment.

REMEMBER

The simplicity of consent among relative equals is this:

>> You know what being treated like an equal feels like.

>> You know when you're at risk because your basic humanity is disrespected or dismissed.

>> You know when you aren't saying what you mean, or need, or want because you're afraid of judgment, or shunning, or losing your partner.

REMEMBER

Consent feels like care:

>> Consent is relational, not transactional. One person isn't just trying to get over on or take something from another.

>> Consent among equals feels like people give a damn about what you say and that none of your opinions or feelings are dismissed as problematic or immature.

>> Consent among equals doesn't mean that you risk your health, job, or housing security to be in this relationship while your other partners are relatively secure and haven't addressed or even noticed that risk.

REMEMBER

The idea of consent among relative equals doesn't mean that you and your lovers are all the same. Your lovers don't have to be the same age or race, have the same level of education, possess the same physical or mental abilities, or be living on identical asset bases for you to be partnering with them as an equal. Relative equals means that whatever differences that exist in that mix of realities — you're able to represent yourself and your needs *on par with your partners*. That none of the differences in arenas where power often plays out irresponsibly or harmfully have rendered you silent or less worthy or less influential in any discussion of how you create your lives.

Full disclosure and transparency

Full disclosure and transparency are core values of polyamory. *Full disclosure* means that each person is informed about all the other members in the *polycule* (another term for poly family), understands the significance of each person, and is fully apprised of any limits or boundaries that arise from those relationships.

A simple way to understand full disclosure is to use the over-the-shoulder rule:

REMEMBER

>> If any other member of the polycule were in the room while you were talking to your lover about the family structure, its members, and your agreements, would they feel loved and respected?

>> Are you speaking about everyone in a way that properly describes their significance, honors them, and honors your commitments?

If the answer is yes, congratulations! You're living the values of full disclosure and transparency.

REMEMBER

Another simple way to evaluate whether a poly constellation is achieving transparency is this: No one shares or withholds information that would betray trust or harm another person in the group.

WARNING

You know you're in a bad polyamory situation when something as simple as honesty becomes mystified or hard to define. No matter how complex your poly constellation is, honesty is simple.

Practicing full disclosure in polyamory

Practicing full disclosure involves a certain level of self-awareness. First, you have to know yourself well enough to know when you're lying to yourself — perhaps as a means of self-protection, or possibly as a means of manipulating others to get what you want. And secondly, you must commit to telling your partner(s) what you know, when you know it. You can refer to Chapter 1 for more on this important concept around honesty in polyamory. This next activity also explores this concept.

ACTIVITY

Use your current or a past relationship to consider the following:

>> Do I refuse to look at relationship difficulties and wish them away?

>> Do I hide my emotions and experiences and create confusion?

>> Do I create hidden intimacies with others as a way to hide out from relationship difficulties?

>> Do I deny what's really going on with me when asked directly?

>> Do I pretend not to know things to hide out or deflect responsibility?

>> Do I decide major relationship issues without consulting my partner, and then just report on or impose my conclusions?

If you answered yes to two or more of these questions, you aren't practicing the *You Know When I Know* activity from Chapter 1 in your relationships.

Handling lies in polyamory

In my polyamorous arrangements, I have a commitment to not connect with anyone, even casually, who isn't committed to full disclosure with their other partners as well. Although this is a baseline value in many polyamorous constellations, it's not universally practiced. For me, if my lover is deceiving their lover or hiding our relationship, that person is a danger to me and my polyamorous family.

And even if that lie doesn't boomerang in a way that hurts me and my partners directly, it's a deceptive fact in some other person's life that I'm party to. It just doesn't align with my core values as a polyamorous person.

TIP

The poet Adrienne Rich has said that a lie is a shortcut through another person's humanity — and that poetic truth has driven my commitment to honesty in my poly relationships for 40 years.

Encountering lies in polyamory

Discovering a lie or lack of transparency can be hard on a poly constellation, especially when a member of your polycule gets interested in someone who is essentially cheating on their other partner. How do you handle this? Each constellation has to figure out what their bottom-line values are and what boundaries or deal-breakers exist for you.

Some of my poly acquaintances believe that a casual or even a core partner's commitment to transparency (or lack thereof) isn't really their business. That's a hard one for me. Lies are everyone's business in a polyamorous constellation. Everyone's choices about something that could rock the foundations of each other's commitments feel like my business.

Being transparent in today's world

A poly friend of mine recently noted that one of their core partners is stuck in a situation where they're exposed to violence and full disclosure would put them in physical danger. Another has shared that their partner is committed to raising her children in her marital household, and full disclosure would bring on displacement and economic ruin.

The structures of economic inequity and social and physical violence often make it hard for people who are the most vulnerable to be fully honest. Given that women, LGBTQ+, and BIPOC people are suffering high rates of economic and physical violence — full transparency is often a privilege.

And yet poly people aspire. Like a lot of things in poly life, living values of openness and honesty demonstrate a yearning for a better world.

The thing I love about polyamorous constellations is that full disclosure and transparency are championed. They're practiced with such care. In fact, a lot of jokes around poly community center on exhaustion from endless processing conversations about transparency and that other key issue — setting clear boundaries, or limits (see Chapter 6 for more on healthy limits).

In a perfect polyamorous world, interpersonal violence would be eradicated; war and displacement and homelessness would be things of the past. In this utopian poly life, there wouldn't be a single lie — by commission or omission — circulating in any poly family because everyone's spirit and humanity would be equally cherished.

Mutual respect

An important part of the mutual respect construct in polyamory is that respect is universal in the poly unit — everyone is respected — even if each lover has a different role, significance, or meaning for you.

POLYAMORY STORY

HONESTY ISN'T ALWAYS THE SAFEST POLICY

I once dated a person who seemingly wanted to spend all their time with me. As a solo polyamorist, I value my alone time and began feeling that I didn't have enough time to myself. I addressed the issue, and my partner shared something they were hesitant to tell me from the start: The partner with whom they were living had been physically assaulting them for months — and they were concealing our relationship out of fear. Immediately, I understood why they wanted to spend so much time with me, and we figured out a plan so that they could stay at my place several times throughout the week and then also crash with some loved ones of mine. —Kamilah

Mutual respect in even a complex polycule has a kind of breathtaking simplicity:

>> Mutual respect feels amazing. You feel amazing.

>> Mutual respect means that you can speak your mind and people listen.

>> Mutual respect means that you're not worrying, rehearsing, or burying conversations that are important to you about how you're feeling or about something difficult that has happened in the group.

>> Mutual respect means that your limits are respected, your basic needs are met, and your wants are of interest to everyone in the poly family.

In the 1970s experiments of polyamory, in some communes and poly arrangements, people who were distressed by some of the free-love practices were silenced. Their opinions were dismissed as false consciousness, and the group or family's leader(s) exerted power over the ways things operated — all while talking endlessly about freedom and free love.

This can happen in any poly family. A way to assess whether mutual respect is upheld in your group is to ask yourself:

>> Am I able to be myself here?

>> Do one or two people's opinions really hold sway over all others?

>> Can I talk about the hard stuff in this relationship? Am I afraid?

POLYAMORY STORY

Polyamory is about much more than having sexual relationships with multiple people at the same time; it's a method of wholly transforming our relationship to ourselves such that we can become partners with a keen sense of self-awareness, the ability to vulnerably and effectively communicate about even the most difficult subjects. —**Kamilah**

How does mutual respect work? Imagine a polyamorous constellation where you have a core partner and you each have lovers that you see regularly, but infrequently. You've set up a monthly date with your *paramour* (another term for lover) and it's on your shared calendar. Two hours before one of your dates, your primary partner says they really want you to come to this social hour with their work colleagues. On your end, you've been jealous of how much fun your partner has with these colleagues, and they've never invited you to this social hour before. What do you do?

>> A. Scold your partner for short notice, say you'd love to come to the next social gathering, and go on your date, which your other paramour has to travel for an hour to get to.

>> B. Think: My primary partner is my priority. I've finally gotten an invite! And text your paramour and say sorry, I have to cancel, my partner is sick, and I'm in the ER with them.

This might seem like an insignificant little lie. However, if you want your poly relationships to work, and if you want to continue to like yourself and come through for your partners, then the answer is an emphatic A.

Mutual respect means that each person's life and well-being have equal value, even if the commitment levels to each person are different.

Last year my mother had a health crisis so I was flying back and forth across the country trying to be there for her. I was exhausted. My partner of three years was seeing someone new and she just wasn't there for me. When I called her on it, she said something to the effect of, "You have a primary partner and isn't this why we are poly?" And I thought, Wow, absolutely no. I'm in a crisis and you have zero time or space to call or text and support me? That's the opposite of poly for me. —Sonja

Exploring Why People Choose Polyamory Today

Monogamy as a relationship form is so universal that you may barely notice it. It's the air you breathe. Prom Night. Engagement reveals. Every romcom you've ever seen. *Say Yes to the Dress. The Bachelor.* And *Love Is Blind.* In U.S. culture, monogamy is monumental.

Foundational to the marketing of monogamy as the only legitimate or functional way of relating is a crazy paradox: This one-true-love experience is the rare pinnacle of love that only so few people will ever get to experience, and yet everyone is compelled to pursue monogamous relationships and marriage *only*. The romcoms and reality shows really don't ever tell you how *that's* supposed to work.

But like all mythologies, this story line has holes. Despite the juggernaut of religious, cultural, and familial messaging on the essential role of monogamy in your lives, your families, and even the survival of civilization (!) — divorce statistics, monogamous relationship horrors in your friend groups, coercive family demands, and the failure of romantic love to *conquer all* as it is professed to do — leave many people wondering if monogamy is right for them.

In these sections you can consider whether you possess some of the relational preferences and personality traits that align well with polyamorous relationships. You can also engage in a brief activity to consider what your poly sexuality and partnerships might look like.

Polyamory may fit better than monogamy

When I think about the people in my life who thrive in polyamorous relationships, they all share a number of traits or ways of being that I describe here. In general,

>> **They have an expansive capacity for intimacy:**

- Loving many people simultaneously feels good, natural, or easy.

- Often they have a group of very intimate close friends.

>> **They're sexual explorers:**

- They want to try out new sexual practices with different people over their lifetime.

- They're open to sexual ways of being that they haven't tried or maybe even imagined yet.

>> **They enjoy novelty:**

- They thrive on new lovers, new intimacies, and new energies.

- New relationship energy is something they want to experience throughout their lives.

>> **They appreciate variety and flow:**

- They embrace flexibility when relationships change.

- They can keep commitments even when experiencing the rush of a new connection.

>> **They define fidelity as a commitment to honesty, rather than sexual exclusivity:**

- They thrive on honest, intimate exchanges even when they involve a lover falling for someone else.

- They can enjoy or feel happy when their lovers find love with others.

>> **They don't need a forever guarantee to create deeply loving and intimate sexual relationships:**

- They're willing to grow and invest in deep intimacy without regard to relationship status.

- They reject relationship forms that link increased intimacy with sexual exclusivity and elevated commitment.

>> **They accept relationship changes without chaos or despair:**

- Relationship changes and endings may be challenging and painful but don't devastate them.

- They can grieve changes without being self-destructive or blaming and destructive to others.

>> **They desire to live in a community of lovers or a team:**

- They have sometimes imagined life in a *throuple* (a relationship in which three individuals are intimate and sexual with each other).

- They thrive on flows of people around them, socially and sexually.

>> **They seek to explore different parts of themselves through and with others:**

- They imagine expressing different parts of themselves with different lovers.

- They want to facilitate the process of discovering new facets of the self for their lovers.

- They imagine new worlds of love beyond what they currently know.

>> **They reject the idea of ownership in relationships:**

- They see romantic ideals of one-and-only as part of a system that creates false scarcity around love.

- They see monogamy as part of a larger system of ownership that drains community love and power.

- They see polyamory as a potentially transformative relationship structure for society as a whole.

If this list doesn't describe you, don't worry. It certainly didn't describe me when I started on my path to polyamory. In truth, I had very little emotional flexibility when I started having sex. The only thing I was clear about was that the men I was having sex with when I was in college were certainly having sex with others, despite professing monogamy. So, I rejected this. I refused to be monogamous in turn, which got me into a lot of trouble with these boyfriends, and marked me as an outsider, a *slut* on campus.

In many ways, being branded a slut freed me to question everything. I wondered why sexual exploration with others was okay for my boyfriends, but social death for me. Throughout this period, I wondered: What might a liberating sexuality look like for me?

And one of the first answers that came to me was: honesty. As I discuss in the section "Full disclosure and transparency" earlier in this chapter, honesty is a pivotal facet of modern polyamory.

Constructing your polyamorous self

ACTIVITY

With this activity you can take a stab at constructing a description of your poly self. You can start where all honest conversation always starts — with yourself. Don't worry — nobody's looking. And none of this is in stone.

1. **Answer this question: What might a more liberating, open poly sexuality look like for you?**

2. **Select six terms from the following list that feel right or feel like they matter most.**

   If nothing fits you, write your own. Write them in a line or a paragraph. Consider organizing them into a hypothetical personal ad or a vision statement.

Gender expansive   Open relationship for kink but no sex with others

No hierarchy of partners   Monogamous with yearly free pass   BIPOC only

My friends are my primary loves   Mental health-centric   Veto power as primary

Lesbians only   Long-term multiple partners, equally significant   Serious cuddler

_____   I'd like at least one partner to also be an introvert

I want to top someone   I want to live with one partner but not all

Primary partner with a rotating mix of lovers   No veto powers in the relationship

Heterosexual only   One big poly household   Open but for long-distance sex only

I don't want to know my partner's other lovers   _____

Queer and trans partners only   My trauma survivorship is supported, not a problem

Asexuality is desired, celebrated   I want specific _____ in my poly family

Not too processy   I don't want to be the only _____ in the relationship

Neurodivergent positive   I must be able to pursue a particular kink or way of relating

I need a dominant/sub dynamic for at least one partner   Mixed-race family like me

I'm in charge of picking my partner's lovers   Role play is a must-have

Someone has to top me   My disability is incorporated, not seen as a problem

We need to create traditions together   Core partners must be open to kids

_____   I want at least one extrovert who wants to talk about everything

Kink positive   I need a lot of alone time   I don't want to have sex at all

---

Your list doesn't have to be a forever thing. Today these six ideas or ways of being or sexual practices mean something to you on your path to exploring polyamory. This kind of exercise can be helpful if and when you sit down and start to map out the poly life you want with your partner(s).

If I were doing this today, my six would be: *Hi, I'm Jaime, I'm a solo polyamorous romantic, my partners are gender expansive, and my friends and lovers have equal weight in my poly life. While I'm a big cuddler, I need a lot of alone time. And I need at least one extrovert who wants to talk about everything.*

While the beloveds in my poly constellation have changed very little over the past 15 years, what my six favorite descriptors would be a year or two from now might be different depending on what's happening in my life and what needs are or aren't getting met. In my 30s, for example, I had to have at least one Dom in the relationship; in my 40s, I had to have partners who were excited about raising kids; over the past decade, my friends and lovers have become equally significant in my poly life. And, when I look at the year ahead, I see romance everywhere.

CREATING A POLY FAMILY

My polyamorous family right now consists of me and my live-in partner, who is also the co-parent to my two children. We share our oldest kiddo with a third co-parent, who is my ex. We both have long-term platonic commitments: Graham to a friend who visits us a few times a year, spends holidays with us, and who our kiddos love deeply. Me to two very dear friends who I've known and loved for more than a decade. One of them helped us to make my oldest kiddo, and now she has a very close Aunt relationship with both of our children. My other friend has a little one who is the same age as my oldest, who entered our lives via adoption shortly after my oldest was born.

We are making decisions with and around these people and are choosing to lean into the value of platonic love and the role it plays in our lives. The time we commit to giving to our family members affects our romantic and sexual relationships just as much as our other romantic and sexual relationships, and we include these platonic loves in the way we configure and share those resources — time, money, space, and so on — that are unfortunately not as infinite as our love. **—Cavanaugh**

Understanding the Surge around Polyamory

For a lot of people who have been living and organizing around polyamory for 20 years or more, the past five years have been a whirlwind of changing consciousness. For decades, major press outlets ignored polyamory altogether. And then, the occasional article would pop up written by someone with no knowledge of polyamory, talking about us as if they were watching the collection of oddities at a 19th century carnival sideshow.

Social media has certainly been a major driver of pro-poly conversation. Around 2010, social media use started to explode, and by 2015 even mainstream media outlets were running the occasional pro-poly feature. But over the past five years, content centering the actual voices of polyamorous people have appeared all over the internet, in the mainstream press, and also in major literary magazines. These sections look at the what and whys of the current surge of interest in polyamory.

Mass media and visibility

One explanation for the rise in conversation and interest in polyamory is simple: poly voices achieving critical mass in public view. All of the non-monogamous experimentation, how-to books, literature, movies, tweeting, picture-posting of poly families, and podcasts over the past decade have added up. Polyamorous relationships are more known, seen, and common than ever before.

In 2023, for example, the city council of Sommerville, Massachusetts enacted the first legal support for polyamorous people in the nation, protecting polyamorous residents from workplace discrimination and police harassment. Such legal affirmation and protections were unfathomable even five years ago.

More polyamorous people being out

Poly people choosing to come out has had a singular, significant impact on poly acceptance and interest. Look to the left and to the right. Check under the seat in front of you. People you know are polyamorous.

For example, when I came out as polyamorous in the early '90s, I got endless grief. No one was happy about it: My coworkers were scandalized (I even survived a witch hunt to get me fired), my acquaintances said that I'd surely grow up and settle down. When I described what I wanted for the lesbian personals section of DC's weekly gay newspaper, they refused to run my ad. Too explicitly sexual, they said — not enough, *love-me-forever*.

But those days are long gone. Many people in my life are polyamorous now. I produce a sex and desire workshop at human rights and pride celebrations all over the world; I've taken it to Beijing, China; Seoul, South Korea; Ho Chi Minh City, Vietnam; Nairobi, Kenya; Cape Town, South Africa; St. Petersburg, Russia; and Nicosia, Cyprus — and polyamory stories and family constellations were shared in all of these spaces.

Social forces behind polyamory's surge

Without a doubt, today's social, economic, and ecological context is driving interest in polyamory. Among Millennials and Gen Zers, the ratio of expenses to resources among people who aren't inheriting wealth is much higher than that faced by the previous generations.

Housing in major cities is prohibitively expensive, job security is minimal, raising children is astronomical, and the world is literally on fire. Within this perfect storm of high risk and declining economic and ecological security, meeting life's challenges with a team of loved ones takes on a different hue. Polyamory has become part of that team outlook.

For instance, in a recent article in the New York Times, *Lessons from a 20-Person Polycule*, one interviewee, Katie, said: "I hope this is a social movement. I hope people will feel more freedom about how they want to live and about pooling resources and living their best life. . . . It's really hard to afford a house. Some of us are thinking of moving into a place with four or five bedrooms where eight or nine of us could live together. We could share the burden of bills. It's just more realistic. And it would be a community space. We would hold events and gather and play and have this endless sleepover. If I get to do this, I will have achieved something great — great emotionally and great in terms of social transformation."

In a time of rising costs and dwindling resources, it's an era of asking big questions and experimentation around sexuality, relationships, and family forms.

Response to monogamy's hardships

Another factor in the rising interest in polyamory is that the truth about the strenuous demands of monogamous long-term relationships and marriage has become much more widely shared. Previous generations commonly joked about the strains of lifetime monogamy, or they dismissed the demands and sacrifices of living with a single lifelong sexual partner as universal and not worth discussion. This generation of seekers is neither laughing nor denying.

HAS MONOGAMY EVER *REALLY* BEEN A THING?

In the 1950s, Alfred Kinsey and his merry band of sexually adventurous researchers interviewed thousands of people in the United States about their sexual practices. And despite this era being widely lauded as championing traditional family values, Kinsey's research found that 50 percent of married men had sex outside of their heterosexual marriages at some point in their lifetime, while 26 percent of married women had extra-marital sex before they reached the age of 40.

Spilling the tea: The era of sharing secrets

Today, many once-hidden family stories about the sacrifices and privations of monogamy have spilled out.

Some people discover that monogamy was a lie in their families, that their parent or parents had hidden relationships, because they've found out they aren't genetically related to the people who were presented to them as kin. Others have painful testimonies from their parents about what monogamy demanded of them and their losses. Others still have stories of violence and harm that were justified in the name of keeping the family together or being a "good husband."

Over time, the formerly outlandish idea of polyamory has become attractive not because of some widespread promotional campaign, but because the closed structure of many monogamous life partnerships was damaging to their parents or grandparents and is currently difficult or draining for peers.

REMEMBER

Polyamory isn't a magic fix. Destructive patterns of relating and coercive practices of power and control can infect any relationship, including polyamorous relationships.

Nonetheless, polyamory and the possibility of a more free-flowing intimate and sexual life sits on the horizon for many people who have felt trapped in the tight enclosure of monogamous relationships, a shimmering possibility.

MESSY MONOGAMY IN MY FAMILY

Unfortunately for many years I was serially monogamous and rather unfaithful; I struggled deeply with concepts of monogamy and had the self-control of the struggling teenager that I was. This was also what I saw happening in my home life, and I believe that my entire family could have been much more fulfilled in themselves and their relationships if they weren't so rigidly allegiant to the idea that monogamy and the nuclear family are the only acceptable ways to be in the world.

When I finally learned about the concept of polyamory at the tender age of 18, I experienced a relief I could never have anticipated. That was the first time I realized how much I disliked everything I thought was supposed to be true about relationships, despite wanting to engage in them so badly. I didn't do polyamory very well in the beginning either (who does?), but that moment was also my first step into writing my own narratives instead of just reading and replicating the stories others presented to me. —Cavanaugh

DNA doesn't lie

If you're obsessed with uncovering your ancestral history (like I am), ancestry. com and 23andme.com have confirmed Alfred Kinsey's exposure of the mythic nature of monogamy. Genealogists coined the term — *non-parental events (NPE)* — for the experience of finding that the relatives in your family tree aren't genetically related to you. In trying to figure out how common sex outside of marriage is in any era, NPEs give a hint by revealing the percent of hidden affairs that resulted in the birth of children. When you think of this in terms of the larger landscape of extramarital sex that doesn't result in births, NPEs actually expose a very small percentage of these affairs. Ergo, NPEs to the Nth Power = extra monogamous relating in any era. NPEs leave breadcrumbs for people looking at how the story of monogamous marriage has papered over a more complex truth in how their ancestors formed their families and conducted their social and sexual lives.

I think it's worth mentioning that this is how so many people currently and historically have lived, whether they were using the term poly or not. It can be easy to buy into the idea that poly is new, and while I think the movement to talk about our relationships this way is currently growing, it's plain to see that families and relationships have always been as complex as we are as a species. —Jack

Chapter **3**

Figuring Out Whether Poly Is Right for You

Because sexuality is so judged and controlled, listening to your inner voice and to your own needs around relationships can be difficult. Your parents have big plans for your future. Your siblings are getting married. Your friends are sharing the various joys of their monogamous partnerships. Your coworkers have those lovely spousal headshots on their desks.

This chapter walks you through several exercises designed to help you throw off the expectations of others and turn down the constant noise in today's culture about how monogamy is the only real relationship form and why polyamory never works.

An old joke in poly communities is: *You think polyamory is impossible? Try monogamy!*

As you move through the exercises in this chapter, try to let go of your fears about telling anyone else about your polyamorous feelings or relationships. Just try to give yourself the space to hear and experience your own desires and dreams. They're yours. They matter.

This chapter also helps you sort through the specific barriers you experience when you consider relationships beyond monogamy. How do your unique family expectations fit into your reservations about creating polyamorous relationships? How do your race, gender, sexuality, and familial history put you in the path of particular stigmas and judgments?

Discovering the Relationship Forms That Are Right for You

A shared experience among the polyamorists I've met is that at some point in their lives, they came to question whether monogamy was really the only workable way of organizing their sexual and familial life. Some found themselves in love with multiple people at the same time, which caused them great distress. Some learned that the story of monogamy in their family was a cover for a more complex web of relationships. Others survived having their lover reveal that they had another lover. And still others found critiques of monogamy in various social justice projects they encountered.

REMEMBER

You may have come upon polyamory through any of these doorways of discovery or another that is uniquely yours. The way doesn't matter. You're here, and I'm here with you, as you make your way as best you can to love the people in your life as fully and freely as possible. As you undertake this journey, look for people who have come to consider polyamory through a process similar to yours. And also appreciate the many different avenues that converge to bring all of us to this journey. You can find polyamory via a million different routes, and you can practice it in infinitely different ways.

TIP

Because here's one of polyamory's boldest promises: There's no singular right way to love. And you can discover and create the right way for you.

POLYAMORY DIDN'T ERASE THE HURTS

My experience of considering polyamory initially came out of an experience of infidelity. My wife had become close to a coworker with whom she had a brief relationship without my knowledge. When I found out, the impact was immediate. My wife and I had a young child together and had been together about six years. As I got over my initial hurt and began exploring what had occurred, I understood that she desired to continue to have a relationship with her coworker, but she also wasn't interested in ending our relationship. What followed was an urgent exploration of *any* relationship framework that could offer guidance or an alternative to our previously monogamous relationship.

Coming to polyamory wasn't the antidote to healing after being cheated on. But it did give my wife and me the ability to agree to a new relationship form and build something together that respected both of our boundaries and provided space for other relationships. —**Rob**

Pursuing New Relationships and Intimacies throughout Your Life

Another very common experience that the polyamorists in my life share is that they value developing new relationships and intimacies across the many decades of their life. In this section, you can consider how your desire, sexuality, sexual practices, relationships, and family forms may develop as you grow and change. You can think through how you may address shifting fantasies, needs, and yearnings over your lifespan. Even though you certainly can go through many changes in sexual practices and pursuits with a singular, monogamous partner, polyamory may offer greater flexibility and a broader range of choices as you embrace your and your partners' emotional and erotic evolutions.

I'm not the person I was in my 20s, 30s, or 40s, even though the core thread of who I am endures. The hypermasculine football player I loved and had great sex with as a freshman in college wasn't someone I could carry on a deep conversation with as a queer human rights researcher in my 50s. But when we did reconnect, decades after our relationship ended, we were still entirely recognizable to each other. I still felt love for him, and I also felt grateful that I hadn't married him, or the person I dated after him, as he did, when he settled into his meaningful life and raised his children.

POLYAMORY STORY

IT'S THE DISCOVERY

I will always want to know more about myself, especially sexually. Poly life is my discovery place. I want to get into those dark corners where we hide ourselves. I suspect domesticity kills the potential for this. We sort of shove more of ourselves down into the dark because of all the sacrifices we face in our daily life with our partners. And don't get me wrong — I'm madly in love with my nesting partner. I love him even more because he trusts me to go find myself and have these kind of soul-shattering experiences with new people.

But then I come home to him with so much more of myself. I come home with love and not resentment. With more energy to put to the task of loving him and raising our kids. I can't believe I've found a partner who is committed to my self-discovery and growth, on this level. It's beyond anything I could have imagined I'd ever get. —**Sonja**

You may also suspect that your sexuality and the ways you want to organize your family life are likely to shift and transform over the course of your life. and you question whether a monogamous commitment in your 20s or 30s or even 40s will be able to hold those changes well and support you. If so, polyamory might present another way forward for you.

Tuning Into Your Desires and Exploring Your Fears

In my work as a coach, I often use reflection questions to help my clients get to the root of what they're struggling with, particularly around other people's agendas for their sexuality and relationships. The following sections present four simple activities to help you push back on inner and external judgments you may be carrying around about polyamory and give yourself room to think.

There's never any right or wrong way to do these activities. You can do them in order. You can pick out the reflections that most interest you. You can do them by just jotting a few notes. Or you can write extensively. You can look at the questions and walk away. Come back later. Take a walk. Sing in the shower. Breathe. These questions are a starting place.

THIS ISN'T A SITUATIONSHIP

These days, I hear a lot about situationships. In general, what's described to me is a murky, undefined thing. Dating while not dating. Hooking up but not in a relationship while forming an attachment. Falling in love with someone who's emotionally or otherwise unavailable while pretending that everything's cool. These situationships are akin to what people in the '10s labeled on social media as: *It's complicated*.

Polyamory is the opposite of a situationship. A polyamorous relationship is well-defined. It's co-created among all the people involved (see Chapter 9). Partners strive to articulate their needs and to be clear about their limits. Everyone understands that they're in a relationship and what their part, role, or function is.

Polyamory often gets lumped in with what people describe as situationships and they couldn't be further apart in construction and aim. Situationships thrive on the unsaid and the unnamed. While in polyamorous relationships, poly lovers are saying and naming all day long — sometimes to our great exhaustion.

Reflecting on the start of your journey

Being at a place of curiosity is exciting, but it can also be daunting. Every journey starts with a first step.

ACTIVITY

Ask yourself these questions:

>> What's happening right now in your sexuality, your life, and/or your community that makes you curious about polyamory?

>> What's scary or hard when you think about polyamory as a possibility?

>> When you imagine your polyamorous life, what does it look like?

- Who's there and who isn't there because poly isn't for them?

- What's day-to-day life look like?

- What's your dating life like?

- What's your sex life like? What are you doing that's not possible to do right now?

TIP

Take your time because these questions are significant. Find some quiet time and a comfortable space to think and write.

Understanding what matters

Like most people, you may have created a story of yourself that doesn't quite describe the full picture. It's like you've internalized bulleted talking points about yourself that hide or downplay a more complex reality. In this exercise, you can uncover or reveal neglected parts of your story.

ACTIVITY

When you're ready, turn to these questions and allow yourself the space to focus. This exercise is just for you and no one else. You never have to share it. Just let yourself discover what deep down you may already know:

>> What matters most to you about your sexuality and relationships?

>> What are you minimizing or denying that *really matters*?

>> Are you hiding something? *Even from yourself?* You can come out of hiding right here, right now. What is it?

Considering how much you're denying yourself around what really matters may be difficult. Writing it down might feel impossible or scary.

REMEMBER

The important part of this exercise is to give yourself permission to say anything you've been denying out of fear or judgment. This step is the beginning to living more honestly among the people you love.

Looking at your name tag

Naming yourself is a way of claiming yourself. For years, I've opened my sex and desire workshops with this fun, simple — yet revealing — exercise. It's fun because you get to describe yourself in ways you may rarely or never do. It's revealing because when you boil yourself down to just a few, crucial descriptors of your desire, you might be surprised who you find.

ACTIVITY

Pull out a piece of paper, or an actual name tag if you have one, and begin:

1. **Choose a name tag and write your name on it.**

2. **Review a list of dozens upon dozens of possible descriptions of your desire.**

   The following figure shows a typical list of desire descriptors.

contortionist Submissive gentle
daddy femme bisexual asexy
hybrid savage
ass-master giver licker
romantic Passion twin-Flame
Cuddler rough eye-contact gender
Romantique pirate
Chatty Porn star
Outdoorsy screamer butch
generous Playful
handsy Vanilla Versatile Weeper
slow-burner
Dyke watcher make-out poly water-sportsy
bandit
body-worshipper Polyamorous
dirty-talker
rope-kilten fairy
silent-cummer

3. Choose three descriptors or another term that isn't included here but that's important to you and write them under your name.

When I conduct this activity in person, workshop participants make their three choices. Then, I ask everyone to turn to the person next to them and introduce themselves by their name tags. Everyone starts out nervously, but within a few minutes the whole room is full of discussion and laughter.

Because you're likely doing this activity alone, you'll be reintroducing yourself to yourself as a purely desiring and desirous being. Look at your name tag. Breathe. Stand in a mirror and recite the words aloud.

To finish the exercise, ask yourself these final reflection questions:

≫ What surprised you during this exercise? How do you feel?

≫ What's not on your name tag that you wish was there? What's missing?

For nearly a decade, when I did this activity I always wrote:

Jaime: *Bossy Femme Bottom*

These three descriptions were fun and made people laugh, but they were also seriously accurate. In my *bossy femme bottom* era, I often had a primary partner who was identified as a Dom; when I sought out play partners, I did so exclusively as a bottom. My femme identity was really important to me in terms of how I connected with my lovers, who were most often butch lesbians, transmasculine guys, or nonbinary people. But over the past few years, my partners' genders became more varied; I no longer exclusively bottom. My friends grew into much more significant social and romantic partners over time, and I stopped organizing my life around a primary partner. So last year, I changed my name tag to look like this:

Jaime: *Solo-Poly Kissing-Monster Cuddler*

These three descriptors have become central to my intimate life in recent years and much more accurately describe how I choose and connect with my lovers today.

What's on your name tag? Like most people, you may never have allowed yourself to consider all the different desires you have. You may have buried some out of shame, or because you believed they were impossible to express in your relationship(s), or because you thought you'd never find anyone who might want to relate to you this way.

Here, at the start of your polyamorous journey, just give yourself the space to uncover who and what you really desire and how you want to connect. These descriptors needn't be permanent. Like me, and most of the people I coach, yours may also change quite a bit over time. If you want to find the people you're actually attracted to and create the kind of relationships you really want, constructing a name tag that artfully and truthfully describes your desire is a very good place to start.

Sifting and sorting out

Here you take all the bits and pieces from the three previous exercises and sort them out a bit, or sift. Many of the reflective exercises in this chapter dig up or uncover new information. Some of your insights will be barely formed fragments. Which is great! You are in a discovery process. When you sift, you take all the scraps and slivers and look for what is emerging.

ACTIVITY

Take out your journal and do the following:

>> Pick out the three most important insights that came out of activity one, two, and three. Your top three discoveries might have emerged from just one question, or they might be spread across all three activities.

>> Write about these three things daily for a week — even if for 5 minutes.

>> Find someone supportive to talk to about what you're discovering.

>> Congratulate yourself. You're on your way.

Sifting can take weeks. Or months. Or years. Keep your journal. You might not be in a place to act on any of these important insights right now. Conversely, you may be ready to take this information and launch yourself into the poly dating scene. If so, Chapter 4 can help you think about some next steps. If you're still wondering whether you're ready to explore polyamory, you can check out Part 2 to get grounded.

POLYAMORY STORY

There is no universal way to be polyamorous. I don't currently have anyone I would call a partner, but I do have multiple people with whom I share deep emotional, intimate, and sexual connections. They're each very important to me, and they all know about each other. I only get to see them a few times a year due to long distance, but we maintain connection throughout and show care whenever and however we can. —**Bishop**

Experimenting with sex and intimacy among different partners

Polyamory imparts the opportunity to grow and experiment with your sexuality and sexual practices over the many eras of your life. These sections get you thinking about whether the imposition of traditional models of relationship is holding you back from even considering whether such experimentation is possible for you or morally right.

Polyamory champions the pursuit of pleasure in the context of expansive love. It's about social, sexual, and intimate freedom.

ACTIVITY

Pull out your journal and may ask yourself these questions:

» What might your life be like if you had the freedom to explore your desire and your sexuality with different people as your life unfolds?

» What if you could do this and not have to break faith with your lovers? What if they could come with you on this journey? What would it be like if they were excited about these discoveries and wanted to support you?

» What if breakups weren't the norm in your life every time you made a new discovery about an important need that your partner can't meet? What if you could make adjustments together and not be forced to choose between either abandoning yourself or abandoning them?

Now imagine the following:

» You have a partner you can talk to about desires that are taboo or needs that you're certain they aren't interested in or can't meet — and they're excited to help you figure out how to meet them.

» You have an open conversation in your partnership about crushes, fleeting interests, or conflicts you have about the kind of sex you want.

» You have thrilling nights of sex and discovery — across your lifespan and into your elder years.

» You bring those discoveries back to your existing partner or partners and grow new things together even after many years of being together.

» You find out things about yourself that you'd never have known but for meeting this surprising person whose desires match up with something inside you that was buried.

» You have a partner or partners you've had over decades who help you resolve conflicts you have about your sexuality and grow intimacies with others so that all of you can meet more of your needs. Imagine

- The laughter between you. The solidarity. The deep knowing. The trust. Imagine the raucous, extended family dinners.

- The expansive space for yourself and the doting attentions of multiple lovers who don't resent you because they're boxed into a relationship that can't meet their diverse and ever unfolding needs.

- The joy.

MAYBE I CAN BE ALL THE THINGS

A lot of work that attempts to give language to expansive kinds of relating and eroticism ends up creating limiting boxes. These terms don't quite describe or encompass the vastness of who you are. They feel jargony and alienating — like they belong to another world of people. The result is that many people don't identify with whatever descriptors are popular and say to themselves: "Ah, that's not for me then."

This is so true in the case of polyamory, which mainstream conversation construes as primarily a space for hypersexual people who are exclusively kinky or emotionally detached. But in my experience, having led sex and desire workshops among thousands of people all over the world, a lot of polyamorous people are asexual. Many are quite joyfully vanilla. Some (like me) are wildly romantic attachers. So as you read this book, remember: You don't have to be a certain way or possess a particular sexuality or gender to form families of multiple lovers and partners. You can find your way no matter the terms you prefer, how you move in the world, and however you want to do it.

Pushing back on the naysayers

You may feel like various forces are working together to prevent you from imagining this joy and freedom. For many people, these forces can be overwhelming.

TIP

Freedom is nothing if not a constantly shifting wrestle. As you grow into yourself, different parts of your being emerge and different aspects of your story become more central to your identity and your self-discovery process.

And while that self-realization is happening, all kinds of authorities are forcing their expectations and conformities on you as the only legitimate path — whether it's how to dress, what you should do for work, or how you are spending your time and money. In the realm of sexuality and family-making, these commandments are often rigid and stifling.

For example, in my life, the naysayers were powerful and many — my parents, religious tradition, teachers, literature, movies, even friends. They all were aligned in the belief that polyamory was unacceptable. Poly life would get me in trouble. I'd wind up jobless, childless, hurt, and alone. Instead, I ended up learning amazing new things about myself in each decade, building a village of friends and lovers and a life that fit me:

>> In my 20s, I learned that I had an intense desire to control or direct a lot of the action during sex with my lovers. This was incredibly hot for me. Naysayers had said that women couldn't be in control of sexual scenarios.

>> In my 30s, I had lovers of many different genders, and being with women, especially, freed me to let go of control. I discovered immense pleasure by turning over decision-making in various co-constructed scenarios. Naysayers had said that women giving up control were only victims.

>> In my 30s and 40s I experimented with pain as a transportive device in my sexuality. I had buried a lot of grief and pain from my childhood, and having lovers hit me repeatedly, and rhythmically put me into a kind of trance that opened up a portal to the pain and let it out. Those decades of sexual exploration were incredibly healing. Naysayers had said that people who played with pain in their sexuality were hurting themselves.

>> In my 40s, my desire for a solo poly life moved me to create a vibrant village of loved ones to support my solo parenting (for more on parenting while poly, see Chapter 14). Years later, when my son graduated from college, dozens of villagers showed up to celebrate him. Naysayers had said that parenting while poly is chaotic and harmful to children.

>> I had suffered debilitating depression as a young person, and in my 50s, partly due to playing with BDSM, the depression went into a remission that has held for more than a decade. Naysayers had said that BDSM is sick and will make you sick.

>> In my early 60s, I find myself with what people call a praise kink — I'm most gratified by lovers and romantic partners who dote on me and shower me with attention. I call this the era of Obvious Love because when someone meets one of my beloveds, they often say: "Wow, s/he obviously loves you!" Naysayers had said that women in their 60s need one dedicated partner to take care of them or they will be lonely and sad.

Could I have discovered any of this if I'd listened to the various authorities in my life? Obvious answer, in this era of Obvious Love: no. Could I have learned all of this about myself with a single sexual partner over these 40 years? It's possible, but highly unlikely.

REMEMBER

One of the unique facets of polyamory is that I'm not relying on one person to love being submissive, or be a skilled top, or have expertise in a particular kink, or want to parent, or be an extreme praise-giver. I'm finding people whose identity or journey of sexual discovery and family-making aligns with mine *in the moment*. I'm choosing people who are actively seeking what I'm currently yearning for.

POLYAMORY STORY

Watching my lovers find what they actually really want in life couldn't delight me more. And that's the gift of polyamory to me. And then it bends back around to me: What are the things I'm going to learn about myself by having this way of structuring my life? And how is that going to make me much more awake to all kinds of experiences and ways of understanding the things that happen between me and the world? Yep, that's such a gift of poly. —**Amelie**

Sorting through Social Stigma and Familial Judgments

One of the stifling underpinnings of intimate life in the United States is the influence of Puritan colonial values on today's social and sexual culture. These values are so woven into daily life that they're almost invisible. The U.S. culture of overwork is a great example (just search "Protestant work ethic" in your favorite browser to see what I mean).

Puritan sexual morality approved of sex only as a reproductive function and only as directed by a Puritan husband in a monogamous marriage. You can see the threads of these ideas playing out today — even as casual sex and hooking up has become so omnipresent in pop culture — the driver of so much advertising, music, and movies.

REMEMBER

A great paradox of sexuality is that because it's so powerful and enlivening, it's also heavily policed and controlled.

REMEMBER

Sometimes your family does the policing around your sexuality. Sadly, sometimes your friends police you. Even in the poly community, you can get messages that your polycule isn't doing polyamory right.

The important thing to understand is that your sexuality *is powerful*. And it's all yours to define and live out.

WARNING

Puritan colonial values echo through 21st century social and sexual life, leaving heavy burdens for people of all races, genders, and sexualities interested in polyamory. Familial and societal expectations often stand in the way of even considering polyamory as a possibility. The following sections point out some specific ways these barriers may play out for you.

Barriers for heterosexual polycurious people

Heterosexual people face a gauntlet of barriers as they consider polyamory because you are monogamy's designated drivers. The whole system is set up to organize and order your future: one partner, one marriage — for life. Pushing back on this system means throwing off deeply ingrained messages and conditioning. Here I explore the specifics.

Among heterosexual men

A man is considered a success only if he can attract and marry an attractive heterosexual woman. A wife's fidelity and devotion are the measure of his masculinity. A man whose wife has lovers is no man at all in this scenario. Additionally, heterosexual men who are interested in polyamory do so alongside a history of men abusing trust in relationships, leaving them to explore polyamory under the cloud of: *all men are cheaters.*

As a man who respects women, how can you even think about polyamory? How do you try on polyamory in ways that live up to your values about equality and honesty?

Among heterosexual women

A core concept of heterosexuality is that virginity and sexual exclusivity are the measures of a woman's worth. Women with many sexual partners lose their system-defined value as the tally goes up. Women who openly pursue their pleasure are a danger to others (as alleged carriers of disease) but also a danger to themselves.

Under these terms, heterosexual polyamorous women are perverse. The very idea that you would center your own desire in pursuit of pleasure and partnership and have many lovers over a lifetime is a threat to heterosexuality and to marriage as an institution.

All heterosexuals

Most straight-identified people form relationships under the weight of the history of heterosexual marriage in your families and intense expectations about carrying on these traditions. Family status, inheritance, and Mom's and Dad's value as keepers of the family name all hinge on your success at finding a high status, appropriate partner to marry. Many families establish a heterosexual coaching process with their children around dating, marriage, and the wedding celebration at a very young age.

Considering polyamory under this intense set of expectations and lifelong training can be extremely difficult.

Barriers for women and femmes who are polycurious

Women of all sexual orientations and gender expressions suffer from sexist Puritan ideas about women's sexuality. Women and femmes aren't supposed to *seek out* partners or prioritize their pleasure. Your sexuality as a woman is only appropriate when it functions as a receiver of the attentions of others; not standing at the center of your sexual story, calling the shots, and certainly not creating a family unit of multiple lovers.

Barriers for polycurious LGBTQ+ people

The unspoken bargain for LGBTQ+ people in the era of marriage equality is this: You have to say that sex doesn't matter; LGBTQ+ people are about so much more than our sexuality. And you must proclaim that "we are just like everyone else" if you want to be worthy of legal equality. The price of belonging is monogamy, a white picket fence, and marriage. Centering pleasure and pursuing polyamory confirms what anti-LGBTQ+ adversaries knew about queers all along: LGBTQ+ equals obsessed with sex. Immoral.

Barriers for polycurious immigrants or children of immigrants

Taiwanese American comic Shen Yang makes a great joke about this. In his standup routine, he says: Can you imagine *leaving your home*, and giving up every comfort so future generations can have more opportunity? And then your kid goes into standup comedy!

Multiply this sentiment one hundred times for children of immigrants trying on polyamory. In a family system where your parents have survived the trauma of dislocation and endured great hardships, polyamorous love may seem frivolous or minimizing of all the family has survived and all your parents have sacrificed.

Barriers for BIPOC polycurious people

For many Black, Indigenous, and all People of Color (BIPOC) seekers of polyamory, healing from the intergenerational trauma of surviving racist discrimination and violence is a fact of life. Accordingly, BIPOC parents often go to great lengths to protect their children. If you're polycurious and BIPOC, you may worry that coming out about your desires or your polyamorous family constellation will add to your parents' burdens.

Common barriers for everyone

All the barriers in the previous sections — across distinct identities and familial experiences — play out in one significant common way: The struggle to reject monogamy as the only legitimate relationship form can be daunting and overwhelming.

BACKLASH FROM FAMILY AND FRIENDS

My brother was the last person to know that Angel and I had opened our marriage and that I identified as polyamorous. This seemed to bring to light some underlying reservations he had always had about our marriage. He was accusatory and dismissive, calling our relationship a "sham." We haven't been able to meaningfully connect since, though polyamory is only part of the reason for that. My brother told my father — who I don't talk to very often — that we were poly, without my consent. My father has never mentioned it when we've spoken.

We've also lost friends with whom we were close as there was a collective reaction, some supportive some not, when we opened and began telling people. Angel and I had very few mutual friends remaining after this took place, though the ones who have been supportive have also become part of the expanding landscape of friends we have made since then. Defining ourselves as polyamorous seems to have been an adverse social experience for some of our friends and family. In a way it has had a pruning effect on people who wouldn't have been there for us through the harder times anyway. **—Rob**

WARNING

If you're having a hard time figuring out whether polyamory is right for you, historic judgments and violence directed at your family, your community, or your gender and sexuality – can really add to the struggle.

REMEMBER

It's okay to do the following:

>> Take time to sift through these historic and ongoing pressures as you figure out the right relationship path for you.

>> Seek support from people who also share your specific identities and histories in sorting through your barriers and options.

>> Get professional help from a polyamorous-positive practitioner of therapy, a bodyworker, or a somatic healer (see Appendix B) to support your journey, whatever the outcome.

Going Back and Forth with Internal and External Barriers

You're likely going to have to manage a mix of internal and external struggles as you consider polyamory. At times, it may seem like a grueling game of table tennis. After you address your internalized shame about your desire, you get hit with worries about your workplace. Then you have a great conversation with a new poly crush, and your mother calls with news of a cousin's wedding and offers the usual suggestions around settling down.

As you read the following sections, think more deeply about what's really in your way as you consider polyamory. Is it internal resistance or external judgment? Is it both? What's holding you back?

Internal barriers: Getting out of your own way around gender and sexuality

Back and forth, forth and back. Maybe it's time to address one of the biggest internal barriers to considering polyamory: your internalized beliefs about gender and sexuality in the world and concurrently — in your intimate and sexual life.

Polyamory means more love. As you venture outside the confines of considering one partner for life, endless possibilities emerge around who and how you might organize your sexual and familial life. Your beliefs about yourself around gender and sexuality can bump up against all of this. Starting this journey of reconsideration can feel like a runaway train.

In 2011 and 2023, I was co-investigator on two major surveys of LGBTQ+ people, and in both cases, more than 800 survey participants couldn't find a box to check that fully described their gender. My study co-authors and I offered a write-in option for: *A gender not listed here* and got an eyeful of the hundreds of ways our respondents think about their genders, including:

Sexy	I reject the premise	Gender is for suckers	Hybrid	Swishy butch
Just a regular lady who expresses a variety	Autistic, folksy, solarpunk	Depends!	All over the map, dyke, jock	Gendergeek
Gender needs to go back to an ugly place from whence it came	Gender atheist	I have no idea	Twidget	Just am
Stem	Very corporate, excu-dyke	Powder Puff Butch	Fantastica	Homebody
Two Spirit	I'm a femme contractor	Demigirl nerd	Futch	Low femme

One of the gender issues that comes up in my coaching practice is that some of my clients express one gender in their day-to-day life and different genders in their intimate life. Another is that if your partners' genders are fluid, what does that mean to you about your sexual orientation?

REMEMBER

Polyamory means you can both pursue different gender expressions among your partners and inhabit different gender expressions with different partners.

There are endless variations here: A client who is the CEO of a health company presents as a hypermasculine heterosexual in his daily life and has two women in his poly constellation. One likes him to top her — to take charge of all her sexual needs — and the other likes him to submit to her, so she runs the show sexually between them.

My client treasures the space that this domme (dominant woman) has created for him, because unlike his highly demanding work life and his relationship with his other partner, he gets to give up control. Unexpectedly, he finds himself thrilled to relate to his domme's other male partner in the ways that the domme — within their agreed limits — directs him to. Accordingly, while he has always identified as straight, increasingly, when he posts profiles of himself online, he identifies as *heteroflexible* (a combination of heterosexual and flexible). Because under the direction of a partner whom he trusts, his roster of desired sexual activities and genders has expanded.

REMEMBER

You don't have to be LGBTQ+ to have a complex relationship to your gender and sexuality. Almost everyone who explores polyamory reevaluates how they think about their gender and sexual practices because — more is more.

Opening the door to polyamory and a more complex intimate life around gender and sexuality isn't a runaway train. You can start and stop this train. You can take time-outs. You can decide you're just perfect as you are and need no revisions. You can decide it's time to date. You can decide you need to build more relational skills (see Chapters 5–7). You can decide you need more polyamorous friends (see Chapter 10). You are in charge.

REMEMBER

Polyamorous life presents the possibility of experimenting with who you are intimately — your genders, sexualities, approaches to sex, favorite practices, roles, kinks, positions — the options are literally endless.

POLYAMORY STORY

I'm a genderqueer woman and dated a pretty awesome straight guy for several years. We had tried a number of things, and I got it into my head that I wanted to strap on a dildo and penetrate or peg him. But what I said was, "Have you ever wanted to try anal?" To which he replied that he had done a little but would be willing to try anal on me *if that's what I wanted.* I was so embarrassed that I hadn't considered that this very heterosexual guy would not even think that I might be asking to peg him. It froze me with embarrassment — and we never talked about it again. I'm still mad at myself. I have no idea if he would have been willing to explore that in any way because I essentially chickened out. —**Robin**

External barriers: Recognizing stigma, shame, and poly life

Stigma and shaming around polyamorous life is real. If you're someone who is deeply affected by external judgments — whether from your family of origin or an internet troll — you're going to need to strategize about how to protect yourself from other people's projections about your poly explorations and identity.

Despite the media fascination of the moment with polyamory, mainstream commentary about polyamory still largely amounts to the following: reckless, slutty, dishonest. Monogamy supremacism is real. Monogamy supremacism says: Monogamy is the one and only way; everything else is fake or childish or selfish.

It's not silly or cowardly to worry about public perception of polyamory. Consider the following:

>> People have and do lose jobs, friends, family, and kids.

>> Polyamory undercuts many myths that uphold deeply rooted traditions.

>> Polyamory disclosures often have an impact on friends and family.

The key question for you on whether polyamory is right for you is: How can you explore polyamory and protect yourself from others' projections?

And, if you're ready to push back on your fears and the monogamy agenda that various people and institutions have laid out for you, it might be time to take those first steps on your path to polyamory. If so, you can check out Chapter 4 to take in so many different ways to organize your poly life, or Chapter 11 for tips on getting the support you need and deserve.

Chapter 4

Discovering the Many Forms of Polyamory

his chapter dives into the wonder and creativity that polyamorous people describe when they throw off conventional ideas about how to build love, sexual connections, and family. Creating sexual, romantic, and familial relationships with more than one partner can be complex, but this chapter isn't about that. This chapter is about sheer polyamorous joy.

Polyamory can be an incredibly freeing, generative practice. It can bring flows of love and partnership into your life that you may never have imagined. How are people remaking the rules of sexuality and family-making over decades of their lives? Here you can find many concrete examples of the seemingly infinite possibilities.

Understanding That the Possibilities Are Endless

For many years in the United States, a standard description of polyamory consisted of a heterosexual man with two women as partners who were often but not always sexual or partnered with each other. This poly-poster-family was usually white, middle class, and had a clean-cut suburban air about them. Of course, such polyamorous families exist and persist in their own wildly eclectic and wonderful ways. And yet, this poly portrait fell very short of describing the depth and breadth of polyamorous practices and partnerships. The following sections attempt to flesh out the expansive range of families and forms that polyamorous people are creating today.

As you can see from the stories that follow, there are literally infinite ways to organize your polyamorous life. And the form that suits you best today, may not be the right form ten years from now. One of the promising aspects of polyamory is that shifts in libido, sexual needs and curiosities, desire, geographic location, life stages, and attractions need not break up your relationships. Of course, that's not a given; change always brings about more disruption than you imagine, but sustaining all kinds of relationships through major life changes and even existential shifts within a polyamorous relationship structure is entirely possible.

Throuples, triads, and threesomes, oh my

For some poly people, three is the magic number for relating. Briefly, here's what these three-centric terms mean:

>> **Triad:** This term tends to describe three-person relationships where one person is involved with two others, and those two may or may not be involved with each other (see Appendix A for a description of the Vee relationship form). The nearby sidebar describes a triad.

>> **Throuple:** This term most often describes a three-person unit, wherein all partners are intimately involved with each other.

>> **Threesome:** A term for casual encounters and hookups that involve three people.

I think of the throuple as the gateway formation for people opening up monogamous relationships — often, throuples feel sort of manageable in the budding polyamorous imagination.

If a throuple is your jam, go get those partners! And if you have other more unruly forms in mind for your poly future, don't worry, your people are out there.

I LOVE A TRIAD

I really like having a triad with two primary partners. It feels very stable and connected to me — and then sure, I can have lots of other lovers who could be long term or short term and are into all different kinds of things. Some might be more vanilla, some might be kinkier, some might be into kissing and snuggling more, some might be more into the romance. You can see these cute little representations in my drawing.

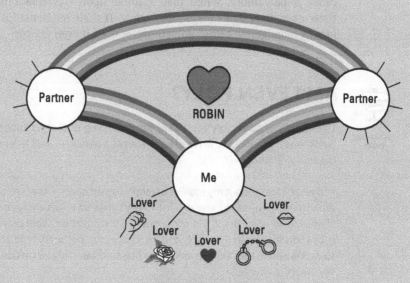

My Ideal Polycule

But this depiction is less *that one is into this*, and *another into that*, but more to indicate a variety of types of relationships with a variety of types of people. I'm *super switchy* (as in, I like to change up roles and who is in control). Sometimes I'm the femme, sometimes I'm masculine, sometimes I'm the top and sometimes I'm the bottom, sometimes I like to punch and spank people, but sometimes I want to be punched and spanked and tied up. So, the variety of partners allows me to experience and express all the various interests I have. Also, there are little spikes off the partners' circles too because they get to have lovers or other interactions as they desire. I don't ever want to define that for my partners.

Gender basically doesn't matter. I am attracted to a wide variety of genders. And any of my partners need to be ready for that.

Lastly my kiddo isn't in this image because, while he is centrally important to me and I love him more than I can express, I don't see my role as parent in any way connected to my extended polycule life, with the exception that the core triad partners are fully in as co-parents. —**Robin**

Ambiguous or ambivalent poly

You're a work in progress when you're ambiguous or ambivalent poly. For many, poly terms and community events don't fit into their worldview, and that's fine. Just be yourself and keep finding your way.

In M'Bwende's case (see the nearby sidebar), they found themselves living relationship arrangements that mirrored the relational forms they grew up in. Nobody called it polyamory. When they stumble upon conversations about polyamory these days, they don't necessarily relate. If their relationships don't fit anyone's idea of monogamy, rather polyamory — does it even matter?

POLYAMORY STORY

AM I EVEN POLY?

Thinking about polyamory specifically didn't come up until my childbearing relationship. But when I think about who I've always been as a person — well, in kindergarten, I had like, two girlfriends.

And when I think about my models of family construction — the idea that family is expansive is in my blood, literally. The family I grew up in has always been constructed of multiple families. But in this contemporary conversation about polyamory, I don't even know that I identify as poly and yet, I have multiple family relationships. And so, if someone said to me, "Do you identify as polyamorous?" My inclination would not be to say, "Yeah, of course."

In trying out polyamory in my adult relationships, what was brought to me and what I could agree with fit perfectly with who I was, so I was like, *Oh, is that what that's called? Great!*

I'm an optimist. I didn't really feel like jealousy was a part of the great ocean that could be our poly existence. That was the ideal, until we came to points where my partners and I departed from what just came naturally to me and then, I kind of wanted it to go my way. So, the poly construction that works for me is: My people are my people. Everything needs to flow from me outward (see the following).

So, it's complicated, and yet it's also very simple. I definitely have challenges. I'm posses-sive. And the simplicity comes when everybody who's involved can be in their lives and not be interrupted by the lives of the other people. I've always been a community per-son, so at every angle, I'm really trying to pull the strands out of what could be — even when it's challenging. — **M'Bwende**

Solo poly with couples play

Solo poly describes poly people who see themselves — rather than a partner or partners — as the central organizing unit of their poly life; some solo polyamor-ists seek out couples as a primary interest. For Mija in the nearby sidebar, finding couples to play with suits their solo poly needs best.

**POLYAMORY
STORY**

I LOVE PLAYING WITH COUPLES; I'M MEANT TO BE SHARED

I love couples. My favorite polyamorous situations are where I hang out, go on adven-tures, and occasionally get sexy time with a couple together or individually (see Mija's adventuring picture). They're both fully aware that they aren't the only couple or per-sons that I hang out, have adventures, and have sex with. I don't feel limited in who or how I get to love within the boundary of consent.

(continued)

(continued)

Printed with permission from Mija

I never understood monogamy beyond it being about possession, and I never wanted to be possessed. I'm meant to be shared. I like that people trust my love enough to share. **—Mija**

Nesting partnership; friends are crucial

Well known genderfluid comic Alok has said that "my friends are my lovers." And by that they mean — their friends are their central commitment — they go on dates and vacations with them, and they celebrate each other as partners, even as these relationships aren't sexual.

In the early days of non-monogamous practices and conversation, poly was often considered exclusively in terms of sexual practices, but practitioners like Alok have changed these ideas. In Elizabeth's constellation (see the nearby sidebar), she has chosen James as her foundational or nesting partner, but she has a lot of intimate partners and supportive love beyond this core commitment — her friendships are a top priority.

I DON'T ELEVATE SEXUAL CONNECTIONS OVER OTHER RELATIONSHIPS

POLYAMORY STORY

My map of connections shows the most important connections of who I consider my family. My daughter is almost an adult and was conceived with a known donor who is STB — one of my closest friends from college.

I do prioritize my nesting relationship with James in several ways: We share finances, a home, parenting, and projects. We're both very independent as well as connected. The beginning of our relationship felt like a game of chicken. "Well I want to go be slutty at this event." "How are you going to feel about that?" "Well, I think that's hot. Have a great time!" It was so refreshing to be with someone who also enjoyed play and friends-with-benefits sex. We also have freedom to experience intimacy, love, and connection with other partners. I look forward to growing old together and continuing to be sexy adventurers and meeting challenges.

I don't elevate sexual connections over my other relationships on this map (see Elizabeth's drawing). DZ, EW, and STB are my best friends from college whom I consider family. AC is a dear friend who I provide care work and financial support for. CK and LL are two longtime sweeties who are family to me. There have been periods where we see each other frequently and others where we don't, but nonetheless I see them always being in my life. We have supported each other in many ways over the last decade. My sister lives nearby and is one of my closest friends; we provide a lot of support for each other and have frequent communication. James and I are both very active in my nibblings' (gender-neutral term for niece and nephew) lives, in the same way my sister and their spouse have supported our daughter. —**Elizabeth**

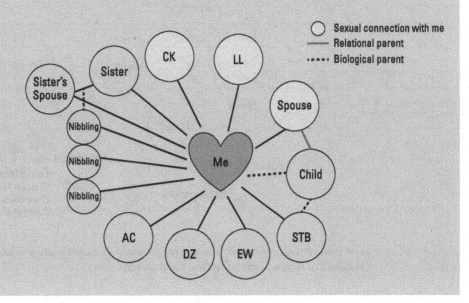

Relationship anarchy and nonhierarchal poly

Relationship anarchists and nonhierarchal poly practitioners affirm and celebrate all kinds of relationships with fervor and respect. Blood and chosen family, romantic and platonic connections, sexual and nonsexual partners all register as crucial and worthy in a relationship anarchist's view.

Ignacio's story in the nearby sidebar gives one example of nonhierarchal poly life — where blood and chosen family, nonsexual, and sexual connections create flows of intimate and family life. Ignacio's daughter and child form the foundation of their familial life, and then friends and lovers float around them. Many of these relationships are long term and very significant, but they're held loosely. There are no expectations around say, showing up for holidays or texting daily.

POLYAMORY STORY

IT'S LIKE A WAVE

In my drawing, I've tried to show that there's no real hierarchy with my friends and lovers — it looks like almost a wave that just goes up and down because sometimes I'm more connected to some people and then something happens, we don't see each other for a while, but then later on, we get together and it's like no time has passed. So, there's movement up and down, but no priority whatsoever.

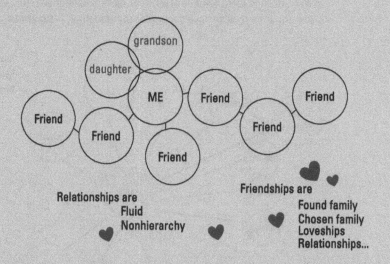

And then I put M., my daughter, and J., my grandson, in a central place — because their relationship is core — my blood family and connection.

I continue to look for lovers and possible new people in my life. But the first thing I think about is friendship. That's what's going to hold it together or build something more significant. I can always take a lover. But this is my more sustainable model. I put my energy into friends who are intimate with me, and I also have friends connected to other friends who are less close. It's like the friend bubble is the root of connection and possibility, even if I'm not sexual with my close friend or their friend.

I see these relationships as fluid and nonhierarchal and that wave can change at all times. —Ignacio

Spirituality-driven poly while keeping sex separate

Among some poly people, their spiritual life drives connection. In the case of A. and C. (see the nearby sidebar), connecting with others goes beyond the physical and sexual for them. In other words, they experience the physical and sexual as a spiritual and sacred ground.

POLYAMORY STORY

THE SPIRITUAL CONNECTION IS PRIMARY

We came across each other in global human rights work; both having left our home countries due to repression. When we met, we had an instant and intense moment of recognition, what we both consider a twin-flame or soul connection. After three years of being monogamous, we opened the relationship so that A. could be more open to flirtation and spiritual and sensual connection with other queer women; C. was in the midst of a gender transition and was interested in sex with other queer people, specifically trans-identified people. Now, after being open for more than three years, we both believe that our relationship is stronger than ever.

For A., her poly sexual life is a portal for drawing in spiritual energies and intimacy, though not necessarily sex. For C., their poly sexual connections are first and foremost about physical intimacy and experimentation that they don't want to bring into the primary relationship with A. (See their drawing.) C. notes: "I want to engage in BDSM role play with my lovers and express my gender in a certain way. It's experimental."

(continued)

(continued)

Our relationship functions as both a home and a bridge. We each feel like we can take more risks emotionally and in the world because of the home and trust we have built together. Very soon, A. is going to meet C.'s new lover and A. is very excited because of the joy the new relationship has brought to C. A says: "This is a new member of the family, I'm very sure of it."

We both are clear that we aren't necessarily going to connect sexually with each other's flirtations or partners. We want to keep our poly sex, flirtations, and hookups private and apart from the intimacy in the primary partnership. Our polycule looks like connected chains threaded through with representations of each other that are significant only to the two of us. This is emblematic of our connection to each other. —**C. and A.**

A rotating banquet of lovers

Some relationships have no escalator, even when these connections are long term. *No escalator* refers to the practice of not creating a formal commitment, even as you're increasingly intimate. You can see in the sidebar about Bishop that they experience their ho'tation as a foundation for their well-being. But they have no plan to form a primary partnership with any of these amazing, supportive lovers.

POLYAMORY STORY

TRUST THE HO'TATION

I found my sexual self in Chicago in my late 20s. I found this love for my body and my femme-ness there in a rotating group of f buddies and intimates (hence, *ho'tation*, as in "ho" plus rotation, see the following). In 2019, I moved to San Francisco and started a job. This was the first time I made a strictly career-based move, and I gave up a lot of my social life.

Planetz/Adobe Stock Photos

I had built these super intimate connections in Chicago with these amazing and beautiful people who I had sex with regularly and then left them all, cold turkey. So when I found myself in San Francisco — and being without them all, I was feeling like not whole — because I'm without this intimacy that has filled my life.

People didn't see my Black femme queerness as attractive in the way people did in my life in Chicago. I wasn't well-received, especially by the gay men there.

And I think people often devalue what I'm talking about, this kind of community of rotating intimates that hold you down — the very specific way you embody and express yourself — and hold you up. In the end, I moved back to Chicago because I missed my ho'tation. Trust the ho'tation! **—Bishop**

Poly while parenting — lovers as just desserts

For polyamorists who parent, creating poly forms that keep major family responsibilities separate from their sexy, explorative relationships can create vibrant possibility. Amelie's poly sexual life was organized for a period around hers and her lover's parenting demands (see the nearby sidebar). Chapter 14 provides more examples of creative poly forms while parenting.

MY LOVERS ARE LIKE MY BEAUTIFUL CAKE

My relationship with D. is an interesting example because we were lovers for six years or so, and she wanted a long-distance relationship at the time because she was raising her young kiddo. She felt like it had always been so intense to have lovers *be right there* in her space. It got in the way of building her business, of taking care of her son, of taking care of her dad, and of staying sober. She wasn't able to manage it. So, we had this one weekend a month structure that was so great for her.

I think it was also great for me, just having moved into my own house, and out of the nesting phase with my lover L. of many years. At that point, L. had a new partner T., who I was also close to, and they were pregnant. So, the summer before their new baby was born, I moved out of the big house we had all shared together and into my house, and we created more of a timeshare, kind of back and forth. The two kids I had had with L. were middle schoolers. And the poly model that I adopted then was this: I have the core unit and they live three doors down, and we parent together and it's very intimate and connected. And my lovers will be my beautiful cake I get to have here in my house when I don't have my kids (refer to the following).

Alexandr_DG/Adobe Stock Photos

And that model suited me really well for a long time, because it allowed me to do all of that relationship labor with L. and T., and love labor with the kids, and then have a weekend a month where I'm just with D. and focused on her and sexy time and not in my parenting space. So, my lover relationships became very separate from my parenting and familial space during this period. —**Amelie**

Waiting for the right time

In monogamous dating worlds, there's often a feeling of now or never. In poly dating life, an attraction and sexy connection can evolve, sometimes over decades as it did for LP (see the nearby sidebar).

POLYAMORY STORY

WE ARE TAKING THE SCENIC ROUTE

I met J. on Mother's Day weekend 2013 when I was living in New Orleans. He was in the Air Force at the time, stationed in Shreveport. I had a friend staying at my house, so we had no place to go, but we decided to just meet up and we'd go have drinks and hang out or whatever.

And we ended up going out and driving to uptown, New Orleans, right off one of the Mississippi River levees. And we parked and made out in the back of my car, and it was the hottest make-out session ever. Then we kept in touch over many years, and hooked up here and there, but he was basically monogamous and in the military and also not particularly verse around sex, which is a thing I really have to have.

We reconnected at a big event in 2022 — and the intensity was still there — and I said, "First of all I could probably give you monogamy for a period of time, but you know I'm a ho', right? Like, I've done all the things — sex parties, groups, whatever."

And he said: "No, I have too." And he started going down a list, which was really different from how he'd been in the past and I got really excited.

So, he said: "I I feel like I would need some time for us to get solid in how we communicate and establish a level of trust and everything else. And then after that I think I'm into however we construct it." And so that's been the game changer! At that point, I told him: "I didn't want to put you in a situation that wasn't okay for you, and I have to admit I've really put you through it! You just keep coming back."

There's something very attractive about that, isn't there? Despite all our differences and the geographic limitations, he's just been earnest and interested, and steady — over a decade (see the following)! **—LP**

(continued)

(continued)

homank76/Adobe Stock Photos

Finding the Right Form for You

I hope seeing all of these forms sparks your imagination. I'm never interested in creating boxes and categories around polyamory, but instead providing building blocks to construct the house or partnership or floating constellation that is going to sustain you. There's never only one way to love or be intimate or create family. In fact, there are endless options. You need only to tune into yourself and your own intimate, social, and familial desires to craft your unique version.

Thinking through your wants and needs

ACTIVITY

In this section, you can turn to your own wants and needs. The questions here can help you make this self-referential shift. Chapter 3 also provides a lot of activities that might be helpful while considering whether polyamory is right for you.

>> What poly forms are most interesting to you in this mix of stories?

>> What feels enlivening and resonates with some feelings or ideas about relationship forms that you may not have been letting yourself consider?

>> What isn't interesting at all — and runs counter to how you want to connect?

>> How might you start to explore some of these possibilities for yourself?

There's no rush here. As you can see from LP's story in the nearby sidebar, he has been living a very satisfying polyamorous life for many years, and now at 50, he's considering moving from an often solo poly life into creating a primary partnership within his poly constellation. He didn't try to force anything with J.; instead he has honored both his own needs, and J.'s limits as they have connected over the past ten years. So now, new possibilities are emerging. This isn't a once-in-a-lifetime, happily-ever-after-story. Instead, it's an over-a-lifetime, honesty-and-care-matter story. Indeed, over a lifetime, honesty and care build trust and possibility.

Defining and accepting your limits

Being clear about your limits is crucial as you're considering poly forms that are best for you. I hope reading about the ways people in this chapter think about love, sex, and family has helped you reflect on the ways you think about how you want to live your life and grow your connections. You can ask yourself defining questions about your possible poly constellation by referring back to these contributors' stories:

>> Are you interested in throuples? You might be like Robin and possibly be looking for two partners as a core unit. (Refer to the section "Throuples, triads, and threesomes, oh my" earlier in this chapter.)

>> Are you ambiguous poly? Like M'Bwende, you might accept that you have just a certain, immovable constitution — in their case, possessive — while being committed to supporting your partners' pursuit of their desires. (Check out the section "Ambiguous or ambivalent poly" earlier in this chapter.)

>> Does *compersion* (the feeling of expansive love and enjoyment you experience while observing your partner being loved or sexually attended to by another lover) come easily to you? Like Elizabeth, you might find yourself to be constitutionally polyamorous — looking expansively at lovers and sexy connections for you and your partners. (Flip to the section "Nesting partnership; friends are crucial" earlier in this chapter.)

>> Do you think you might be a relationship anarchist? If so, your friends might be as central to your well-being as your lovers, like Ignacio. (Refer to the section "Relationship anarchy and nonhierarchal poly" earlier in this chapter.)

TIP

Claiming and articulating what you want is a great way to define your limits, because going after what you truly desire is extremely clarifying. Inside all of these contributors' descriptions of what they have said *yes* to, and brought into their lives — there are very clear *nos*. For example:

» LP didn't create a more serious relationship with J. when J. needed monogamy and wasn't identified as versatile sexually, which was one of LP's core needs. (Refer to the section "Waiting for the right time" earlier in this chapter.)

» Bishop moved back to Chicago because they realized that despite a great job in San Francisco, the sex and hookup culture didn't support them. (See the section "A rotating banquet of lovers" earlier in this chapter.)

» Amelie didn't move in with D., or have D. move in with her, because that didn't work around their parenting and other familial commitments. (Refer to the section "Poly while parenting — lovers as just desserts" earlier in this chapter.)

I love the process of figuring out my no list by concentrating on my emphatic yeses! You can use this set of stories and the considerations these contributors sift through to start thinking about your big yeses and absolute nos. Look at Chapters 2 and 3 for help on listening to or discovering your yeses and to Chapter 6 for defining your limits and setting boundaries to further develop your ideas about your ideal poly constellation.

Dreaming Bigger in the World: Vibrant Sexual Intimacies Can Help

How you decide to live your sexual and intimate life is a pivotal decision that has far reaching impacts. Critics may tell you that your interest in polyamory is a superficial obsession with sex, a kind of immature selfishness, or a belief that *you can have your cake and eat it too* (to be honest, I've never really understood what that even means).

But anyone who lives and loves in poly community can tell you that taking risks to be who you are and love who you want can have cascading affects around dreaming bigger in your life — whether that pertains to building more intimate friendships, pursuing more meaningful work, or fighting for a better, more just world.

Bravery begets more bravery

The kind of freedom that polyamory promises can open up a lot of other joyful and experimental avenues in your life. Throwing off the constraints and expectations of authority figures and the ideas of the majority in your intimate life can grow your imagination and bravery across many other arenas. Many of the polyamory contributors in this book have made significant, singular contributions to their fields of work or activism — whether in the law, education, public health, or violence prevention.

The freedom that doesn't get talked about enough in polyamory is freeing yourself from the need to lock down your partner — or any lover. Being more gratified by your own openness and willingness to not know — what's next, or how your lover is going to be affected or changed by the love of another. That's not a love they promote in the movies. It's a grounded self-love, a security in yourself that says: I'm worthy and amazing even if I'm not one-hundred-percent everything in my partner's life.

Polyamory offers a giddy kind of freedom from that life of emotional and social surveillance of your partners, and not being enough.

When you commit to acting boldly in your intimate life, speaking up at that difficult work meeting isn't as difficult. It's not so far-fetched to strike out on that business idea you have always wanted to pursue or to get more serious about your art or another source of joy.

I often think people criticize polyamory because they're afraid or shut down. They sacrifice a lot to monogamy and seeing you break out of that system and become a more fully realized, joyful person brings up their grief. In this next activity, you can consider how pursuing polyamory might open up your vision of family and your larger world. Honoring your truths is the first step to finding and building the love and relationships you want. Answer these questions:

>> How might the fuller embodiment of your desires impact your vision, risk-taking, and energy in your work life? In your family?

>> Do you consciously or unconsciously draw on your erotic integrity/desire in your work in your community? Your desire for a better world?

>> How does the failure to embody your desire or the effort to avoid and suppress your desires impact your vision, risk-taking, energy, and dreams of family and community?

REMEMBER

As you complete your reflection, being unclear or unsure about how your desire is relevant to life in your family or community is okay. You may have been taught to keep any discussion or thoughts about your sexuality or your desire in a tiny box in a dark room, disconnected from your larger life.

TIP

These questions may start to help you consider whether the suppression of your erotic and sexual desire is impacting your vitality and vision for your life beyond the bedroom.

After you complete your journaling on these questions, take a breath and congratulate yourself. Review your work. Then write down one or two steps or actions you can take to move toward committing to pursuing your desires in an effort to better embody your values and grow your dreams.

POLYAMORY STORY

In the '90s, when we were fighting the AIDS crisis, I remember my aspiration was that I was in the center, and I had two lovers, and I had my work, right? During that period, my work was deeply my most intimate relationship because I felt like we were caught up in changing the world. And I remember that this kind of triad structure was sort of ideal. —Amelie

Some of my best friends are monogamous

I hate a hater, which is to say, having been targeted for pursuing various kinds of outside-of-the-box dreams and ways of being over the course of my life, the last thing I want to do here is give any grief to the happily monogamous people of the world.

Because I absolutely do have people in my life who have stayed the course with a single lover and partner for more than 20 to 40 years. These incredible relationships have been foundational to my friends' bountiful personal growth and the significant contributions they have made to their communities over the long and winding course of their lives together. These people were incredibly lucky to come upon a rare match early in their life, and with the abiding love of their partner, they've grown and morphed and built a deep, vibrant connection that has endured against the odds.

REMEMBER

The keyword for me here is — rare. *It's not monogamy per se that's problematic but enforced monogamy as the one and only way.* For, just as long-married folks find polyamory wildly improbable and even an offense to their deeply personal ways of relating, so do I experience monogamy.

Some people consider monogamy or polyamory foundational to their sexuality, as fundamental as their sexual orientation, or their gender. Other people have a more fluid view, living out polyamory and monogamy in different phases of their life.

What's important is that you tune into your own experience, so that you can pursue the intimacies and relationship forms that make sense to you — that will make you happy and bring you the lovers and the life that you deserve.

TIP

Some of my best friends are monogamous. And some of my other best friends are wildly, unapologetically polyamorous. There's room for everyone in the pursuit of their true selves, pleasure, and abundant joy.

POLYAMORY STORY

It's okay to step back and analyze. Are these boundaries and values that I've set for myself — do they still apply? Do I want those things moving forward? I think so often we just get stuck and say, *Oh, these are my values.* I may have had these values since I was 10 years old, but haven't done any reflection on whether they still work for me. And you know, it's really okay, especially after a breakup or a change, to take a moment and step back. Do these things still work for me? Or do I need to create something new? —**Rox**

Trying on Polyamory

You may be wondering what it means for you to try on polyamory right now. What obstacles are you facing? Do you need more knowledge? More conversation? Polyamorous role models? Poly social spaces? Do you need to talk to your partner? Or the person you're dating? Do you need to approach a crush? In this section, you can find ways to put yourself out there as a potential polyamorous date.

ACTIVITY

This activity that I call "I am, I want" is one of my favorite exercises in my book *Great Sex: Mapping Your Desire*, where you start to articulate who you are and what you want by creating a dating profile or personal ad. Just follow these steps:

1. **Take all the knowledge you're gaining about yourself in the reflection exercises you've done in this chapter.**

    Identify what stands out. Figure out what you're discovering about yourself that's different from any way you've described yourself before.

2. **Put all the information you have and cast it into I am and/or I want statements.**

    For example, "I am a highly romantic, aspiring relationship anarchist" or "I want to start hooking up with people, but I'm terrible at flirting."

    Be bold, specific, and clear.

3. **Read the statements aloud to yourself.**

    Gauge how they sound. Is this you? Could this be you?

4. **Use these statements to re-create and anchor a new dating profile.**

When I do this activity in a workshop, I have people walk around a room of 50-120 participants, stop randomly, and then turn to the person next to them and try out their new I am/want statements or profile. After having spent some time in the workshop discovering theirs and others' poly desires, it's exciting to get these ideas out of their heads and into the open air, into the room. The whole place gets noisy and giggly and filled with emphatic gestures — an eruption of joy and relief.

Testing the waters

You can test the waters of polyamory without committing or blowing up your life. Often, the first step is the hardest. You have to ask yourself how you can support yourself while you attempt to share these tender new understandings and desires.

One of the reasons the *I am*, *I want* exercise is so popular in my workshop is that participants are trying out or articulating these new parts of their identities with strangers. It's a very low-stakes environment and everyone is taking similar risks. Suddenly, people who have felt so alone and trapped in their heads with seemingly outlandish ideas about how they want to love or organize their sexual lives have many peers on their journey.

And they often find that some of the things they believed were outrageous or unattainable are perhaps middle-of-the-road compared to some of the wants shared by others. It's so much easier to dream and listen to yourself in a community of like-minded dreamers. If you're the only person in your life even considering polyamory, stretching out and imagining what your poly life might be can be very hard.

TIP

Just as hard is posting that profile when you aren't in a community that can receive it or you don't know where to look to find your people. Appendix B provides a lot of reading, podcasts, spaces, and places to connect to poly people and ideas and to find community. Here are just a few places to start:

>> Post a polyamorous-positive profile on a dating app. Feeld is a great app for experimenting and flirting with poly candidates. Many more polyamorous people are on the old-school dating apps as well.

>> Invite two to three close friends over and brainstorm how to get you out there into poly circulation. Maybe someone could throw a coming out brunch and invite polycurious and poly-interested people.

>> Go to a sex-positive conference, retreat, or sex/hookup gathering. Bring a supportive pal if you're nervous. Go to workshops and learn about things. Go to the parties and look at all your amazing options.

>> Try a local poly brunch or happy hour. Have your *I am, I want* ideas together. Try sharing them. Flirt.

>> Find an online group or conversation to join. Look for like-minded or hot participants. Share your new self-discoveries and see what happens.

The keyword in all of this is try. Another would be experiment. Another: flirt! And finally — enjoy yourself! Get out there! A world of poly fun awaits.

SET YOURSELF FREE

For a few years, I ran a leadership center at a small Midwest college. The students were absolutely wonderful and hailed from all over the world. Many of them, though, had been raised in Michigan where abstinence-only sex education had been a barrier to learning about sexuality and experimenting with pleasure. When I gave my Desire Mapping workshops there, students often expressed frustration about the campus sex culture, which was driven by keg parties hosted off-campus by seniors.

This created some serious drawbacks for everyone. A lot of underage drinkers attended these parties, which meant they were vulnerable to predators because they couldn't call for help should anyone assault or harass them, because their illicit drinking would jeopardize their academic standing. It also meant that most sexual exploration was happening while people were drunk, so consent conversations were often blurry, and even when consent was freely given, many people's capacity to be present and attentive as lovers was compromised. Across all ages and gender, students reported suffering under these conditions, wanting something different.

I said: "If you hate your sex culture, why not change it?"

At first, people couldn't even imagine what that might mean. The campus sex culture had always been this way. But after a series of workshops, a group of senior women took their responses to the *I am, I want* exercise (see the section "Testing the waters" earlier in this chapter) among others, and posted them in the foyer of their house. They sent out invitations for make-out and hookup parties and outlined practices of consent and engagement on the invites. They created ground rules around drinking. When they came to me with the idea, they thought it likely that no one would respond. I assured them they were underestimating the power of their creative intervention. I said: "Going after what you really want is sexy." And I was right.

Ask yourself this important question: Are you living in a terrible sex culture? If so, leave it. Change it. Throw a party. Go find more like-minded people. Discover and speak your truth. Create the connections you actually want, that will sustain you. Set yourself free.

2

Building Relational Skills for Polyamory

Assess your communication and attachment styles and find out how to use boundaries to level up for the challenge of having multiple lovers.

Note your strengths and vulnerabilities as a communicator and find new tools for dealing with fight, flight, freeze, or fawn reactions to emotionally taxing situations.

Understand your history of abandonment and harm and consider how trauma might be impacting your ability to solve conflicts or be present with your partners.

Build your communication toolbox and appreciate who and where you are at as a communicator.

IN THIS CHAPTER

» Discovering your
communication style

» Understanding how your style
impacts your relationships

» Figuring out your strengths as a
communicator and building on them

Chapter 5

Understanding the Importance of Communication

Successful polyamorous communicators sit atop a three-legged stool of solid relational skills. These are

» **Communication-style knowledge:** Introversion/extroversion, fight-or-flight reactivity, neurodivergence/neurotypicality — understanding these and other key facets of your relational makeup strengthens your ability to communicate. This chapter focuses on communication styles.

» **Sustainable boundaries:** Growing your capacity to set and sustain boundaries helps you level up as a communicator. (I spend more time on this in Chapter 6.)

» **Attachment awareness:** Thinking about your attachment history and how it affects your ability to trust is a crucial awareness to bring to your communication practices in your poly life. (You can get much more information about attachment and trust in Chapter 7.)

Drawing on your strengths and being able to identify which leg of your stool might be compromised is a key skill for polyamorous communicators. You can imagine that if one leg of the stool is underdeveloped, your balance is altered, and your communication might be off kilter. For example, if you have become caught up in your attachment issues and are responding to a present-day difficulty with the pain and intensity attached to a childhood wound, you can fall off the stool altogether.

How do the three legs of your communication stool come together to support you? Where are its strengths and weaknesses? What do you bring to the table as a communicator that will help your poly constellation succeed when getting through conflicts or crises? In this chapter, you can take your inventory as a communicator and consider what's in the way of connecting with and supporting your partners.

Identifying Your Communication Style

The following sections describe the kind of skills you need to develop to enjoy your poly life.

Differentiating between introversion and extroversion

An important thing to note in terms of communication styles is the introversion/extroversion mix in your partnerships or polycule. Introverts and extroverts approach social and intimate interactions differently, and they also need different kinds of support to stay present and enjoy themselves. Appreciating rather than denying or judging these differences is a strong step toward connecting with your partners.

REMEMBER

The simplest way to identify an introvert or extrovert is not to assess how you operate at a party — some introverts are wildly chatty among the people they love best, for example — but rather how you refuel and recoup. Consider the following:

>> Introverts thrive and revive on alone time and the power to define their space. Introverts tend to need a *lot* of space and time alone to take in sensitive information, process its meaning, and respond.

>> Extroverts thrive and revive on feedback, engagement, and the energy of others. Extroverts tend to solve problems out loud, in the moment, through active conversation and engagement.

Taking alone time to reflect upon a high-conflict relational problem makes no sense at all to an extrovert, whereas it may feel like the only way to survive for an introvert.

REMEMBER

THE MEYERS-BRIGGS INVENTORY AND THE WORKPLACE

Mother-daughter team Katherine Cook Briggs and Isabel Meyers created the world's most popular sorter of introverts and extroverts in the 1950s, known as the Myers-Briggs Type Indicator or MBTI. These two trained psychologists were motivated by Meyers's experience in World War II, where she often saw the impacts of mismatched personality types on teams that were charged with extremely sensitive war projects. Together, Meyers and Briggs hoped to shine a light on the very different ways that workers experience each other and the tasks at hand. They also aimed to de-pathologize analyses of the personality spectrum that often pit one communication type against each other, as in: extroverts, good; introverts, bad.

A lot of workplaces have come to understand the power of using the MBTI to identify styles of engagement to improve the productivity of their teams. I remember one work retreat when introverts were encouraged to say everything they'd ever wanted to say to the extroverts and vice versa. For example, they said something like this:

- **Introverts:** "Stop acting like I have no social skills. I'm choosing not to talk — I'm not a child."

- **Extroverts:** "Appreciate me for my engaging conversational skills at all of these demanding public events. And stop acting like I'm ruining your day when I'm just happy to talk to you."

The airing of these grievances surprised everyone on either side of the introversion/extroversion spectrum. Who knew we were carrying such resentment? The session helped us recalibrate and appreciate ways we'd been hard on our colleagues. This learning has been very useful to me as I've watched introverts and extroverts struggle with each other in poly relationships.

Eyeing the MBTI and how you can use it

Today, managers use the MBTI inventory to assess the introversion/extroversion mix in their teams as well as other traits such as sensing/intuiting, feeling/thinking, and judging/perceiving.

Inventories like the MBTI and others like the Enneagram or DiSC can help you see that your ways of communicating might not be well-matched to the ways your lovers or partners operate. In some cases, this information can help you let go of resentments, building greater appreciation for your differences as you develop solid communication practices.

If you've taken the MBTI, you may already have a sense of your profile and its possible meanings for you as a poly communicator. If you haven't or need a refresher, Figure 5-1 looks at the 16 different MBTI typologies, which can give you a snapshot of who you are and how you move in the world:

For many years, various experts suggested that MBTI results were a definitive and unchanging assessment of character, but then people who took the inventory over time saw their results shift as they aged. In my case, I found that when I took the inventories at work, I scored differently from when I took them in relationship contexts. I'm an ENTP (the Debater) or ENTJ (the Commander) at work and an INFP (the Mediator) or ENFP (the Campaigner) at home. This makes so much sense to me — the parts of my personality that take over at work and at home are suited to the tasks at hand. Wrangling my coworkers versus wrangling my lovers and children brings very different strengths of mine to the fore.

If you think that your persona or engagement strategies change between work and home, answer the MBTI questions thinking about how you operate in your poly family rather than how you solve problems at work (look online to take the MBTI). Your home-based inventory might give you insights into poly family issues that recur or seem to be unresolvable points of conflict.

REMEMBER

The inventory you use doesn't matter; the practice of coming together as a poly family and working to identify different ways of filtering experience that might impact communication and solving conflicts is the goal.

Communicating while neurodivergent

Over the past ten years, many more people who identify as neurodivergent have become visible in the larger culture and shared their stories about how they experience the world. Accordingly, awareness about neurodivergent and neurotypical differences in communication styles has increased greatly, improving people's abilities to collaborate and hear each other while processing inputs and relating to the world very differently. This kind of understanding can be especially helpful in communication loops involving multiple lovers or partners.

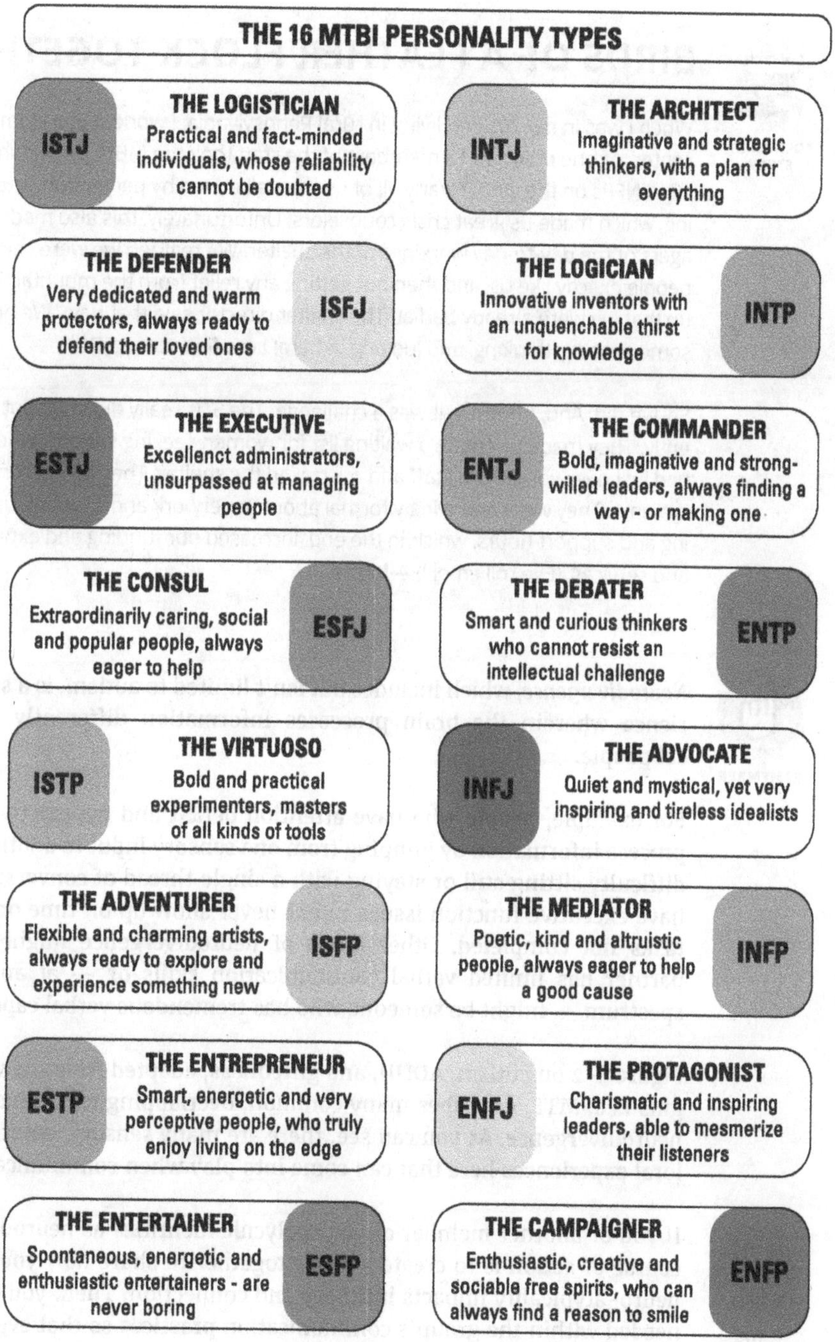

THE 16 MTBI PERSONALITY TYPES

THE LOGISTICIAN
ISTJ
Practical and fact-minded individuals, whose reliability cannot be doubted

THE ARCHITECT
INTJ
Imaginative and strategic thinkers, with a plan for everything

THE DEFENDER
ISFJ
Very dedicated and warm protectors, always ready to defend their loved ones

THE LOGICIAN
INTP
Innovative inventors with an unquenchable thirst for knowledge

THE EXECUTIVE
ESTJ
Excellenct administrators, unsurpassed at managing people

THE COMMANDER
ENTJ
Bold, imaginative and strong-willed leaders, always finding a way - or making one

THE CONSUL
ESFJ
Extraordinarily caring, social and popular people, always eager to help

THE DEBATER
ENTP
Smart and curious thinkers who cannot resist an intellectual challenge

THE VIRTUOSO
ISTP
Bold and practical experimenters, masters of all kinds of tools

THE ADVOCATE
INFJ
Quiet and mystical, yet very inspiring and tireless idealists

THE ADVENTURER
ISFP
Flexible and charming artists, always ready to explore and experience something new

THE MEDIATOR
INFP
Poetic, kind and altruistic people, always eager to help a good cause

THE ENTREPRENEUR
ESTP
Smart, energetic and very perceptive people, who truly enjoy living on the edge

THE PROTAGONIST
ENFJ
Charismatic and inspiring leaders, able to mesmerize their listeners

THE ENTERTAINER
ESFP
Spontaneous, energetic and enthusiastic entertainers - are never boring

THE CAMPAIGNER
ENFP
Enthusiastic, creative and sociable free spirits, who can always find a reason to smile

FIGURE 5-1: The 16 MBTI types.

badproject/Adobe Stock Photos

BIRDS OF A FEATHER FLOCK TOGETHER

When I was in my 20s and living in rural Pennsylvania, I worked at a women's crisis center. At one point, all 13 members of the staff took the MBTI. To our shock, we had 12 I/ENFPs on the staff. Nearly all of us were all driven by perception, intuition, and feeling, which made us great crisis counselors. Unfortunately, this also made us poor managers of the day-to-day workings of the shelter. We realized we were constantly hiring people exactly like us, and then not getting any relief from the mountains of tasks piling up that we were already bad at. The shelter director said that day: "We need to get some sensing, thinking, and judging in here! Let's find some STJs!"

So, we did. And, honestly, it was a challenge. The STJs really did go about things differently. They made us create a waiting list for women seeking support when before, we had just overworked the staff and overtaxed the shelter. They talked constantly about systems. They were annoyingly formal about paperwork and counting up our counseling and support hours, which in the end, increased our funding and expanded staff and services. (Eye roll emoji!) —**Jaime**

Neurodivergence, which includes but isn't limited to autism, is a spectrum of experience wherein the brain processes information differently from neurotypical people.

For example, people who have attention deficit and hyperactivity (ADHD) often process information by jumping from one sensory input to another; they can have difficulty sitting still or staying with a single thread of conversation. People who have executive function issues might never show up on time or arrive with their tasks not completed. Other kinds of neurodivergence might mean that your partner has limited verbal communication skills or — at another end of the spectrum — might be someone who has tremendous verbal capacity.

Figure 5-2 on autism, ADHD, and giftedness, adapted from the work of Katy Higgins Lee, MTF, describes many common, overlapping experiences of people with neurodivergence. As you can see, there are many sensory, emotional, and behavioral experiences here that can come into play when communicating.

If you or another member of your polycule identifies as neurodivergent, the best course of action is to create a space together to share how your or their specific neuro-atypicality impacts intimacy and connection. Then, you can decide what's needed within the group's communication practices so that everyone feels heard and supported. In the absence of this kind of sharing, you're setting yourself up for communication miscues and blunders.

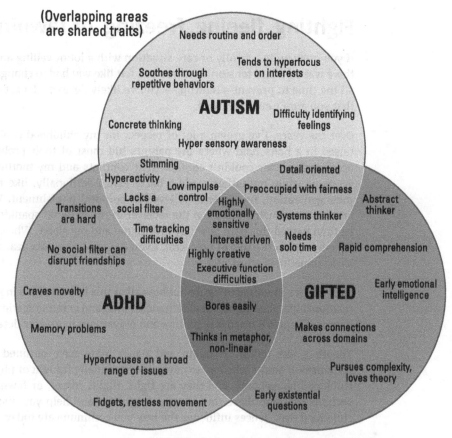

(Overlapping areas are shared traits)

AUTISM
- Needs routine and order
- Tends to hyperfocus on interests
- Soothes through repetitive behaviors
- Difficulty identifying feelings
- Concrete thinking
- Hyper sensory awareness

ADHD
- Stimming
- Hyperactivity
- Lacks a social filter
- Low impulse control
- Transitions are hard
- Time tracking difficulties
- No social filter can disrupt friendships
- Craves novelty
- Memory problems
- Hyperfocuses on a broad range of issues
- Fidgets, restless movement

GIFTED
- Detail oriented
- Preoccupied with fairness
- Abstract thinker
- Systems thinker
- Needs solo time
- Rapid comprehension
- Early emotional intelligence
- Makes connections across domains
- Pursues complexity, loves theory
- Early existential questions

(center overlaps)
- Highly emotionally sensitive
- Interest driven
- Highly creative
- Executive function difficulties
- Bores easily
- Thinks in metaphor, non-linear

FIGURE 5-2: Autism, ADHD, and giftedness Venn diagram.

Kathryn H. Lee / https://www.katyhigginslee.com/giftedness-autism-adhd-venn-diagram-pdf-free-download

For example, a neurotypical partner may interpret an autistic partner's lack of eye contact during an intimate discussion as indifference. Or a neurotypical partner may receive a neurodivergent partner's excitement about a particular topic, which includes lengthy description and a cascading series of facts, as overwhelming or insensitive.

REMEMBER

You don't know what you don't know. Making assumptions about the meanings behind a partner's communication practices is never a better course of action than hearing directly from them about their experiences.

TIP

If a partner's communication style seems disconnected or at odds with yours, speak up. Investigate. Your best results as a communicator come when you put yourself in a position to share, learn, and grow.

Fighting, fleeing, freezing, or fawning

If you grew up in a family or care situation with a lot of yelling and arguing, or if there was constant tension — where you felt like you had to change your behavior all the time to prevent a blowup — you've likely developed a set of coping skills that you aren't even aware of.

Over the years, I've grown a lot of respect for my childhood coping skills. I was raised in a household where my parents hid most of their problems, and then occasionally, they couldn't contain their conflicts and my mother would yell at everyone while my father made a hasty exit. Additionally, like many people of their generation, my parents believed in corporal punishment. While my older brother was much more often the receiver of my parents' spankings and hitting, he then passed this pain down by hitting me and my sister. When this happened, I often took on the role of protector. Even though he was six years older, I'd fight back, sometimes physically.

So, when it came time to figure out how all of this impacted me in my present-day relationships, theories about childhood trauma and communication helped me see myself (Chapter 8 discusses trauma and polyamory in greater detail.)

Theorists like Judith Hermann and Gabor Maté have outlined the four basic responses of adults who had to navigate emotionally fraught or physically abusive childhood households, and they are fight, flight, freeze, or fawn. The following sections examine these four trauma responses and help you discover how your childhood experiences influence the way you communicate today.

Assessing what the four Fs mean

Finding out which mode of communication (or noncommunication) you slip into when conflict arises is important, so you can get support from your partners and take care of yourself. Check out the following:

>> **Fight:** When the going gets tough, you come back verbally swinging. Your partners say they never win an argument with you. Once activated, you're going to defend yourself to your last breath.

>> **Flight:** As the voices rise in the room, you slowly disappear. By the time conflict is high, you've probably got your hat and coat on and are out the door.

>> **Freeze:** As the argument unfolds, you're here, but not here. Maybe you're on the ceiling watching a heated volley of complaints between your partners. What's being said? Who knows. You're frozen.

>> **Fawn:** You might tell jokes when emotions start to heat up, trying to distract one partner from their pain, while tamping down another's fury. Or maybe you're telling everyone how wonderful they are and that everything is going to be okay because they're just perfect. Everything is fine, just fine.

THE FIGHTER IN ME WAS SCARING MY KIDS

Although I had read all kinds of trauma theory, when I started family therapy with my co-parent and our two teenagers, I was in for the shock of my life. As we went around the circle and each identified our communication style in times of conflict, all three of them said freeze or flight and I was the only fighter — and by that I mean vociferous, argumentative, and loud. Suddenly, the unproductive ways that our family arguments played out became crystal clear to me.

And for the first time, I could see that the heroic fighter who had helped protect my sister in my childhood was making it hard for my parenting partner to stay engaged — and much worse — was actually scaring and hurting my kids.

Mind blown. After I recovered from my deep regret and shame, I was able over many months to sincerely apologize and to repair communication avenues with everyone in the unit. And in our family, the definition of apology means: *I'm not going to do this anymore.* And I don't. The freezers and fleers in my family unit do much better when I lower my voice, make eye contact, and give them space for their feelings rather than make rapid-fire, strenuous arguments or yell.

Throughout this really challenging therapeutic process I learned that deep healing is possible. Behavior change is possible. But nothing is possible if you can't see yourself or if you refuse to take hold of your story. **—Jaime**

WARNING

Not being able to communicate in the moment when emotions run high or when trust has been breached is okay. However, sabotaging or abandoning the process altogether isn't okay.

REMEMBER

Being a good communicator means knowing how to inform your partners about what's happening in your body, brain, and heart. Then, you can take a break if you need to, and eventually move from traumatic activation due to childhood events, back into the present, where you can face whatever issue has arisen, as a full-grown adult.

Discovering the ways you communicate

ACTIVITY

Here are a few key reflection questions when you're ready to discover how your childhood communication story is impacting your present-day communication with your partners:

>> On a scale of 1 to 5, with 5 being very often, how often did you experience conflict in your family of origin or childhood household?

>> How was conflict resolved?

>> How did you react to conflict in your family? What was your role during family arguments or violence?

>> Did anyone else take care of you when you were scared or upset? How?

>> How did you take care of yourself when you were scared or upset?

>> When you reflect on these answers, do you see yourself as a person who fights, flees, freezes, or fawns?

That's a lot to take in. Breathe. This activity might be helpful to do with partners. Like me, you can get a picture of yourself within the mix of communicators in your unit. Consider whether you need a trained professional to help sort through these questions. Looking at how old hurts are still driving how you operate today with people you love may be difficult.

REMEMBER

The good news is that nothing is set in stone. As long as you're open to the truth of your story, seek support to heal and make changes, and then take responsibility for yourself and the impact of your behavior — you can grow. And all of you can grow together.

Dealing with mental health challenges

For many people, their ancestors and parents survived poverty, violence, and displacement, which has had a significant impact on mental health over generations. Recent advances in the field of *epigenetics* demonstrate that the impacts of intergenerational trauma and mental illness are literally encoded in a person's genes.

And that doesn't even account for people's day-to-day experiences.

Many people are direct survivors of multiple systems of violence, which has had a massive impact on their mental health. The mental health advocacy organization National Alliance on Mental Illness (NAMI) estimates that 20 percent or 1 in 5 people in the United States experience some kind of mental illness every year.

If you're part of that 20 percent, the important thing to remember is that people with significant mental illness fall in love and make family of all kinds, every day, just like everyone else.

Some mental illnesses present particular hardships around relationships — borderline personality comes to mind as does narcissistic personality. In both cases, people struggling with these conditions may have a hard time stepping outside of themselves and their intense needs for security. People suffering from dissociative disorders and addictions have a difficult time showing up and being consistent; people with complex post-traumatic stress disorder (PTSD; see Chapter 8) struggle with unpredictable reactions when they're intimate or vulnerable. The list goes on.

As a person who has been diagnosed with mental illness and who also has managed to sustain an expansive, loving poly life over decades, all I can say is this: If you too are part of the 1 in 5, you deserve all the love in the world.

TIP

If you have significant mental illness, you may need a lot of support and a serious commitment to your health and recovery to enjoy polyamory.

But nothing thrills your wronged and deprived ancestors like your healing and success. *Go get it.* See the pod mapping discussion in Chapter 11 to think about and how to build the support system you need. And go get that love!

Developing Communication Pathways That Work for Everyone

Communication practices that work for everyone involve dealing with the partners you actually have, not the ones you imagine. And by that I mean, here are your beloveds! You've chosen them! They've chosen you! This is miraculous and wonderful and is also bound to come with communication challenges. Embrace them. Embrace your different communication styles and commit to improving your own communication skills as best you can. In this section, you can think about relatively enjoyable options for assessing your polycule's relational capacities. Then, you can start to craft communication pathways that work.

Having fun with assessment tools

You can use personality inventories lightheartedly to think about your communication needs, strengths, and challenges. In South Korea, the MBTI has become so widely used in workplace settings and casual conversation that the rapper Tablo recently released a song with the lyric: "My MBTI is IDGAF" (consult your favorite search engine if you need help).

Take what's useful in terms of what assessment tools reveal to you. Ask the following types of questions:

» How does communication go awry in your poly constellation?

» What's working?

>> Where does everyone get stuck?

>> How does this tool help you understand these challenges and point a way toward taking better care of each other?

Appreciating and adjusting for differences

The poet Audre Lorde has said that it's not differences that divide people, but the pretense that these differences don't exist. Take this perspective to heart as you analyze communication problems in your polycule. Answer these questions to figure out your communication roadblocks:

>> Are you taxing the introverts by scheduling long face-to-face conversations and demanding immediate answers?

>> Are you denying your neurodivergence and masking your true ways of being so that you can fit in with neurotypicals?

>> Are you a freezer and having trouble remembering the substance of important conversations, leaving everyone to think you aren't listening?

>> As a person managing PTSD, do you panic when voices get raised during a disagreement and tend to either escalate or abandon the conflict?

>> Are you judging your polycule members rather than being curious about their communication challenges and needs?

>> Are you fully aware of your own communication strengths and weaknesses so that you can get to the root of what's not working for you?

When I think about myself as a communicator in my polycule, one of my biggest assets is that I've done a lot of mental health recovery work, so I know a lot about my strengths and challenges:

Here are my strengths:

>> I'm an E/INFP, so I'm very chatty and emotive with the people I'm closest to, but I also need a lot of alone time.

>> I'm great at staying connected, even when a conversation covers painful or difficult topics.

>> Having had a lot of success with my polycule, I'm optimistic when there are serious arguments or breaches.

>> I can see my part in problems. I know how to apologize (see Chapter 13 for how to make a great apology).

>> I'm good at asking for help when I get stuck in a bad communication loop.

And here are my challenges:

>> My leftover burden from childhood is that I'm a fighter if I get activated (see Chapter 7), so when I feel my blood pressure start to rise and my heartbeat accelerate, my self-care step is to ask for a time-out.

>> People find it difficult to win an argument with me. I'm stubborn. I don't let go of my point easily, so to compensate for this, I try to stop a lot during disagreements. I try to listen better and breathe more. I tell myself: "I'd rather solve this problem than be right."

>> A part of me doesn't believe this at all. But saying it to myself always improves the outcome of the discussion, even if only by a little bit.

TIP

Your goal here is to make your own self-assessment so you can illuminate differences rather than deny them, uncover the roots of conflict rather than bury them, and celebrate the great mix of communication strengths and challenges your polycule is holding rather than disdain them. That's the dynamic, challenging road you're on.

Relying on communication forms that work best for each person

Considering what forms of communication work best for you and your partners is essential. Everybody in a poly constellation will have their favorites. For example, I text all day long with mine, but these relationships are all at least ten years old. My beloveds get me: They can hear my voice and read my intentions on text in a way that people I'm just meeting can't.

Here's a simple communication ladder to support good communication:

REMEMBER

WARNING

>> **Text:** It's generally best for logistics and keeping up with each other in daily ways; it's for sweet, caring, connective shorthand.

Polycules love a group chat/text to check in and share parts of the day with each other. Just be sure you don't use it to solve problems.

Working out mistakes, breaches of trust, or otherwise highly sensitive subjects by text is the worst. Don't do it.

>> **Phone:** If you've made a mistake, missed a commitment, or had a glitch, get on the phone so your person can hear your voice and intention and the sincerity of your apology. Phone is also great for lively longer exchanges that text just can't cover or to offer comfort to a partner who is struggling.

>> **Video:** If you've had a breach of trust, you need to show your face. You need your partner to see the impact of their behavior on you or vice versa. You need to read body language and tone. You need to connect closely to begin a process of repair.

Alternatively, if you have something wonderful to share or something vulnerable and amazing, make a video call. Share the amazingness.

>> **Face-to-face:** All the really big poly conversations should be in person. Do you need to change some of your bottom-line agreements? Do you want to start having deeper relationships outside your primary partnership? Neither text nor phone work for this level of discussion. If you live hundreds or thousands of miles apart, video can work, but only when getting together isn't possible.

When I mess up with my polycule, face-to-face conversation is always my best option. If that's physically impossible, a video call is a must. A simple way to think about which one to use: The higher the emotional content of a conversation, the closer you need to be.

Along with communication vehicles, think carefully about the best forms for engaging with your partners. A lot of polycules have a weekly business, logistics, or calendaring meeting (refer to Chapter 9.)

WARNING

Try not to have your poly relationship meetings stir up the dread of a Monday morning staff meeting.

POLYAMORY STORY

I think there's a tendency to overprocess and over discuss rules, parameters, and feelings about the whole thing. I think it's important to do all of that as much as is necessary, but also not to do more of it than the involved parties find to be necessary. I think sometimes people feel like that's the only way and it's an obligation, and I don't necessarily think that's the right operating assumption for everyone. —Jack

Eyeing fun ways to communicate

Think about ways to remind yourself that communication and meetings are all about being in service to a vibrant, sexy relationship. Here are some suggestions:

>> Meet while you have your favorite takeout delivered.

>> Have meet-ups in significant locations that are relationship hallmarks.

>> Travel to fun retreat settings for your annual relationship agreement tune-up (see relationship agreement-making in Chapter 9).

>> Create meeting forms that are maximally accessible to your poly constellation members. Access is love.

>> Use art projects to solve relational challenges. Bring out the colored markers and make messy art projects out of various inventories.

>> Build big collective maps out of your inventories or explorations; create collective poems from what you've learned about your polycule.

>> Plan to watch your favorite movie, read your favorite story, or have a sexy adventure afterward!

Figuring out big stuff in poly world should always include time to celebrate each other and your audacity.

POLYAMORY STORY

HOLD REGULAR CHECK-INS WITH YOUR PARTNER(S)

Having scheduled or at least frequent check-in conversations about how the relationship is going can be a really helpful way to ensure that everyone feels they have the space to share, be heard, and gain understanding.

Nobody is a mind-reader. In the romantic comedies the love interest frequently engages in some grand romantic gesture that totally surprises the protagonist and turns out to have been the perfect thing. But in real life, it doesn't work that way. If you don't tell the people in your life that it's important to you to have a big party for your birthday, they may not know it matters. If you like grand romantic gestures, tell your partners! If you want to try a new sexual position or practice, you have to tell them. If something doesn't feel good — physically or emotionally — you need to communicate — and not just with moans or other body language! **—Robin**

IN THIS CHAPTER

» Exploring the basics about
boundaries

» Considering what kind of boundaries
you need in poly relationships

» Distinguishing healthy boundaries
from the need to control
your partners

» Assessing and adjusting boundaries
along the way

Chapter **6**

Setting and Sustaining Healthy Boundaries

Boundary-setting is one of those terms that has become so overused it can become meaningless. What *is* a boundary? How do you set and sustain them? This chapter examines the basics about creating boundaries that work for you in your polyamorous relationships. Here, you can find a lot of concrete tools and ideas about how this concept fits into polyamorous world-making.

Discovering the Importance of Boundaries

Boundary-setting basics all revolve around tuning into yourself and deciding what's workable for you as you create relationships with multiple lovers. Setting boundaries entails deciding what your core values are *personally* and — as you create agreements with your lovers — *collectively*.

When thinking about your core values, I suggest you read Chapters 2 and 9. These chapters have activities that can help you get centered on fundamental beliefs and desires that are driving your interest in polyamory.

In this section I define boundaries and also give you some activities to start to think about how to define and sustain limits in your poly relationships.

Eyeing boundaries: What they really are

Somatic practitioner Prentis Hemphill has said probably the most famous and apt quote about boundaries ever: "Boundaries are the distance at which I can love you and me simultaneously."

This idea is so simple and yet revolutionary. Embedded in it is the possibility that every person in your life is potentially loveable and that your relationship to everyone in your world of friends and lovers would be more functional, caring, and enjoyable, if you could just figure out the appropriate distance at which to keep them.

REMEMBER

In other words, *boundaries* are something you create and set for yourself, not someone else. By identifying and positioning your limits and needs in conversation with your polyamorous partners, you can literally define yourself to your partners. Your limits and needs speak to your values and desires. They tell your potential lovers how you want to move in your intimate life and in the world. If you've chosen your partners well, they'll be excited to learn about your boundaries and want to listen deeply so they can understand and respect them.

You may have people you talk to every day, even several times a day — the distance you need to thoroughly enjoy them is nearly zero. Some people you struggle with could be a lot more enjoyable if you stopped engaging with them so often, especially on topics that may draw you into arguments. Others could be more fun to be with if you only saw them in certain contexts and put limits on the amount of time you spent together. Others still would be easier to love and hold in high regard if you stopped seeing them at all.

You may be reluctant to create and sustain boundaries like these because you're afraid of people's reactions. You may let boundaries lapse that actually improve your relationships or make being with certain friends or family members more enlivening because you don't want to seem mean or demanding. That's often the biggest obstacle to sustaining boundaries that clearly work — the fear of someone telling you that you aren't being nice.

Tuning into yourself versus people-pleasing

People-pleasing is a common adaptive behavior among people who were exposed to a lot of chaos or shaming in their childhoods (refer to Chapter 7 for more details). In this section, you can think about how people-pleasing behaviors may prevent you from listening to yourself — about your true experiences of your loved ones and your needs in relationships.

If you aspire to vibrant, loving poly relationships that minimize drama, being able to identify your core needs in set boundaries is imperative.

ACTIVITY

In order to move away from people-pleasing and begin to get centered in your values and your wants, find a private space to do this freewriting session. Freewriting means you're writing just for you. You need never share it with anyone else. There's no editing in a freewriting session. You write whatever comes up, in a stream of consciousness. Let yourself stretch out into thinking about your hypothetical poly life and tune into your feelings:

>> Think through what you really want to do — what you want the flow of polyamory life to be like

>> Think through what you reasonably can and can't do

>> Think through what you reasonably can and can't manage — emotionally, physically, socially, and sexually

Brainstorm away. Write, write, write. Put on your favorite playlist if that helps. Draw pictures or diagrams. Think about the limits you'll need to set to hold this vision in place — to take care of you so that you can take care of your partners.

TIP

If your boundaries are working, you're not struggling.

If you've given too much of yourself away when making polyamorous agreements — capitulated to a partner's needs over your own — you're likely going to have a lot of internal turmoil and pain.

WARNING

If you've been too rigid — given in to your fears by perhaps letting your childhood abandonment wounds drive your boundary-setting (see Chapter 7 on attachment) —you're going to be living in a state of hypervigilance and surveillance.

POLYAMORY STORY

A big issue in one of my nested relationships was that my anchor/nesting partner didn't want to have boundaries because they didn't want to hold me back from dating or from my happiness. I was trying to get away from mind reading and so I trusted his yes. But then there would be big meltdowns where he was very hurt that I did what he said was okay with him. I have to say — this often comes up in my relationships. If boundary confusion leads to hurt feelings, I like to come back to it a couple of times to keep processing it out. —**Sonja**

The *Primacy of Nice* is a sprawling territory where people-pleasers live. It affects all of us who have survived childhoods where rules changed arbitrarily and we were often fearful, and scrambling for our footing. It's a construct especially foisted on women and *femmes* (I use women and femmes together because many femme-identified people don't necessarily identify as women, but women and femmes are often targeted by similar prejudices.) When women set limits about how available they are for any kind of interaction, they often find themselves on a conceptual tightrope that says: defining this interaction isn't ladylike. It's ball-busting. It's bossy. And on the flip side — failing to define a boundary and becoming exhausted and overextended renders you unattractive. You're not game. You're no fun at all.

BIPOC people suffer a parallel tightrope in the Primacy of Nice. Defining your availability gets interpreted as anger. Asserting limits around conversation is branded as not being open to differences. The demands of making everyone else comfortable are constant and drain attention away from what you actually need.

Becoming successful at polyamory requires throwing off the Primacy of Nice — the imperative to deny what your needs are in service of others, or in service of everyone getting along.

REMEMBER

Stretching your boundaries — to decide to try things outside of your comfort zone — is okay. Just don't lie to yourself about it. Own that you're stretching and if it gets hard, reach out to your loved ones for support.

Understanding what setting and keeping boundaries mean

Setting and sustaining boundaries means coming to fully understand and own your limits, and then sharing these limits with partners who are grateful that you've chosen them to confide in. I discuss the how-to of boundary-setting in the section "Defining your limits when setting your boundaries" later in this chapter.

To give you some ideas about how to consider what boundaries might be useful to you, here are some examples of good boundaries in my life:

>> I'm not on my ex's social media.

>> My son and I don't discuss politics.

>> My cousin and I don't talk about her brother.

>> A childhood friend and I rarely talk about his partner.

All these boundaries help me love my ex, my son, my sister, and my childhood friend better. It keeps us out of territories that are fraught and frankly none of my business. The idea that if we love each other, we are in each other's business is about enmeshment (see the nearby sidebar) and about needing validation from or controlling the other person, not love.

Here's how I think about these boundaries and why I'm so pleased I've been able to articulate and sustain them:

>> When my ex and I broke up as lovers, we were very enmeshed. We were raising kids together, and we had hurt each other. We had a lot of anger, and so we mutually agreed to block each other on all social media. It was a sanity-saving step. It helped me stop thinking about them; it helped me define my own social and emotional life separate from them. Over time, this boundary helped us become better co-parents and caring friends.

>> My son and I have wildly different political views. He often tries to engage me about this because I'm his mom, and he's in his early 20s and growing into adulthood. But there's no good outcome for these discussions. He knows where I stand, and it's time for him to create a life separate from me and the way I think about things, without my approval.

>> My close cousin has a brother who has been hurtful to me at different times in my life. She has a different experience of him. I don't need her to have my experience of him. If we were enmeshed, we would be fighting about why she doesn't see him the way I do and thus take on my battles with him or keep the same distance I keep.

>> If my childhood friend is with a partner who bugs me, that's my problem. I adore my friend; my friend is making the life they want with this person. This boundary isn't so tight that we never speak of their partner; we just minimize this to take care of each other.

Applying boundaries to polyamory

How you conduct your social and familial life around boundaries is the blueprint for your capacity to assert boundaries in your poly life.

If you can't be honest and express your needs with the people closest to you *outside* of your sexual and intimate life, you're not going to be practiced enough to do this in the high stakes emotional theater of your polyamorous sexuality. As you assess your current capacity for boundary-setting in your life, the simple question you need to ask yourself is:

> What is the appropriate distance you need from your lovers so that you aren't a fish on a line, hooked to their every move?

Identify what limits you need so that you can *maximally enjoy* your poly life together. What's the closeness/distance ratio you need from:

>> Exposure to their sexual and romantic life with others

>> Discussion about their sexual and romantic life with others

>> Interaction with their other sexual and romantic partners

What limits do you need to set so that you aren't working too hard on your polyamorous life, or perpetually seeking validation, or constantly trying to control your partner?

For some people, the answer is — *none!* The more info the better! For others, it is *total* — I never want your romantic and sexual life with others to pierce the veil of my consciousness. For most people, the answers lie somewhere in between.

REMEMBER

A boundary isn't a fortress, instead it's like that half wall or island in the kitchen; you can still see everybody over there in the living room while you cook, and you can decide how you want to interact. It creates a delineation, a space so you can do your business and everyone in the living room can do theirs.

ENMESHMENT VERSUS VIEWING YOURSELF AS A DISTINCT BEING

Enmeshment is the failure to understand yourself as a separate being from another — a parent, a sibling, a lover, a friend, or a child. When you can see yourself as distinct from others, you don't try to control them. You can love them and allow lots of differences to exist in the field of life that you traverse together. You can be apart. Have separate friends. Live differently. Love differently.

Here are some examples of enmeshment:

• A person who can't make simple decisions without their partner

• A family member who feels betrayed when someone else in the family moves away

- A parent who relies on their child as a confidante to navigate family arguments or crises

- A person who takes on the interests and social life of friends or lovers and abandons or never develops their own

- A person who is always in waiting mode for a partner to act on something so that they can be okay, move forward, or decide something

Generally people who struggle with enmeshment:

- Don't have a strong sense of self, which may be masked by having a very strong personality

- Depend on others for validation and their self-esteem

- May have a hard time being alone

- Have difficulty maintaining a healthy level of independence within a relationship, especially romantic and familial relationships

- Believe that a friend or lover or family member thinking differently from them is an act of betrayal

- Either always look to others to define what the group or couple should do or overexert themselves as a partner/planner of events and experience perennial disappointment

Seeing the links between enmeshment and codependency

There's a very old joke that when a person's life is coming to an end —some kind of highlight reel or regret sequence of their life story flashes before their eyes. But in the case of a person with codependency — when a codependent leaps off a building — *someone else's life* flashes in front of their eyes.

In the codependent's final moments of life, only the person or people they've been obsessing over come into view.

REMEMBER

Codependence is the abandonment or denial of self for the needs of others.

I once had a client, Larissa, who was moving through a terrible breakup. She was devastated and physically looked sunken for many months. Her ex was traveling around the country following a band and dating up a storm. Every morning, she'd wake up alone, in the middle of an argument that she'd been carrying on as she slept, her mind racing through a rehash of all the things she'd groused about when she and her partner were unhappily together.

This was beyond grieving a breakup, which generally improves over time. This was about failing to accept the end and continuing to fight the fights that brought about the breakup in her unconscious every night.

In one of our sessions, I said to her: "This *is* going to pass. Not because Terry is going to come crawling back to you or realize the error of her ways, but because you have decided to work on letting go, every day, and one morning you'll wake up and this resentment and despair will be gone."

And that's what happened. One day Larissa finally stopped adjudicating the relationship in her head and started talking about what hadn't worked in the relationship. She attended a grief group and minimized her drinking. Over time, she found herself talking about other, new things with her friends. She went to work, paid her bills, made small attempts to socialize, and bit by bit, her obsession with and focus on her grievances with Terry fell away. She was able to regain herself as the center of her life.

REMEMBER

Codependency is dreadful. It's exhausting. Taking back the power you've given someone else to define your happiness and your success as a person can be a very strenuous job. Your best move is to not give that power away in the first place and to notice when you're growing so wrapped around another person's every breath that you've lost your own.

TIP

Melody Beattie's classic work *Co-dependent No More* stands up over many decades as a fantastic audit of codependency and a helpful guide out of the toxicity and desperation so many get caught in. If you find yourself caught in codependency's net, check it out.

Defining your limits when setting your boundaries

Here's a good boundary checklist that might help you start figuring out what limits (if any) you might need in your poly partnerships.

Ask yourself this important question: What boundaries do you need to ensure the well-being and functionality of your polyamory constellation? Consider the following areas:

>> **Friend group/proximity**
  • Who do you want in your polycule in terms of the social worlds they will bring to you?

- Is it cool if your lovers are lovers with your friends?
- Are you okay if your lovers are lovers with people in your broader supportive community?
- Do you want to keep your friend group to yourself?
- How much overlap is there among friends and lovers in your ideal polycule?

» Physical/sexual proximity to other lovers

- Do you want to know your lover's lovers?
- Are you sexual with them?
- Do you all go to parties together?
- Do you hang out at home together?
- What do you think about collective sleepovers?

» Emotional proximity

- Are you emotionally connected to your lover's lovers?
- Are you confidantes?
- Are you BFFs?

» Time and space boundaries

- What kind of time do you want to spend with your lover's lovers?
- What kind of space do you want between you and them?
- Would you prefer it if your lover had out-of-town lovers?
- Do you prefer never to meet your lover's lovers?

» Boundaries for conflict/communication and privacy

- What kind of information flows do you want in a polycule?
- Is it okay to relay conversations you've had with one lover to another?
- Will you talk about difficulties you have with one lover with another?
- How do you think about privacy?
- How do your lovers think about privacy?
- Is everyone in the polycule out at the same level? How do you handle different levels of outness and privacy?

» Financial/resources/assets boundaries

- How do you want to manage your expenses/resources/assets?

- Do you want to share all resources and take care of everyone's needs collectively?

- Do you want to maintain financial independence?

- What does financial interdependence mean to you?

- Do you envision having one nesting partner that you share resources with? How?

- How will you balance differences in income and asset bases?

Clarity around your boundaries here helps your partners understand your values and also forestalls confusion and arguments.

POLYAMORY STORY

I'M NOT CODEPENDENT; I JUST DON'T WANT TO HURT YOUR FEELINGS

The ugly underside of codependency (raising my hand) is that when I was at my worst in this lane of thinking and doing, I told myself that I was motivated by kindness — that I loved my partner so deeply and I never wanted to hurt their feelings. But in truth, I desperately wanted to control my partners. I was driven by feelings of insecurity. I thought I wasn't hot enough for my partners, and all the overfunctioning and overextending myself to meet their needs at my own expense was a way to lock them in and keep them in my constant sights.

I wanted to control their experience of me. As long as I was overdoing it, they wouldn't be able to see how lacking I was. Then, it would be impossible to leave — they'd be overwhelmed by my kindness, and if they left, they'd seem like a total jerk.

Over the course of my life, I've been fortunate to recover from addiction and major depression. But recovering from codependency was harder than both of these. Intergenerational family trauma and patriarchy had a terrible grip on my self-esteem — there's a reason codependency impacts women and femmes more often than men and masculine-identified people. The cultural conditioning to abandon myself for the needs of others *because I wasn't enough* is intense. If that's your story, be gentle with yourself. This is hard. And if you can come out of denial and face this truth, you can recover. There's another whole life waiting for you on the other side. **— Jaime**

Sustaining and Adjusting Boundaries

Setting boundaries can be hard — especially if you're new to it. Coming to understand the limits of your current capacity for openness and intimacy in your relationships can be distressing, particularly if your capabilities don't match your aspirations around polyamory. And sharing these with your partners — especially if you're judging yourself — can be a big challenge. In the following sections, you can move into the work of sustaining boundaries, which in my mind, is really next-level work.

I wish I had could say that sustaining boundaries is easier than setting them, but the truth is — sustaining boundaries can also be quite challenging.

Reassessing and making changes when boundaries are breached

After you identify your needs, articulate them respectfully, and co-create structure in your relationship, having to reiterate boundaries if you feel attention to them slipping — can be difficult. For me, all of my shaky self-esteem stuff comes roaring up when I have to reassert a boundary. "If I say that they aren't respecting my boundaries, they'll be angry. I won't be a fun poly partner, and they'll leave me."

REMEMBER

That's why an important piece to put in place when establishing boundaries is an outline of consequences or changes that will happen in the event that someone disregards a boundary. If you make these consequences clear as you establish your agreements, then when boundaries are breached, you're just executing a co-created plan, rather than making a solo intervention while in crisis.

Different boundary disruptions prompt different levels of response, from reevaluation of the existing boundary — because it's possible you've outgrown the need for it and that's what this place in the road is telling you — to a rupture so serious, a partner needs to move out, or you need to create a significant shift in your relationship.

Being clear

Defining all of these parameters and consequences when you're doing well, not when you're in highly emotional jam, is so important. Your future self will thank you. Table 6-1 shows a hypothetical table of values, needs, boundaries, and consequences for a polycule.

TABLE 6-1   Values, Needs, Boundaries, and Consequences

I Value	So I Need	I Will Act on This by	In a Breach of Agreement
Honesty	You to be honest with me	Modeling honesty with you	Time-out
Time together	Date nights	Keeping dates	Check-in/reevaluate
Sexual experimentation	Safer sex agreements	Keep safer sex agreement	Full stop/STI tests
Emotional intimacy	No falling in love with others	Not falling in love with others	Inform/adjust/break
Sharing experiences	Openness	Being open	Reevaluate
Privacy	Commitment not to speak for me	I won't speak for you	Reevaluate
Leisure time	Leisure with you, not just kids and work	Saving time for us	Reevaluate
Not being overscheduled	See my other lover once a week	Not overscheduling	Reevaluate
Time with the kids together	You involved	Planning fun stuff together	Reevaluate

Use Table 6-1 in the following way:

>> **I value:** This column centers on your core needs.

>> **So I need:** This column provides an example of how to operationalize this need. It sets limits and helps your partners see some bottom-line behaviors that support you in your exploration.

>> **I will act on this by:** This column brings the focus back to you and demonstrates the ways that you'll live out the values in first column.

>> **In a breach of agreement:** This last column is so crucial to the exercise because this is what you and your partners agree will happen.

For example, in the first row, honesty is so important to this person, that if there's a breach of this agreement, there's an immediate poly time-out. What does this mean? If this is a solo poly person, it likely means that they need a break from contact with their lover(s). If this is a polycule where the primary partnership is prioritized, it may mean taking a break from all lovers beyond the primary partnership.

TIP

You can see that you may need to seek more clarification or detail, depending on your situation.

REMEMBER

You may notice from Table 6-1 that breaking safer sex agreements has the highest level of consequence for this polycule — full stop. But falling in love with another person, which is outside of the bounds of how these poly partners conceive their poly life only prompts informing, adjusting, or taking a break. This polycule doesn't seem to define falling in love with another partner as a necessarily problematic breach; it's just not on the horizon as they begin their poly exploration.

That's important because it highlights the difference between setting a boundary around behaviors that are acceptable and unacceptable — lies are a deal-breaker — as opposed to setting a limit around emotional investment and intimate connection — your or our poly life is over if you fall in love with someone else.

More and more, conversation in polyamorous communities centers around the difference between holding boundaries that take the best care of you and model integrity versus enforcing limits that constrain a partner's emotional and intimate connection to another person.

Handling a boundary breach

When you recognize and address a boundary issue, don't apologize for yourself. You've co-created agreements and worked hard. Noticing and calling in partners when boundary breaches happen is a core skill for sustaining polyamorous life (refer to the nearby sidebar).

TIP

Don't wait for a thousand small breaches. When you first feel boundary erosion happening, don't deny it; notice it and name it.

I work on small boundary breaches with my son all the time: "Oh, no, we're veering into another political discussion." And he might say "But you brought up this issue!" And that might be true, so I say, "Sorry, my bad," and reassert the boundary.

Checking out your capacity to hold your boundaries

It's useful to assess where you are on your boundary journey at this point, so you can better communicate with your partners about challenges you foresee in setting and maintaining boundaries. Table 6-2 offers an excellent, practical assessment tool.

TABLE 6-2   ## Comparing Boundaries

Porous Boundaries	Healthy Boundaries	Rigid Boundaries
Has difficulty saying no to other people	Accepts it when others say no to you	Avoids intimacy and close relationships
Over-involved in others' problems	Seeks support when appropriate	Unlikely to ask for help
Dependent on the opinions of others for self-esteem	Values own opinions and perspectives	Uses the silent treatment to ensure compliance
Fears rejection if you disagree with others	Doesn't compromise values for others	Cuts people off over disagreements
Over-shares personal information	Shares information appropriately	Withholds personal information
Accepts abuse or disrespect	Communicates wants and needs clearly	Aloof and detached even with partners

Look closely at these categories and think about where you are on your journey to identifying and establishing boundaries. When you look at your close existing relationships, which column in Table 6-2 describes you?

Where you are on this spectrum in your existing relationships gives you a good idea about where you're starting in terms of your capacity to establish and sustain boundaries in your poly life.

CALLING IN YOUR PARTNERS DURING A BOUNDARY BREACH

Calling in is a practice established by transformative justice activists, among them Loretta J. Ross and adrienne maree brown. Calling in your partners when there has been a breach of trust hinges on the idea that calling out or canceling is a stigmatizing and marginalizing practice when there has been a violation of trust or boundary breach — a finger-pointing and distancing action. Calling in gathers your loved one into a circle of care to address grievances and issues that have caused harm or pain. Sisterlove's founding director Dazon Dixon Diallo said in the '90s, when she was trail-blazing AIDS prevention and care programs in Atlanta: "If you have something hard to tell me — if you are going to call me to account — I better feel like you are holding my heart in your hand."

Holding your boundaries versus constraining others

Here's a really hard question to ask yourself as you identify and communicate boundaries to and with your poly lovers: *Am I trying to take care of myself or am I trying to control this person?*

In this section, you can get help distinguishing between boundaries that are focused on self-care versus boundaries that attempt to control your partners.

Reactivity versus responsiveness

Often, when you're *activated* (refers to being caught in your attachment wounds, see Chapter 7), you may deflect or deny what you're feeling. If you knock against your attachment wounds and become reactive, you may then fail to ask for the reasonable boundaries you need, and then act from one of two polar opposite places:

>> **Denial/minimization:** I don't need this boundary. I need to hide this insecurity. I'm a terrible poly partner. My partner is excited about *XYZ* possibility and now I'm going to ruin it. I can't show him how needy I am.

>> **Projection/blame:** I'm vetoing this! My partner wants to pursue the one thing I said I couldn't deal with. My partner doesn't care about me. They're so selfish, they've always been selfish.

The third way

Amazingly, there is a third way, beyond reactivity, which holds the honest truths of the moment. These truths may be about a lot of different issues, but they generally emerge from the same foundational space in your psyche: *the feeling that you aren't enough.*

If you can stop reacting — minimizing your fears and/or projecting blame onto your partner — you may be able to hear yourself in this moment of scarcity and panic and speak from the third way. It may sound like this:

I'm feeling vulnerable about this choice you want to make because:

>> This is my favorite kind of sex with you, and if I let someone else experience it with you, they'll steal you.

>> I don't have the physical or emotional capacity to have this kind of sex with you, and if you experience it with someone else, you'll leave me.

>> This person is the opposite of me, and if you date them, it confirms all my suspicions that you've never been attracted to me and you're just waiting around for someone you're really hot for.

>> This person is too much like me — but better. Hotter, smarter, more — something.

>> We said we would go slowly and now this feels like a runaway train.

REMEMBER

The third way is always about exposing your vulnerability and taking a risk. Often, when a poly conflict surfaces, people grandstand about honesty and talk circles around political or community issues for hours on end when the real issues lie in realm of the short stack of incredibly vulnerable disclosures on the preceding list.

The amazing thing about telling the truth about what you're feeling is that you have control over you and your willingness or unwillingness to be vulnerable. You can decide the following:

>> **A hard truth:** Imposing sexual and emotional limits on your partner often amps up the desire for these things. It's the paradox of sex taboos: that you can't do X with Y makes X+Y impossibly attractive. Taking yourself and your fears out of the equation leaves your partner with just their feelings about the new person, no barriers, nothing in the way of just seeing this person and the possibilities as they are.

>> **Another hard truth:** If you can't get to the third way — if you decide that your partner can't be trusted with your vulnerable, insecure feelings, it's unlikely that having a polyamorous relationship will work for you. Having multiple partners by definition increases your risks of getting hurt or hurting someone because more people are involved.

>> **The hardest of the hard truths:** You can't really prevent your partner from falling for someone else. People in monogamous relationships can't do it. People in polyamorous relationships can't do it either. The difference in poly relationships is that together *you can decide what falling for someone else means to your relationship with each other.*

You can consider what kind of changes you're willing to make and whether you want to accommodate another big love in your poly constellation, or if this is some kind of deal-breaker for you in your relationship to the person who has fallen in love.

And if your partner pursues your worst fear — and abandons you to this new love, then you know something that's really hard to know — this partner didn't come through on their commitment to you. And that's a moment in any relationship — monogamous and poly alike — to gather all your loved ones around you for maximal support. Chapter 9 delves deeper into the third way.

Practice Makes Almost Perfect

A great question to ask yourself as you start identifying and setting boundaries in your poly relationships is: What kind of practices can you put into place to make this less arduous, more enlivening, and an exercise that builds intimacy rather than dread? In this section, you can find questions and insights to help you establish new practices.

Here are some helpful guiding questions and ideas based on the work of transformative justice activists Mia Mingus and Dean Spade:

>> What can we do in the polycule to reward people for saying what their limits are and what they absolutely can't handle?

>> Be intentional in the day to day — being aware of your tone, practicing daily acts of care, communicating clearly, being encouraging, having faith in your partners — so that boundary conversations aren't so heavy.

>> Model owning your mistakes — be proactive, so that this becomes a practice everyone steps up to, instead of having to call each other in.

>> Align your actions with your values — you want to be loved, so be loving. You want people to be honest with you, so be honest. You want to be generously cared for so offer generous care.

>> Share success stories around resolving conflicts beyond the polycule. How did you work out that conflict with your best friend? What steps did you take in healing that rift and owning your part with a difficult family member? Lift up practices of repair rather than stories of shunning and broken relationships.

Another place of practice for your polycule might center on integrating the information you've gotten having gone through the reflections posed in Tables 6-1 and 6-2.

Maybe your capacity for boundaries in the group is more in the porous category than the healthy boundary column at present (refer to the section "Checking out your capacity to hold your boundaries" earlier in this chapter). Maybe you're recovering from having rigid boundaries because you just got out of a dangerous relationship or family situation. As you take in what your abilities are at present, the question for you and your poly partner(s) is:

> What can we reasonably do given the current state of our relationship and our skill level around setting boundaries and taking care of ourselves?

Here are some of Dean's and my ideas around building capacity and taking care of each other:

>> Have discussions where you aren't trying to decide things — it's just a time to dream up possibility or talk through a new poly concept.

>> Talk about scarcity and fear in your childhood stories. How is this impacting what you think is possible? What scarcity actually exists between you and what is a holdover or echo?

>> Dream up new ways of being together.

>> Suggest new practices that will build trust and fun with each other.

>> Appreciate where you are instead of thinking about it as something to fix.

>> Practice asserting boundaries with new ways of talking to each other: "I appreciate that this is something you really want, and this is what I'm capable of right now."

In Chapter 10 you can look more deeply at practices and possibilities for growing your capacity for new poly relationships and setting boundaries that work for you.

POLYAMORY STORY

You have to be honest with yourself about your desires before you can be honest with partners. And it may take time to come to know your desires — just because you're changing doesn't mean you were dishonest. This is really about investing in your own self-knowledge, as much or more so than negotiating with another person. —JD

Chapter **7**

Identifying Attachment Styles and Building Trust

This chapter helps you explore your formative attachment story for clues about your challenges as you build intimacy and trust in poly relationships. You can also look at your adult relationship history for patterns of connection, conflict, and breakups. Ask yourself these questions while reading this chapter:

» Were your parents or caregivers consistent in caring for you when you were very young?

» Were there disruptions in your care due to illness or family crises?

» Did you have a traumatic birth?

Answers to these questions offer breadcrumbs on the path to investigating your attachment story.

Looking at your adult history can also provide you with important insights:

>> Have you had a lot of conflict in your intimate relationships?

>> Have you developed a strong set of tools for conflict resolution in your friendships and romantic relationships?

>> Has conflict ever escalated into emotional or physical abuse?

Looking at this history can give you a strong idea about your current capacity to support multiple-lover relationships.

REMEMBER

An assessment is a starting place, not an ending place. Looking honestly at your attachment history reveals the ground you're standing on, but it doesn't define you or what's possible for you. Even if you have a lot of disruption in your attachment story, you can have good love in your life.

Examining Your Attachment Story

Research suggests that what happened when you were an infant up to age 5 has a significant impact on your ability to trust and attach as an adult. *Attachment theory* investigates the connection between your formative attachments — those with your parents and other close caregivers — and your patterns in relating intimately as an adult. The following sections explore attachment theory and consider how it applies to you.

In 1958, psychologists John Bowlby and Mary Ainsworth developed a theory of attachment based in part on experiments wherein a mother and infant established a play space in an observational setting, and then the mother exited the room. Researchers monitored escalating anxiety in the child, and the mother returned to offer comfort. This test established the psychological term *separation anxiety* and created categories of attachment based on the baby's connection to the mother and its ability to reestablish a secure bond.

While becoming one of the most highly referenced work on attachment and mental health in children and adults in the world, Bowlby's and Ainsworth's work had significant flaws. Their ideas about attachment hinge on a sole caregiver, a mother, and have been used like much work of the era to suggest that a mother's relationship to a child is singular and all-determining. The experiment fails to consider that a child may have more than one significant caregiver of any gender and also doesn't consider what kind of systemic stresses might impact a child-caregiver bond, such as poverty, violence, displacement, and so on. Bowlby's and Ainsworth's work is aimed at one mother's success at connection or empathy in an isolated situation.

Despite these flaws, this research has provided a series of worthwhile containers to consider the effects of disruptive attachment on children as they move through crucial early stages of development. Accordingly, as you look at the attachment categories that I introduce in the "Looking Closer at Attachment Style" section later in this chapter, you can think about your attachment story in terms of your closest caregivers through your formative years, but also at whether your family were targets of state violence or discrimination or poverty. All of these factors come together to influence your attachment story.

Investigating your early childhood attachment story

Here you can undertake activities and reflections that help uncover your attachment story. How does the past impact your present? How do unconscious burdens get in the way of being close to your lovers and resolving conflict? Here are some reflective exercises to help you sift through your history and understand your present-day challenges.

Uncovering your attachment story

ACTIVITY

Use a dedicated journal for your exploration of polyamory for this activity. If you don't have one, you can answer these questions anywhere — on paper, in a digital file, or as notes on your phone. Be sure to give yourself time and private space to answer them because they may bring up memories you haven't visited for a long while. Perhaps bookend this activity with a phone call or text thread with a dear friend if you need emotional support. Answer these questions:

>> What do you know about your early attachment story? Can you ask a parent or caregiver about the circumstances surrounding your early childhood? Write down what you know about the environment. Some areas to consider:

- Was your birth uneventful? Were you able to be with your parents or separated from them at the start of your life?

- Did your family have enough resources to care for you?

- Was anyone in your household very sick or otherwise in crisis when you were young?

- Were people in the family targeted by police or the government?

- Was your family ever displaced from their housing?

- Was there violence in your home? Were any of your parents harmed?

- Were you harmed?

>> When you think about your earliest memories as a baby, toddler, or pre-schooler, what is the emotional content of these memories?

- Are you laughing?
- Are you crying?
- Are you frightened?
- Are you wrapped in the arms of someone who loves you?
- Who in your earliest memories created a place of comfort?

>> When you think about times that you were scared or hurt as a very young child, who is there for you?

- What happened in this memory?
- Who intervened?
- What was your connection like?
- Do you remember being comforted?
- How would you describe the resolution of this hurtful experience?

Taking your time

REMEMBER

Investigations like this can be multilayered and take some time. You may have to revisit these questions again and again. Just allow yourself to move through your memories and know what you know. You may want to get information from siblings and family members to round out your inquiry.

Take all these clues and keep them together; having this information handy can be helpful as you look through the attachment categories that I discuss in the section "Looking Closer at Attachment Styles" later in this chapter.

I once had a caller on a sex-positive radio show ask me for help because she had never had an orgasm. She was in her 40s and in love with her partner of many years. We looked at the following areas:

>> **Her physical situation:** Did she have any physical conditions that might prevent orgasm? Had she experienced sexual trauma as a child or youth? Did she have pain while having sex, or had she been diagnosed with high blood pressure or diabetes? Was she on a depression medication that made it difficult to orgasm? She answered no to all these questions.

>> **Her social environment:** Was she an exhausted parent? Did she have money worries, or had she been displaced from her home or moved away from friends? Was she isolated? All no.

>> **Her partner situation:** She reported that she loved her husband, but was she harboring a resentment? Did she have something she was hiding from him that made it hard to be vulnerable? Nothing there.

>> **Her attachment story:** She told me that she had grown up in a very rigid religious environment and that nobody had held her as a child. She could remember lifting her arms to her parents, and both of them refusing to pick her up.

"Ah," I said, "this is the place to begin." I congratulated her. Given how painful her attachment story is, it was amazing that she had persevered and attached to a wonderful partner. The way her parents had withheld love was likely a barrier to experiencing pleasure with her husband. She possibly felt unworthy or exposed when she and her partner were intimate — the early attachment wound coming between them.

As we ended the call, I noted that therapy might help her untangle the ways she had internalized her parents' treatment of her and could help her find more pleasure in her sexual life with her partner. I also noted that not everyone has orgasms when they're sexual. Therapy might help her recognize the pleasure she was already experiencing without orgasm and also give her ideas about what she wanted to seek and give in intimate relationship to her husband, irrespective of her capacity to achieve orgasm.

REMEMBER

Discovering your attachment story might be difficult. But denying your attachment wounds cripples your ability to attach.

POLYAMORY STORY

WHO'S THE PARENT HERE?

I have a vivid memory from long ago when I was on the phone with my mother. She told me she was moving — I was looking at this big atlas in my kitchen — this must have been in the 1990s. She was telling me she was getting back with her husband. She had often used me as a confidante in her life — as a supportive ear on the difficulties she had in that relationship and then she'd make whatever decision she wanted. She was like this throughout my childhood — terrible boundaries and an inappropriate dependence on me — and then I had no control over what she did.

Her behavior was disturbing, always inconsistent and unpredictable. What popped into my head when she told me this was: Where is my partner, P.?

(continued)

(continued)

In that moment I clearly was upset with her lack of constancy, so I was projecting this onto my partner, P.

I hadn't had any clarity about how one thing was related to the other until that moment. I was in a triad at the time, where we were all three altogether and there were dyads within.

We had an undoable list of rules with a lot of attachment stuff floating around. P's emotional orientation at the time — he seemed to get off on duplicitousness and setting people against each other. Both of my partners were breaching agreements and cheating on me.

All of these insights came much later. But I had this flash of insight on the phone that day. I'm looking at the atlas — and literally saying, where is P.? And I realize this insecurity and worry is really about my parent, not my partner. —JD

Facing the complexities of your early attachment story may be difficult, but not facing them is harder. Pretending that you don't have early attachment wounds won't make them go away and in fact will make addressing attachment challenges more difficult as you deny and deflect your attachment barriers onto your partners.

In JD's case (see the nearby sidebar), they were able to make a direct connection between the pain and disconnection in their attachment story and the panic they suddenly felt about not knowing where their partner was. Making this connection didn't magically solve the problems in their polycule, which was burdened by broken agreements and dishonesty, but it certainly gave JD a crucial insight about their own attachment challenges that was useful to them throughout their life — in this polycule and in all their other future partnerships.

Integrating your attachment story can be hard work

As you gain important insight about your attachment story, the next step is integrating the information and taking care of yourself. Many people have been discouraged from thinking too deeply about their attachment stories by parents and caregivers — "the past is in the past," they often hear. Some of this misdirection may have been the result of a misguided protectiveness. In previous generations, a lot of parents were advised to hide hard truths from their children.

REMEMBER

Investigating your attachment story can be difficult. Among many of my clients, their parents have lied or withheld significant information thinking that they were shielding them. But these truths live on in your body and your psyche. Regardless of whether your parents reveal the honest narrative of your early childhood, experiences of early attachment and disconnect persist in your adult capacity to connect, be intimate, and sustain your close friendships and partnerships.

Going back there and finding the truth of your experience is okay, even if nobody in your family wants you to do this.

In my case, when my mother died, I went into a deep depression and had to seek psychiatric help. One of the first questions that my psychiatrist had for me was about the environment I experienced as a child. My mother had been an alternately very loving and very volatile presence in my childhood, and I didn't see what help it would be to ask my dad for more information about this. He was grieving the loss of a partner of nearly 40 years, and I was sure I had all the necessary pieces of the story. Nonetheless my psychiatrist insisted that I call him. When we finally connected, my dad explained that my mother had been a survivor of major depression (news to me) and had been hospitalized against her will after my brother's birth in the late 1950s. The doctors had forced Mom to undergo electroconvulsive therapy (ECT), which at the time was a much more brutal treatment than it is today.

This information was shocking, but it also explained a lot. I asked if Mom took medication after her hospitalization, and he said, "No, the depression never came back." In just this short phone call, my mother's lifelong rigidity and harshness as a parent came into an entirely new light. She hadn't been arbitrary or harsh with me, she had been scared witless, so much so that she let everyone around her believe she didn't need any further treatment.

Getting this part of my attachment story helped me do two important things:

» Reevaluate my mother as a person in an isolating, heroic struggle to stay out of the hospital and stay with me. She wasn't being harsh or dismissive; she was sick and struggling fiercely to function so that nobody would notice her pain or force her to go back into treatment.

» Reevaluate myself as a child who had a compromised primary caregiver. My attachment environment was full of anxiety, fear, loneliness, and anger. A lot of the struggles in my adult intimate attachments suddenly made sense. This one piece of information cemented my commitment to getting a therapist who understood family systems and trauma. It also helped me put some of my mother's most painful and damaging behaviors into context so that I could love and appreciate her on a different level, building a new, more honest story of my childhood and charting a new course for my future.

This activity can help you dig deeper into your attachment story:

>> Ask your parent, caregiver, siblings, or even an aunt or uncle about attachment disruptions that you remember. Ask them if they remember what happened. Try to uncover new details from others' perspectives in the family.

>> Ask if the family member recalls how you responded to this disruption. Again, get any details you can gather. This person's memories may not be entirely accurate, but they're recollections based in your family system and can give you important perspective.

>> Make a list of three new insights you've gained about your attachment story. They can be helpful clues as you figure out your attachment style.

Looking Closer at Attachment Styles

In this section, you can look through some established categories on attachment and identify where you may sit on the attachment spectrum. These classifications can give you some insight about common challenges that arise from your attachment type. From there, you can consider what kind of support you might need to build the kind of closeness and intimacy you want.

Recognizing your attachment style

Researchers have observed four core attachment styles over the years. The following sections delve into each one:

Secure attachment

If you have a secure attachment style, you likely had very abundant and consistent caregiving when you were young. Your family's economic and social situation was likely stable and supported. When you reached out for comfort, your parent or caregivers often affirmed your experience and held you close until you felt better.

As adults, secure attachers tend to be comfortable with intimacy and have confidence in their relationships. They find it relatively easy to be vulnerable and take risks. And although breakups might be painful, as they are for all people, secure attachers are less likely to beat themselves up or to fall into deep, prolonged regret or depression.

Anxious-preoccupied attachment

If you're an anxious-preoccupied attacher, you likely experienced judgment, avoidance, or even ridicule from your caregivers when you expressed a need or showed vulnerability as a child. (Some of this may have been shaped by a highly distressed or hostile context versus an intentional choice by your parent.)

As an adult, this attachment style may leave you often feeling insecure and worried about your partners' availability and commitment. You may become overly concerned about the relationship and seek constant reassurance. As anxiety and preoccupation escalates, this attachment style can move into toxic surveillance and a cycle of arguments about imagined infidelities or slights. The anxious-preoccupied attacher's biggest worry is to be left, and their behavior often alienates their partners, pushing them away.

Dismissive-avoidant attachment

If you have an avoidant attachment style, you likely experienced something similar to the anxious-preoccupied attachers. Your parent may have been unresponsive or rejecting when you expressed your needs, but as a child, you acted as if that didn't matter to protect yourself. You suppressed your response, and this suppression has followed you into adulthood.

Adults with a dismissive-avoidant attachment style aren't comfortable with emotional expressiveness in their partners and also reluctant to expose their vulnerability. You may distance yourself or require a lot of space when emotions run high in your relationships. You likely will have difficulty responding to your partners' stated needs or expressing your own.

Disorganized or fearful-avoidant attachment

If you have disorganized or fearful-avoidant attachment style, your primary caregivers were likely significantly traumatized people, and they passed this trauma onto you with frightening, harmful, and inconsistent behavior.

Accordingly, your attachment style as an adult is often inconsistent and unpredictable. You may yourself have become frightening and harmful to your partners. If that rings true for you, getting help and healing from your childhood attachment wounds is possible. Healing can make it possible to improve your connections in your intimate relationships and also enable you to create limits for yourself so that you don't harm your partners.

Identifying your adult attachment style

Considering your attachment history can be emotionally taxing. Take your time with your story. Breathe. When you're ready to think about how your attachment history is impacting your present-day relationships, the following activity can help you connect the dots between the clues in your formative attachment story and your adult challenges.

ACTIVITY

Work through the following steps and figure out what your childhood attachment clues tell about you and your adult attachment style:

1. Review the two activities in the "Investigating your early childhood attachment story" section earlier in this chapter.

2. Review the attachment style descriptions in the previous sections.

3. Think about a recent argument you had with a lover or think about a particularly bad conflict you had with a partner at any time in your relationship history.

4. Ask yourself what you think your actions during this conflict are revealing to you about your attachment style.

5. If you can't figure this out, what similarities do you notice when you look at your story and the attachment categories I list in the section "Recognizing your attachment style" earlier in this chapter.

6. If you had to make a guess, ask yourself what attachment style you think best fits you.

REMEMBER

Stop and breathe. You are more than your attachment style. These categories can help you see your challenges and figure out what kind of help you might need. They aren't meant to confine you; they're meant to help you take your next steps toward healing and intimacy.

POLYAMORY STORY

I CAN HAVE THE FEELINGS BUT NOT REACT

I'm just reading about all of this attachment theory in my graduate school program. And it's clear that I'm an anxious-preoccupied attacher — I'm always wondering when the next bad thing is going to happen, waiting for the other shoe to drop.

I don't love attachment theory because most of it is so individualized. In my family, legacies of slavery and ongoing experiences of police violence are so present — what does secure attachment even mean under these systems? My people all raised me knowing that there was a daily likelihood that I could be killed.

And my grandparents have been preparing me for their deaths forever. This is such an echo of slavery — you may have a year or two with your child. They may be sold off when they're ten. These systems disrupted any notion of a secure attachment, and the legacy of those terrors get carried through generation to generation.

The healthy attachment history I do have comes from my grandparents — despite the fact that there was physical violence in the household — really the echoes of slavery — practices that aren't core to our ancestral traditions of childrearing.

So, despite the critique I have of attachment theory and psychology in general for failing to look at systemic violence — looking at the outcomes of disruptive attachment — I thought, well this is info that's helpful. For example, I didn't have a name for why I want to be open and live a poly life — while I still experience such intense jealousy.

And then I see, oh, literally, I have a father who wasn't around, a mother who would say I'll be back in an hour, drop me at my grandparents, and then would be back in like two weeks. As a result, my agency and autonomy have become very important to me around how I live my life and my relationships.

Interdependence is a choice — it's the goal. On openness in relationships — I don't want to feel trapped. And yet, sometimes when I experience that agency and autonomy *in others* I'm deeply activated. Mostly I don't know why sometimes when you kiss someone it bothers me and sometimes it doesn't. Maybe I'm just having a bad day. Maybe I feel disconnected or abandoned.

Now that I've got this attachment theory framework I can make different choices around my behavior. I can have the feelings but not necessarily react. There's an explanatory framework there. I'm not broken. Nothing's wrong with me. This intense feeling is partly a result of how I grew up. **—Romeo**

Building Trust Is an Attachment Practice

There's a very old joke about a lost musician on the streets asking a passerby how to get to the legendary performance venue, Carnegie Hall — and the random New Yorker replies: *Practice, practice, practice!*

The same is true about creating vibrant and caring attachments in your polyamorous relationships. How do you get to a place of being ready for intimacy with multiple lovers? *Building trust in relationships takes practice.*

If your formative attachments involved inconsistency, volatility, or abandonment, you'll need a lot of practice. Start by owning your anxiety or avoidance about attaching and getting support when your old history is driving you into a state of panic.

Likely you've already had some practice. Perhaps you've noticed patterns in your relationships that you've tried to change but keep getting stuck in. Maybe you deflect your partner's requests for intimacy. Maybe you cheat. Maybe you run when you get too close to anyone. Maybe you swear to yourself you won't lose interest in your next partner and check out, but then you do.

The following sections look at your patterns for clues about how your attachment style is playing out in your adult relationships. Here, you can find activities, contributor stories, and reflections that can help you sidestep the fearful reactivity that prevents you from connecting with your lovers and find ideas for trying out new trust-building practices.

Reflecting how your attachment style impacts trust

If you've had a few or several crushes or romantic/sexual relationships, you have a track record that's likely working for you in some areas, but not in others. Your interest in polyamory might have been piqued by your distress over conflicts or difficulties you've had in previous relationships. In this exercise, ask yourself these questions as you consider your new insights about your possible attachment style and how your formative attachment story might be playing out in your adult attachments.

>> What are some of the recurring problems you've faced in your intimate relationships?

>> How have your partners described you when they're frustrated or hurt?

>> Does your attachment style explain some of these recurring problems? How?

>> Do you see your issues in a different light when you consider them through the lens of attachment theory and these categories? What insights do you have?

>> What does attachment theory tell you about how you might be sabotaging or hurting your chances at sustaining intimacy in your adult relationships.

You're getting a lot of information here and possibly making connections that are new and potentially unsettling. Nobody's perfect. Very few people have highly secure childhood attachment stories or smooth attachment histories as adults.

The important thing about this information is that it can be useful. You can observe your behaviors in the context of attachment theory and identify what your issues are and what you want to do about them.

I CAN LIBERATE MYSELF THROUGH THESE CHANGES

Last summer I went to the beach with my nesting partner of six years. We were hanging out, and I was having some anxiety or tenuousness because this nesting partner is now committing to one other full-on significant relationship with another partner for the first time in our relationship, rather than being more open.

While at the beach, when I used the term "primary partner," they informed me that they hadn't and don't use that word. So that was a lot. And in the moment, I could really feel myself struggling with jealousy and fear.

I just tried to tune into myself and the reality of our relationship — every bit of me wanted to get right with this, because this has been and is a great relationship. We've been poly for a long time and we don't have a ton of rules and it really works.

I think to myself (over the fears running around loudly in my head): I can live into this.

So, right there, I just thought: I'll be spending less time with my nesting partner so I can try to get rid of some of the things I don't really like in the relationship — the things that irritate me — and just enjoy my partner more. I thought: I can liberate myself through this changed circumstance around the stuff I like the least and orient myself toward the things I love the most.

I remember that I drew an illustration — just a little thing with arrows in a tiny notebook. I thought: Let's get rid of petty household arguments. I'm going to let go of the small stuff and areas of friction where we aren't compatible. Because now they could take some of their needs somewhere else, perhaps where there were new compatibilities, and there won't be so much to rub up against.

I decided to orient myself to opportunity rather than falling into an abandonment fear. And I opened myself to getting more intimate with my other two partners.

It's a year later — and it's really worked. Our nesting relationship is just as strong and important to me, and I have become more intimate with my other partners. My immediate reaction was to kind of contract with fear, but instead, we've expanded. And it's still so good. **—Sonja**

Aiming for secure-enough attachment

Attachment theory can help you aim for what I call *secure-enough attachment*. While your attachment wounds might present challenges, you can still press on and do your best to connect with and be intimate with your partners. You don't have to do this perfectly, and you can expect that attachment issues will arise when you're being intimate — especially with people you care deeply about — and then you can figure how to address them together. In this section, you can look at what kind of resources and support you might need to form secure-enough attachments, regardless of your attachment style.

Given my family story, I'm often (though not always) an anxious-preoccupied attacher in new, romantic situations. You may find yourself in a similar situation. If so, consider these options to take care of yourself when you're crushing on someone or going on a date with someone new (refer to the section "Getting Help" later in this chapter for more details):

>> Use a weekly support group to dump your anxieties. Let them hold all of that for you while you enjoy the sparkly new energy of a crush.

>> Talk to one of your besties about how wonderful you are and that you aren't bound by history.

>> Draw on these avenues of support so you can meet this person with openness, rather than under the weight of old baggage.

>> Get excited if you've done a lot of work with your attachment story; it doesn't have to define or limit you anymore.

Along with needing help stepping out and meeting new crushes, you might need support with your long-term partners and lovers. There's nothing wrong with that. Secure-enough attachment doesn't mean your issues will never come up again — it means that you and your partners accept and work with your attachment histories.

In my existing relationships, my best defense against the activation of my anxious attachment responses is to just tell my partners when I feel myself getting into trouble. I'll say things like: *I'm getting activated. I need to stop,* or *I have to sit down and breathe for a minute; my old story is getting in the way.*

This too, has taken a lot of practice. For many years, I'd get activated with no understanding about what was going on. I was experiencing a kind of terror of being abandoned without realizing it. My heart would race and physically, I'd literally have a hard time hearing what was being said. I'd automatically reject what my partners were trying to tell me. My voice register would raise, and sometimes I would become accusatory and yell.

Now I can feel it when my attachment wounds start to get activated. My lovers and intimates also know what this looks like because I've shared my attachment history with them and also my new self-knowledge about how my attachment anxiety plays out. In my family and polycule, when anyone notices that I'm deep in my fears, the key support intervention is to ask: *Are you okay?*

This simple act of care — asking if I'm okay — has an immediate, supportive effect. It counteracts what happened when I was a child, when I was definitely not okay, and my parents were unable to be emotionally present and offer comfort. It signals concern for me rather than anger or rejection; it lets me know that the people in my life want to be there for me. They aren't going anywhere. And I can relax. I can stay in the moment and figure out what's going on with me — why am I so fearful or distressed? I can step up to the issue at hand without creating chaos, fighting, or pushing them away.

POLYAMORY STORY

I ENVISION A HISTORY WHERE WE ALL GET TO LOVE

When I got to college and started taking women's studies and Black studies — I had always understood the systems that my people were suffering under — but now I had a whole discipline to examine it through. I was like, oh wow. My family really did try their best. I come from such loving people. And even as I know they tried their best, I also know that what they were able to give was still wildly insufficient for what a child needs.

My mom, for example is so clingy! She's ten times the anxious-preoccupied attacher that I am.

No one taught me how to work through things. Nobody taught me to sit down and say to a partner, "Okay here's a feeling I'm having." My mother told me this story about her parents: My grandparents broke up every summer so they could go be with other people. My grandfather had multiple children with other women, but if you ask my grandparents, they don't know anything about polyamory. When I talk to my grandparents about it, they wave it away.

My mother witnessed all that. She had no name for any of it. So, I feel like I come to my poly identity honestly. I feel the same way about the summer that my grandparents did! It's time to go out and find all the people. They had no resources or language for this.

I envision an alternative history where they were poly and open and we all learned about navigating complexity in relationships; and where we all get to love expansively and not feel trapped by love. **—Romeo**

Practice, practice, practice. You're more than your attachment wounds. You can do this.

Dealing with toxic attachment

Your next step is to consider what proactive steps you might take to improve your attachment practices and relationships. In this section, you can consider whether you have toxic — and by that I mean harmful —attachments in your close group of friends and lovers and consider how you can improve or let go of these draining entanglements.

Previously, a lot of emotional harm in my adult relationships just appeared to be a mass of swirling chaos — *things kept happening to me*. After learning more about my attachment story and understanding its impacts, I could see that I had a role in these depleting interactions and involvements. I could see my part, which was really painful and humbling, but also hopeful, because I could see that some part of this chaos was under my control. If I could grow and heal, my relationships could be more loving and sustainable.

Identifying traits of a toxic relationship

You may be unsure about whether you're in a toxic relationship. Some signs that you are in one include if you:

>> Often feel unsupported

>> Don't trust your friend or partner or feel trusted by them

>> Experience a lot of controlling behavior — your friend or partner is often correcting you; they monitor food, friendships, how you spend your time, your job, how you spend money or even dress — and expect you to change these things to suit them; your partner or friend talks you down in subtle and not so subtle ways, sometimes publicly

>> Suffer a lot of angry and judgmental conversations or often find yourself angry and judgmental

>> Find there is disrespect everywhere — in the language between you; your limits are often dismissed, your trust is broken repeatedly

>> Constantly walk on eggshells, trying to prevent a blowup

>> Have a lot of neglected needs — for care, comfort, the food you like, sexual or intimate connection, your basic sense of safety and security

Eliminating toxicity in your relationships

The good news is, with greater awareness about your attachment wounds, and by undertaking more healing work, you can make your relationships more loving and sustainable. Here are some of the steps you can take to eliminate toxicity in relationships:

» End some relationships — whether friendships or romantic partnerships — that have become mired in your old story and have created a lot of hurt. Take responsibility for your part in this and let go.

» Find a new, short-term therapist with expertise in building internal resources for people with anxious, dismissive, or disorganized attachment styles. There you can develop some new tools and set new standards and limits for yourself and your relationships.

» Commit to a few new practices: No raised voices. No name-calling. No arguing after 10 p.m. Instituting a few new, constructive practices can have a big impact.

» Tell the people closest to you about your attachment wounds and how you struggle with them. You aren't telling them so that they take them on as their responsibility. You're letting them know you're a work in progress and trying to improve your ability to address your anxieties and work through conflicts. Create a support phrase they can use when you're distressed. Mine is: *Are you all right?*

» Make sincere apologies to people you've unwittingly hurt when you were deep in attachment distress (see Chapter 13 for how to make a great apology). Make amends to ex-lovers whom you have blamed for everything in your breakups because you were unable to see your part. Apologize to friends and to your children.

WARNING

Being stuck in a toxic attachment loop can be hard to recognize. You can think: I just need to convince my lover of X, and they'll love me again. Or, I just have to get them to stop doing Y, and everything will get better. But working on yourself rather than trying to change your friends or partners is your next best constructive step in addressing your attachment wounds. As an anxious–preoccupied attacher, I can tell you that being obsessed with or focused on changing your lover is never a good sign.

TIP

A hallmark of mental health is being centered in yourself and your reality. If you're mired in obsessive thinking about your partner and find yourself in a constant cycle of conflict, get help.

Getting Help

There's no shame in having a complex or fraught attachment story, and nothing's wrong with seeking help so that you can build the communication tools you need to have the intimate relationships of your dreams.

You can find a lot of help in developing communication tools and relational skills for better intimacy in Chapters 5, 6, and 8. These chapters work together to help you get grounded in the story of you, so you can move into the world of polyamorous dating and partnering fully supported, reaching out with curiosity and expansiveness instead of fear.

Fear-based attachments are controlling and painful. Digging up the abandonment fears embedded in your early attachment story is a powerful step toward owning your truths, healing, and moving forward. In these sections, you can consider what kind of help you might need to improve your capacity for intimacy and creating sustainable, enlivening relationships.

Finding professional support

One of the best resources for support is a counselor or therapist who has training in attachment theory. If you don't have insurance or your insurance doesn't cover therapy, look for a local university training program — often they offer free therapy as they train their students.

Many therapists are now available by video call. You can choose from a more expansive list of options among people who are a better fit in terms of race, gender, culture, and therapeutic specialty.

When looking for a therapist, keep the following in mind:

>> Make sure your therapist-candidate has a systems framework as well as an individual framework on attachment disruptions. If they don't have this, they'll likely miss important systemic factors in your story.

>> Ask them what their approaches are with their clients. Listen to how they talk about their clients and what kind of work they do to assess whether their approach, language, and respect for their clients meets your needs.

>> Be sure to tell them that you're looking to build your skills so that you can better pursue polyamorous relationships. Check out whether they have prejudices about polyamory. That's usually easy to detect.

>> Ask them if they have experience working with polyamorous clients. Inquire about what kinds of outcomes they've had with poly clients.

>> Explain your goals for your therapy and see if you can create short-term goals together.

>> Explore what more long-term work might entail and if you're interested.

Seeking online, anonymous, and free support

Finding sustainable support is such a gift. Free online and in-person support groups can be a crucial supplement to other resources in your life like friends and paid professionals because there are no financial or interpersonal barriers. These groups and organizations can be your port in an emotional storm, a backdrop of constancy when other things are harder to sustain. Consider the following when seeking a group:

>> **Look for daily mindfulness or meditation apps that can help you stay grounded.** Like everything these days, *there's an app for that*. Check out free apps that look at somatics, which can help you get more centered in your body, or practices that support de-escalating your nervous system (your body's emotional command center, which consists of pathways to and from your brain, spinal cord, and nerves).

>> **Seek outside-of-the-box, creative ways to build secure attachment.** An article I read a year ago detailed the experience of an anxious-preoccupied attacher downloading an AI girlfriend and building a consistent relationship with the AI over many months. This strengthened her relationship with her actual lover, because she didn't have anxiety or preoccupation that the AI lover was going to leave her. In turn, she was able to take a calmer, reassured self into her life with her partner. Consider what other, creative avenues you can pursue to try out more secure attachments.

>> **Pursue free support groups.** A support group is any gathering of like-minded seekers on a path to self-improvement or health. The 12-step model isn't for everyone, but if you have a family history of addiction or codependency, it can be a steadying lifeline. The program's emphasis on sharing your story and making amends in a supportive environment can be helpful for people with attachment wounds. Beyond 12-step groups, you can find a lot of other free support group options out there, including sexual assault survivor groups, cognitive behavioral therapy groups, and grief groups. Checking out your local mental health services agencies can lead you to listings of anonymous and free support groups.

Connecting with polyamorous peers and other friends

Friends are a crucial supportive resource as you build your poly life. Having the feedback and counsel of someone who knows your history — whose only agenda for you is that you find happiness — and who is a good listener, is one of the great gifts of life.

Having friends who are experienced polyamorists is also a huge plus. As you come upon your attachment wounds in particular polyamorous situations — as you meet your jealousy and find yourself reactive or in some ancient funk you can't shake — a polyamorous friend who has been through the same situation is a precious resource.

If you don't have intimate friends who have your back and can tell you the truth about yourself, it's a good idea to work as diligently on getting them as you are on finding your romantic partners. Friends are life-savers and mental health boosters.

Keeping a commitment to self-discovery and growth

After years of *practice, practice, practice* at addressing my attachment wounds, I live in a relatively calm, engaging, and supportive emotional and social world now. I'm not afraid that the people who love me will abandon me. I don't think my friends and lovers are telling me lies when they tell me they love me or that if they really knew me they would leave. The fears that ruled a lot of my intimate life when I was unconsciously acting from my attachment wounds are much less present, and amazingly, the people who are closest to me can really see and enjoy me.

If it feels like this is impossible to imagine, don't worry. If you take time with the activities and information in this chapter, you can *practice, practice, practice* and expand your capacity for intimacy and connection. Self-discovery never ends, and if you embrace your story, you can work with it all your life and discover new meanings and uses of it to help you grow.

The emotional capacity and relational skills I have today aren't something I could have imagined as a child, when I was weighed down by parental trauma I didn't know about or understand. It's not a life my distressed mother ever had (see "Integrating your attachment story can be hard work" earlier in this chapter). When I feel the bounty of the love I have today, I am so grateful to my mom — for sticking it out when her life had so much hardship. And for somehow, against all odds, passing onto me the strength and depth of the love she had for me.

REMEMBER

Assessments are a beginning place.

Take in all the information offered here, and all of the new insights you've gained through the activities, and decide what you need to work on, and how you want to grow. Chapter 6 on setting and sustaining healthy boundaries might be helpful to you, and Chapter 4, which describes different poly family forms, might help you keep imagining that expansive, sexy future of your dreams.

Chapter **8**

Surviving Trauma and Exploring Polyamory

rauma survivors often encounter prejudice when exploring intimate relationships as though their experiences of harm disqualify them from the possibilities and joys of sex and connection.

If you're a trauma survivor considering polyamory, here's the good news: Like all people, survivors are capable of intimacy and expressing your sexuality on your own terms. The nature of your trauma and how much support you've been able to gather to pursue healing will impact your capacity for being vulnerable and close in social and sexual situations.

In this chapter, you can explore how survivors of emotional, physical, and sexual trauma think about and engage in polyamorous relationships. The stories, tips, and tools in this chapter can help you consider where you are on your healing journey as it relates to navigating polyamorous intimacies.

REMEMBER

Because polyamory literally means more love, it also has the potential to mean more healing for survivors of trauma and abuse.

Understanding How Trauma Impacts Attachment and Communication

Nearly everyone survives negative experiences at some point in their lives. *Trauma* is a term that describes what happens in your body and your psyche when these experiences are so overwhelming and intense that you can't fully process them in the moment. Traumatic experiences dig in, like a psychic splinter, and take up residence in your body in ways you can't predict or control.

REMEMBER

Post-traumatic stress disorder, or PTSD, refers to the intrusive ways that present-day experiences connect to and activate an emotional or embodied response to traumatic events in your past. For many who have survived negative experiences that endangered their lives — like a car accident, rape, or physical assault— and those who have survived negative experiences that have shattered your safety — like being forced from your home or country, getting fired from a job, confronting a stalker, or leaving an abusive spouse — your body and mind may have locked down these traumatic events and stored them to help you get through the period of crisis.

However, the legacy of trauma and whatever you have yet to process lives on in the ways you interact with others and build your life, especially with your intimate partners. Because your closest friends and lovers are the people you take emotional risks with, they're often the people who encounter or trip over your traumatic history. It seems incongruous or illogical that the internal territory where your deep trust, joy, and ecstasy live are often pressed up against or situated atop of your stored pain and terror. But there you have it. Stepping up to love, stretching your emotional capacity, and being vulnerable and open — all these incredible, wonderful pathways to growth can be littered with traumatic potholes from the past.

The following sections help you sift through the specifics of surviving traumatic formative and adult experiences so you can start to consider how they might be impacting your present-day ability to express your needs and navigate conflict in polyamorous relationships. (To look deeper at attachment issues specifically, Chapter 7 presents key information and activities for you to explore.)

REMEMBER

An important term I use often in this chapter is *activation*. When trauma survivors experience an event in the present that recalls or connects to a past event that involved abuse or harm, they can get triggered by that event or *activated*. When you're activated, you're no longer responding to the present situation. Instead, you're in survival mode, which often features an outsized panic response of fighting, disappearing, becoming frozen, apologizing for yourself, or overly attending the person who has set off the trigger. This response is called fight, flight, freeze, or fawn.

ADVERSE CHILDHOOD EXPERIENCES IMPACT ADULT RELATIONSHIPS

In the mid-80s, an obesity researcher and treatment specialist became frustrated with his poor results. Dr. Vincent Felitti found that no matter how much education he provided his patients around nutrition and behavioral modification, they didn't sustain weight loss. He decided to interview them to see if he was missing anything important and was shocked by what he found: A very high percentage of his patients had experienced childhood sexual abuse.

This finding was the starting point of a massive arena for study — adverse childhood experiences (ACEs) — and the creation of ACE scores by Felitti and his research partner Dr. Robert Anda, which calculate the load of adverse experiences on a child's formative years. These researchers were shocked to find a direct connection between high ACE scores and adult disease and mental health issues. Children with an ACE score of 4 or higher, for example, were found to be more likely to have chronic bronchitis, emphysema, stroke, or heart disease as adults. High ACE scores are also associated with higher rates of alcoholism and drug addiction, and, as Felitti observed when he started — obesity.

What does the ACE measure? The ten key experiences that make up the score are listed here. Place a check beside anything that you experienced and earn a score of 1 for each checkmark:

❑ Did you experience frequent emotional or verbal abuse by a parent, including put-downs, humiliation, and threats?

❑ Did you experience frequent physical abuse by a parent or other adult, including pushing, grabbing, slapping, or throwing objects?

❑ Did you experience sexual abuse by someone five years or more older than you in your household, including a parent or sibling, including touching, fondling, or penetrative sex?

❑ Did you experience emotional abandonment? Were you on your own emotionally? Did no one care for you or have your back?

❑ Did you experience economic precarity? Did you not have enough food or clothes? Did no one protect you? Did you not go to the doctor when you were sick?

❑ Did you experience divorce or breakup between your parents?

❑ Did you witness violence against your mother or stepmother?

(continued)

(continued)

❑ Did one or more of your parents drink or drug excessively?

❑ Did one or more of your parents have a mental illness that impacted you?

❑ Did one or more of your parents go to jail?

Many researchers have built on Felitti and Anda's work, which although imperfect, has established a highly impactful field of inquiry. In the years since the development of the original ten questions, researchers have noted that divorce in itself isn't necessarily a bad experience for children, depending on how the parents manage it. And the construction of the sexual abuse question isn't great — many people survive sexual abuse from siblings less than 5 years older than them. The questions miss witnessing violence against siblings and they entirely miss sexual abuse from people not living in the household. Other researchers have added tangential disruptive experiences for a longer list of concerns to measure such as experiencing frequent displacement or periods of housing insecurity, being in foster care or having your family surveilled by the child welfare system and being exposed to police violence.

Nonetheless, even without these improvements, the original ACE measurement provides crucial information for anyone trying to measure their exposure to traumatic experiences in their formative years.

Digging through your childhood story can be painful

Perhaps you've never considered how your childhood experiences influence or impact your adult attachment patterns. If so, this territory can be fraught, and that's okay. In this section, you can consider how your childhood story is playing out in your intimate life and get some ideas and tools for healing and staying present with your partners.

Take your time with this information. If you survived any of the brutal or disruptive events that I describe in the nearby sidebar about adverse childhood experiences (ACEs), the good news is that they're over. You're an adult. You can decide how you want to relate to your history of trauma or abuse. If you're like me, sorting them out may take years.

When I was growing up in the 1970s, my understanding was that sexual abuse was extremely rare. The girls in my hometown who endured sexual assault in their teens were stigmatized to the extreme. People hurled insults at them. No one invited them to social or celebratory events. The message was clear: Only bad girls got assaulted.

Recognizing and sorting out my own experiences of emotional trauma and sexual assault at that time was difficult. I was traumatized by loving parents who were each emotionally absent in their own ways and also extremely controlling about my body and my sexuality. I encountered daily, contradictory commentary about my body and my sexuality. On one hand, I was told I was beautiful and needed to guard my virginity strenuously. On the other hand, I was told I was fat and ruining all my chances at a good life. This kind of conditioning made me self-conscious and ashamed of my body and my desires. It led me to hide my feelings and my sexual exploration from everyone, leaving me vulnerable to sexual abuse by peers in high school and college. I was in my 30s before I had any awareness of how my childhood conditioning and experiences of sexual assault in my teens had impacted my ability to form adult relationships and take care of myself.

Today, there's a great deal more understanding about the prevalence of emotional, physical, and sexual abuse in childhood. In the United States, 1 in 9 girls experience sexual assault before the age of 18, and this prevalence is higher for LGBTQ+ and BIPOC girls. The prevalence of emotional abuse in childhood is much higher, across all genders, and is often reported as between 36 and 44 percent.

And research has largely contradicted the idea of a stranger as most likely to commit these abuses. Most sexual abuse is committed by people known to the survivor; emotional abuse of children is most often perpetrated by a family member; teen assaults are most often committed by friends and romantic partners. Great advances have been made in understanding and treating childhood trauma, while also understanding that it leaves the survivor at risk for abuse in adulthood.

Although treatment for trauma has improved tremendously since my childhood, finding appropriate healing resources, acceptance, and good love can still be a hard road. If that has been true for you, then you're in good company. Healing from trauma is a lifelong process. The work gets a lot easier when you find others who share similar experiences. In community with other survivors, recognizing and appreciating the sacredness of your survivor journey is often easier.

Connecting the dots between past trauma and your present realities

Making connections between your childhood emotional, physical, or sexual abuse and the way you feel around your crushes and partners is a crucial skill in navigating intimate relationships. In the nearby sidebar Cavanaugh describes how echoes of the past can make taking risks and seeing your partners as they are in the moment difficult.

ACTIVITY

What can you do when you find yourself activated by simple, everyday behaviors among your potential partners? This activity helps you track and de-escalate your trauma responses.

Referring to Table 8-1, create your own table with the following headers so you can track your activation. In this example, the table details the triggering behaviors that a hypothetical client, Polly, has identified in her three partners. In each of these cases, Polly goes on to note her reactive responses, and what steps she took to de-escalate her emotional state and take care of herself.

TABLE 8-1　　**Tracking Your Trauma**

Partner/ Date	Activity	How I reacted	What's the parallel?	Care/De-escalation
A. 3/24	A. touched my neck	Shut down and felt scared	Abuser used to rub my neck	Called therapist Had cup of tea
A. 4/2	A. raised voice watching basketball	Got fearful and anxious	Dad drank and yelled at the TV	Reached out for A's hand
C. 5/3	C. interrupted me because they were excited	Shut down; got angry	Mom talked over me — dismissive and angry	Told C. about Mom, cried with them
B. 6/15	B. got tipsy and handsy at my birthday party	Shut down — terrified	Assaulted by boyfriend at high school prom	Removed myself; later, discussion about boundaries and drinking/sex

You can see from this table that Polly is at a place in her healing process where she is activated by her three partners' behavior fairly often. That's hard on Polly. But the good news is, she's done a lot of work on her trauma history, and she has great insight about the sources of her activation and what she needs to do to support herself when she finds herself thrown back in time to past events.

You might not yet know much about your history or be able to identify what activates your panic or shuts you down or know which action steps would help you come back to the present and feel grounded and connected with your partner. And that's perfectly okay. The usefulness of Polly's table is that it demonstrates what's possible. You can survive multiple traumatic events and heal. You can come to identify your triggers and develop ways to reconnect to the present and communicate with your partners.

This table can even become an important tool for your healing process. By keeping track of moments when you're thrown back into past events that were upsetting or abusive, you can observe what kind of trauma load you're carrying in your day-to-day poly life and consider the bigger picture of your healing path.

PLEASE PICK ME; PLEASE DON'T PICK ME

So, I finally agreed to go out with my crush, K., just as friends, and we went to a sports bar. We got there and had great conversation. They mentioned in passing that they're polyamorous — and I had a panic meltdown. *Oh my god am I on a date? What do I do?*

The meltdown wasn't discernable. I just tried to stay present and get through the conversation. At the end, they asked if they could give me a ride home. Everything inside me was screaming: No!

An absolute flight response. I felt like a deer in headlights: *I don't want to handle whatever this is. What am I even hoping for?* I find myself swinging between obsessing and reminding myself that I've sworn off relationships — it was just a *huge spiral.*

Then in therapy, I could see that this all was very much connected to my childhood. It was a direct response to enduring a lot of abuse or neglect as a child from the age of 6. It's a point of pride that I don't need anyone else. It's a sense of accomplishment. Little me was saying: I don't want anything to do with this. It's a risk that I'm not going to take. But K. just kept talking to me. And I just kept showing up. —**Cavanaugh**

TIP

If and when you create your own table, don't be hard on yourself if you find that you're getting activated a lot. Instead, appreciate the level of crisis and strain you may be carrying in your relationships. Others in the polycule may also share a trauma history. Or others may have little to no traumatic history and have a limited understanding of what you're going through as you move through events that throw you back into crisis. The function of the table is as a tool to help you figure out the best ways to take care of you.

I REALIZED THAT THESE ARE JUST THEIR THINGS

When I think about two of my partners — M. and K. — they both remind me that at the beginning of our relationships I was constantly activated. M. nerded out on topics that were my Dad's topics. It would trigger my activation around my father and sometimes I'd find myself incredibly anxious around him. K. had stuff like my mom. K. would do something simple — like take a deep breath in a certain way and it would remind me of my mom when she was giving me the silent treatment. Neither of them were doing anything wrong. My own track record around having a lack of healthy intimacy and my

(continued)

(continued)

challenging relationship with my parents made it hard for me to relax around both of them.

But as I came to understand my own story — how I hadn't received enough emotional support as a kid, including the negative and intense messaging I received around my body and sex — I came to understand how I was impacted in my adult relationships. I could see that my relationships with K. and M. were an opportunity for healing.

I could say to myself: This trigger is bringing me back to this wound from my childhood, in these cases around my parents, *but this is not that.* Now, it's three years later, and I'm noting how those things are no longer triggering. My partners are still doing those things; these are just their things. I'm not activated by them.

Here's the amazing bonus: The way I relate to my parents has also shifted! I've been able to look at my activation. I'm not constantly burdened by these triggers — it's a parallel healing. It has improved how I deal with being activated around my parents.
—Aredvi

De-escalating your responses

This section focuses on de-escalation, or working to contain or lighten a past trauma-induced, crisis-level response to a present-day situation. The resource list that follows may be helpful if you're looking to build skills in self-care and de-escalation when your emotional reactions feel outsized or out of control. As you look at the Care/De-escalation column in Table 8-1, two important questions you might ask yourself are as follows:

>> What are your strategies for de-escalation during difficult moments?

>> What resources can you draw on?

Many survivors have found this following list of strategies to be helpful for de-escalating fight, flight, freeze, or fawn responses:

>> Breathe. Inhale deeply for a count of three and exhale to a count of five.

>> Identify whether you fight, flee, freeze, or fawn (or some mix of the four) when activated so you can talk about it with your partner(s).

>> Tell your partner(s) when you're activated or triggered.

>> Report on the feelings rather than act from them: "I can feel my anger rising up; I need a break." Instead of "I can't believe you just said that!"

>> Decide not to argue when you can feel that you're activated. Practice maintaining this as a boundary.

>> Have one or two close friends you can call for support when your feelings are escalating.

Ground yourself in the present by doing the following:

>> Take your partner's hand if you can.

>> Make a cup of tea.

>> Literally put your feet on the ground and note where you are.

>> Look around the room at your favorite things or colors.

>> Call a time-out.

>> Take a walk in nature.

And after you're out of the critical moment, think about building more resources so that you have more support the next time you are activated:

>> Build your survivor community.

>> Look for therapeutic help.

>> Consider online and in-person free support groups.

>> Find joyful things to join or attend, like a pottery class, sports or community event, live music, plays or dance performances.

>> Identify alternative therapies like

- Acupuncture

- Herbal medicine

- Bodywork or massage

- Sports teams or dance classes

- Swimming or walking

REMEMBER

If you work at it, and have a lot of great support, you can identify your triggers and develop your own strategies and resources for de-escalation. Multiple partners create multiple contexts and opportunities for self-reflection and growth. Refer to Appendix B for a list of resources.

THE BEAUTY OF POLYAMORY IS WE GET TO DEFINE IT

Another partner B. who I've known for years — we used to date, but he was in an intense relationship that I couldn't be a part of, so we didn't see each other for a while — came back into my life last year and was single. He said: "I don't think I can have a full-on relationship." The beauty of poly is we get to define it.

So, we started what I think of as a relationship-light. We hung out once or twice a month, but no involved planning or big discussions about what we were doing, the future of our connection, or otherwise intense enmeshment. We just were with each other. And he's become a part of my community — he's getting a lot of supportive community time through his relationship with me, among people whose relationships are light and joyful and playful. His capacity for engaging more emotionally and more deeply is growing. His emotional capacity is also increasing because of the way we have been able to be together to accommodate and support his healing.

I can see that in monogamy, many of us are trying to lock down one person and create a single relationship to rely on. In many ways it might feel comfortable to minimize our activation — like maybe I can be safe here in this little locked room. But I think we may actually need the opposite. **—Aredvi**

Accepting how trauma is operating is key so you can appreciate your strengths

Acknowledging to yourself that you have a history of childhood or adult trauma can be hard. The narrative you have created around your childhood is often a foundation for how you move in the world — how you introduce yourself and how you talk about yourself to colleagues and friends. Even if that trauma doesn't seem so present in your day-to-day life, the stories you've told yourself about how you grew up, or about your first love, or your college experiences are like a river flowing through you, part of your life force. Reconsidering them with an eye on harm and abuse can create monumental shifts in how you see yourself and who you keep close.

Many people have survived traumatic events that were beyond their control. Very often, the situation or events were denied, so the story was buried. If that's true for you, it's likely you didn't get appropriate care for years, or maybe ever. And all of this may have added up over time, making your adult intimate relationships fraught or hard to navigate.

SOLO POLY LIFE DOESN'T MEAN I HAVE TO LIVE ALONE

For a long time, I was solo poly and really valued independent movement and intentionality around keeping my space to myself. My politics are grounded in the idea that merging households doesn't mean your relationship is more real; I had a lot of trepidation and judgment about merging space.

But when I was planning to get pregnant, I sought therapy and looked at my childhood and it unearthed a lot of fear. It gave me clarity.

A lot of the reasons I kept things so separate was a trauma response. The desire to never need anybody. If I never need anybody, then nobody can hurt me. I have complete control over my physical and emotional safety. My trauma was bolstering this fear that I'd be hurt or disappointed if I ever lived with someone or allowed them into my space. —**Cavanaugh**

But this doesn't have to be the end of your story. After you accept your trauma history and start to take a look at how it's operating in your adult relationships, you have options. You can start to heal and grow. You can identify the strengths that surviving such difficulty has forged in your adult coping strategies and also let go of what isn't working.

ACTIVITY

This activity helps you appreciate your strengths as a survivor. Enumerating the hardships you've endured and the problematic coping strategies you've developed may be easy. But surviving abuse as a child or adult also leaves you with gifts that can be hard to recognize or easy to dismiss. If you're not sure what that means for you, you can take a minute with this checklist of common strengths that survivors report:

>> I have great intuition and can often sense impending trouble or argument.

>> I can tell when people are lying.

>> I'm an excellent de-escalator of other people's activation.

>> I'm a great crisis manager.

>> I can walk into any gathering and read the room — I have hyper-perception of people and situations.

>> Because I can dissociate, I can endure boring or terrible situations — like a horrific staff meeting — better than most of my peers.

>> I'm good at distracting people from their distress because when my parents fought, I did this with my siblings all the time.

>> I can endure tough times.

>> I show up for my friends.

>> My strengths are _____.

As you start to consider polyamory, remember to take in your strengths as well as your challenges.

For example, I once had a client who went into treatment for alcoholism and an entire team of psychiatrists and physicians gathered to talk about her family history of neglect and abuse. My client was outraged. Her parents had done the best they could with a terrible set of circumstances. She rejected their diagnosis of depression, and when she left rehab, she returned to work with me on her persistently absent libido.

And we had a very challenging series of conversations over many months that eventually boiled down to two key insights:

>> Your parents can work monumentally hard to provide for you in terrible circumstances and you can still be left traumatized by what you were exposed to and what you didn't get around safety and comfort.

>> The things you can see in your adult landscape — in my client's case alcoholism, a despairingly low libido, consistent sadness that made it hard to get out of bed and go to work, a lot of ruptures in her friendships and family relationships, a number of exes who were mean or abusive — are breadcrumbs that lead back to a formative history of trauma.

You can look at the activities and inventories in the chapters in Part 2 to start to get a sense of your relational skill level and what kind of healing work you might want to pursue so that you can live your best poly life.

Drawing on Polyamory as a Healing Practice

Although you can find articles or conversation about how logistically difficult polyamory is or how painful it can be around navigating jealousy and insecurities, not enough ink has been dedicated to exploring the healing possibilities embedded in polyamorous relating — for anyone engaged in multiple-lover relationships —but especially for trauma survivors. In the following sections, you can read about survivors who have made leaps in their healing processes and grown their capacity to address their trauma triggers through polyamorous partnership. And then you can start to consider whether polyamory might present healing possibilities for you, too.

Creating new worlds of possibility through poly relating

The core tenets of polyamory — full disclosure, consent among relative equals, and mutual respect — pose a tremendous counterpoint to childhood experiences of abuse. They're literally the opposite of abuse, which thrives on secrecy, denial, power imbalances, and contempt.

Trauma survivors who explore polyamory can find it tremendously liberating to openly discuss things like desire, sexual practices, intimacy, jealousy, insecurity, bodily autonomy, ecstatic experiences, and lust with multiple partners, sometimes while all together. Consider Ignacio's story, for example:

POLYAMORY STORY

I was always very invested in the negotiation part, the communication part. Let's talk about it all, let's put it out on the table. Let's talk about what we want, what we don't want, what's good, and what's bad because in my family of origin, I never got to have that agency or any kind of communication whatsoever to shape my reality. None at all. It was just given to me — imposed — and I had to accept it with physical punishment, emotional punishment, and my sister's sexual abuse. So that's where poly and kink negotiations really became a healing practice for me. —Ignacio

Trying on new parts of yourself with different partners

Any time you enter into a relationship with a new lover, you enter into a new realm of possibility. You put yourself in the path of someone else's worldview, ways of being, and circles of loved ones and passions. Your world gets bigger and often reorients itself as you attempt to accommodate the wildness and wonder of loving this new person. Polyamory multiplies this space of disorientation and reorientation.

In poly configurations and social worlds, the bigness of love can extend outward into groups of intersecting or parallel circles. In Chapter 4, contributors have drawn their polyamorous configurations and explained them. There, you can start to get a sense of the seemingly infinite nature of polyamorous possibility.

This expansiveness has special significance for trauma survivors, especially if you've compartmentalized parts of your trauma history as a way of managing it. As you heal, survivors can spend a lot of time compartmentalizing experiences and carefully reintegrating them on the path to wellness. In many ways, polyamorous relational practices create very similar pathways as you manage multiple emotional investments and a complex intimate life.

POLYAMORY STORY

Examine these examples where contributors report on dreaming big and building new worlds through multiple-lover partnerships:

>> **From Aredvi:** I'm gobsmacked by what it means to be healing in relationships and in community. The wounds happen in community — in our families, in the communities we live in. People around us all see what is happening to us. And so, the healing happening in community is just incredible. There's so much possibility there.

>> **From Ignacio:** The way that I tried to rework my emotional and sexual trauma in my poly world was through role play and family re-creations —that was huge for me for my healing. Before I even had language for it, I was recreating my family dynamic, in all kinds of relationships. I was trying to fix the lack of communication, the lack of connection, the fear. I found myself constantly recreating scenarios. My brother had been my protector in my childhood and my sister was my abuser, so in my poly families, through kink role play, I'd create a brother and a sister and put everyone into specific roles when I played with them. I'd re-create all kinds of scenes that hurt me, but here among people who love me, I could create better ways for these things to occur that are pleasurable and joy-producing, rather than the fear and secrecy and pain.

Ignacio notes here that both their *poly constellation* (their expansive mix of lovers and partners) and their *kink practices* (erotic activities that play with power and control, like consensual role play, domination and submission, and bondage, see Appendix A) helped them role play toxic family dynamics and transform them into new, healing experiences. This is a common strategy for many survivors, and one that has often been stigmatized or judged. How can you heal if you're drawing on abusive stories in your intimacy, sexuality, or play? The answer is simple: In abusive situations, your choices are stolen from you. In your chosen poly families, you're the author of your stories. You can create what you want. You can criticize without harmful repercussions. You're free to leave. Many survivors draw on the love and expansiveness of their poly families to rework and transform painful family-of-origin stories.

REMEMBER

As I note in many other places in the book (see Chapter 2), polyamory literally means *more love*. Accordingly, in a polycule, you literally have a potential cast of complex, intimate characters with which to create, re-create, and heal family dynamics.

FIGURING OUT WHETHER YOU'RE TRANSFORMING OR DOING HARM

Critiques of polyamory and kink scenarios that rework past trauma are many. So many people find this kind of intimate re-creation and exploration terrifying and so designate any such play as fundamentally toxic. But survivor testimonies over the past few decades have soundly refuted this analysis.

Of course, re-creation and role play that delves into territories that mimic your abuse is risky. So is dating. So is falling in love. Do you trust your partners? Do they respect you deeply? Do they honor your journey as a survivor? Then they may be candidates for this kind of connection.

Or not. Only you know what is transformative in your journey toward meaningful intimacy. Only you are the expert on your healing. A simple litmus test about the value or efficacy of this kind of play is to simply review how it is impacting your life:

- Are you falling into depression? Or are you uplifted and experiencing joy?

- Is trust and love growing in your polycule? Or are boundaries being crossed and disrespect and conflict emerging?

- Can you take care of your basic responsibilities — getting to work, paying your bills, parenting? Or is your life unraveling — are you unable to take care of the business of life as you did before?

- Can you take care of yourself? Or is your basic ability to get out of bed in the morning, face your day, groom yourself, and attend to your friendships and your passions slipping?

Transforming your trauma through role play and other re-creation scenarios can make life better, more spacious and more joyful if you have a strong healing foundation and are ready for it and if you have chosen worthy partners. If the opposite is true, and this kind of intimacy and play is creating pain and chaos in your life, then it's time to take a break and get more support for your healing process.

I'm loving fumbling around these days because it's nice not to know where everything is going. It feels great to just let myself be in the moment and not know what's next. —**Ignacio**

Honoring Your Story

You may have spent a lot of your life hiding the story of your childhood or adult trauma. It may have taken you many years to even recognize what happened as real or wrong. That's true for so many people.

Coming to honor your story, to uncover and know what you know, may be difficult — to stand by it, and in doing so, to stand with your survivor self. These sections explore what it means to grow respect for your survivor story and keep faith with yourself.

Honoring your limits is a strength

Continually feeling yourself at the edge of your limits around emotional capacity, flexibility, and intimacy is difficult. As a trauma survivor, you may want to make everything be okay for everyone else. You may be tired of having to speak up and say what's really happening for you, especially if your lover or your lover's lover are excited about a new crush or a new sexual or social practice that they have proposed. You may wonder: Why do I always have to be the one to set limits or introduce a concern?

But the truth is, people who love you want to know and respect your limits. They want to know *you*. As you move through your healing journey and become truly intimate with others, you'll find it easier and easier to speak your truth among your loved ones and:

>> Know when to stop or tap out.

>> Understand that it's okay to be overwhelmed.

>> Tell anyone, and especially yourself: I can't do this.

>> Know that it's okay to be done trying.

It's okay to be honest with the people who love and are in relationship with you. You're responsible for setting limits that take care of you, and in the end, taking good care of your partners as well. (See Chapter 6 on boundaries for more resources for how to set and sustain healthy limits.)

It's not your job to:

>> Heal others

>> Please others at your expense

>> Make it work if the effort isn't mutual

>> Constantly compromise, without reciprocity

>> Anticipate others' needs

>> Change yourself to fit in

It *is* your job to:

>> Heal as much as you possibly can

>> Listen to yourself — to your needs and desires

>> Respect yourself and your time

>> Be honest with and true to yourself

>> Protect your energy by setting limits

>> Leave when you're not being valued

>> Say no when you need to, and say yes when it's good for you

Taking care of yourself, in community

Chapter 11 introduces the concept of the pod map, a creation of Mia Mingus and the Bay Area Transformative Justice Collaborative. Pod mapping can help you look closely at your community of friends and confidantes as you pursue polyamorous relationships. Do you have a lot of support? Is your pod full of highly judgmental, anti-poly people? Mapping your pod can help you see what kind of community-building you need to do to create an environment where you can explore polyamory with joy and expansiveness.

ACTIVITY

As a trauma survivor, ask yourself these specific and important questions on your journey to taking care of yourself in community:

>> Do I have other trauma survivors in my polyamorous social network?

>> Are there other survivors in my polycule or constellation?

>> Am I out as a survivor in my poly family? Why or why not?

>> Is conversation about survivors hushed and whispered in my community?

>> Is there an open conversation about healing and resources and growth?

Living in a community where there's open, engaging conversation on survivorship is an unparalleled, foundational support in any survivor's healing process. When you can freely share your resources, experiences of growth, mistakes, funny stories, failures, and major milestones in recovery, then life is fuller and possibilities abound.

Keeping faith with yourself and other survivors

When you're struggling to understand your survivor story and to get a handle on how your traumatic history is impacting your relationships, you can easily lose faith in yourself. The daily climb toward wellness can seem insurmountable at times. You can become exhausted and think: I'm just going to stop having relationships altogether. I'm fine on my own. I can't do this.

I've certainly had those days. And if I'm really honest, I'd say I've had a whole year that felt like this. And the thing that got me through was the love of good people, many of them other survivors. Therapy, support groups, and a lot of other professional help certainly have made huge contributions to my recovery process. But there's nothing that compares to the practice of actually relating to other people informally or socially, of trying out newfound trust, and sharing parts of yourself that have been hidden out of shame.

POLYAMORY STORY

WHAT CAN COMMUNITY OFFER?

It's making me think of someone whom my partner K. got interested in and they were starting to date. This person reached a place of confiding that they had avoidant attachment and were feeling activated (see Chapter 7). They let K. know that they hadn't done enough healing to be in this relationship, which is so very common and real. There was so much sadness — K. was really sad — and had to accept that this person just wasn't at a place of healing to be available.

And I thought: I wonder what the community can offer to someone in a moment like this? I'm interested in polyamory as a way of holding this kind of moment; to think about how we heal as a community. I thought: Is there anything I can do with people I'm in community with — to make this process of getting ready to be available for love and intimacy as people surviving so much relational harm? I do think there's something in here that can be explored together. **—Aredvi**

You can do this. You can grow. If polyamory is what you want in your adult relationships, you deserve to explore and discover these possibilities just as much as anyone else. You can keep faith with your survivor self by believing in your ability to try, to fail, to do your best, to learn, and to keep trying. You deserve a life full of the best love you can give and the most bountiful love you can accept.

POLYAMORY STORY

Trauma shows up in my poly life in all kinds of ways, but if there's one specific thing I'm unwilling to cast aside, it's my belief that people can grow, we can change. I'd collapse under the weight of it all if I stopped believing this. It's as much for me as anyone else. It guides all my work with my clients, as well as with my lovers, my children, and myself. If I can't believe that — I have a feeling that if I can't continue to hold this unwavering truth —I'll die. And I have children who need me, and I have a life I deserve to live. So, I hold onto my faith in us and our ability to grow beyond all of these harms. We are proof. —**Cavanaugh**

3

Living Polyamory, Loving Polyamory

Figure out what you really want from a polyamorous relationship.

Create agreements that work rather than constrain and complicate your life.

Discover what your bottom lines and deal-breakers are.

Think carefully about how you will structure life, especially your time and attention.

If you're opening an existing monogamous relationship, find out how you can avoid common mistakes.

When deciding if and when to come out as poly, identify your core vulnerabilities and concerns.

Consider ways of growing support and community as you explore polyamory.

Chapter 9

Creating Your Poly Family Agreements

I n this chapter, you get to dream a little about what your polyamorous family constellation might look like through discovering and trying out different creative poly organizing tools.

Family mission statements, poly family organizational charts or maps, and boundary-setting agreements all can help you and your partners and lovers create a structure that works for you. Here, I go through processes and forms that have worked for me and worked for many of my clients and collaborators. Take what's useful to you, and leave the rest.

Crafting a Family Mission Statement

When I had my second child, I sat down with my polyamorous co-parent and created a family mission statement. It was an intensely busy time: I'd given birth to two children eight years apart. I had a demanding job. I'd been a solo parent by choice of the eight-year-old for many years, raising him in an expansive village of lovers and chosen family. I had been a very intuitive parent with my son, rejecting sleep training, and leaning into free-range practices where whatever was happening in the moment drove us.

And now, I found myself with an elementary schooler and an infant, with a new parenting partner who loved structure. They had a million ideas about how to manage our overwhelming responsibilities and take great care of the kids (as a gender *nonbinary* person, they use the pronouns they/them). They pulled out calendars and chore wheels and reward charts — all of which terrified me. And, as I glanced at all of these tools through my breast-feeding exhaustion, I understood that we had to find a new way together.

Crafting a family mission statement was part of that process. The following sections explore what a family mission statement is, how one might help your poly family, and how you can craft your own.

Declaring who you are and what you're creating together

Family mission statements describe the foundational values and operating assumptions that underlie any family project. They can help guide you in times of stress or conflict. Family mission statements don't solve differences by picking one way of being over another. My poly co-parent and I remain on fairly opposite ends of the free-range to highly-structured scale, and today that baby is choosing colleges. Instead, the mission statement grounds you in your values as a unit. For me, it was a helpful statement to return to whenever we were struggling. I'd re-read the statement with a little sigh of relief: *Ah yes, this is who we are.*

So, when we sat down to create the mission statement, we brainstormed some of our key values:

>> Demonstrate care in small daily ways. We believed that small acts add up.

>> Avoid yelling during arguments. We're both trauma survivors and yelling wasn't something we wanted in our or our children's lives.

>> Respect the babies. We believed our job was to respect and nourish the kids, not control them.

>> Commit to nonviolent resolution. Nobody gets spanked or hit.

>> Dedicate ourselves to personal growth and sharing love to the greatest extent possible.

For years I carried our family's mission statement around with me. It was a guide but also a limit-setter. When our son was in college, I realized I had long lost the mission statement, and also, that we had lost our commitment to some of these values. I had become an intermittent yeller. Our acts of care had fallen away.

We agreed to go to family therapy with the kids — to recommit to the values and practices that had been foundational to us.

POLYAMORY STORY

With two of the people I have the most intense relationships with (one being my live-in boyfriend) we have an agreement to try to have the relationship be a contest of generosity. This has been a really helpful mission — the opposite of the competition and resentment and withholding patterns that are so common in romantic relationships that last any period in a culture that pushes hierarchy, scarcity, insecurity. **—Dean**

Co-creating as a core polyamory skill

If there's one skill that will serve you best as a polyamorous partner, it's being an artful co-creator. The foundational value of full consent in polyamory is a driver of poly life. *Co-created agreements* are easy to consent to because you've made a deep investment through careful deliberation.

REMEMBER

This doesn't mean you all have to sit down and write agreements word for word together. Getting to consensus on a statement of values or a document that sets out the structure of your relationship can mean a lot of back and forth and fine tuning. But it shouldn't feel like you're having a root canal or dragging a sack of rocks up a mountain.

TIP

A first step in co-creation might be to create a simple list of guidelines for your work together. I call them *community agreements* and I use these in every workshop I give on desire and sex. Creating a clear, loving container for the conversation you're undertaking together sets the tone for everything going forward. How you start is how you finish.

REMEMBER

Here are number of my favorites. They can function as family guidelines, for when you're co-creating any kind of agreements or having a hard discussion. Or, you can embed them in your mission statement:

>> **Use I-statements.** *I-statements* describe where you are at and what you are experiencing. They are entirely self-referential. For example, "That comment was very hard for me to hear because I. . ." is an I-statement. "I think you're wrong" isn't an I-statement because it's actually a you statement — a judgement about someone else.

>> **Speak one at a time.** This guideline helps avert explosive runs of speech when emotions are escalating and disrespectful interruptions.

>> **Listen attentively.** Try to stay out of your head about what you're going to say next and put all your attention on the speaker.

>> **Stay off your phone.** Better yet, agree for everyone to put their phones away to give every person speaking the full attention they deserve.

>> **Avoid speaking when activated.** Generally, you can tell when you're activated because your heart is pounding and a furious or distressed commentary is flying around in your mind. Wait until you're back in the present, your pulse rate has returned to normal, and you have had a moment to think before you comment or ask a question.

    When you're upset at something a partner has said, call in, don't call out — and by that I mean, remember that you love this person as you present your comment or critique (refer to Chapter 6).

>> **Think well of each other.** When a conflict arises, remember the love and hope that brought you here. You have all come together to do something extraordinary and out-of-the-box in terms of relationships.

>> **Create time limits for the meeting and for each commentary.** Stick to them. Doing so limits oversharing by the more extroverted and verbally inclined. It also ensures that you don't exhaust yourselves by endlessly spinning around on one topic or issue.

>> **Remember that tears raise the spiritual level of any meeting and laughter saves.** Adding a guideline that references the way your constellation of loved ones gets through hard things can help set tone.

REMEMBER

In creating guidelines for engagement, try to ensure that everyone has their favorite on the final list. Guidelines hold boundaries while creating culture and possibility. They help everyone contribute and guard against targeting and marginalizing any member of the group.

Making a poly family agreement or map

After you've co-created your guidelines, you are ready to take on building a poly family agreement. An excellent poly family agreement or map serves as a joyful container for your unit — it clearly lays out boundaries and limits, and the love and verve that has brought you together is also apparent.

REMEMBER

When you're ready to co-create your own family compact, here are my suggested steps:

1. **Bring everyone together and brainstorm terms, values, and family forms that relate to the agreement you're trying to create together.**

   This part is maximally generative – you want to get everyone's ideas into the room.

   - Triads, quads, floating waves of relationship might emerge
   - Ideas about time, space – who, where, what, and when
   - Deal-breakers and hard limits can be shared here
   - Hopes, dreams, and wild ideas can come into view

   No editing yet. Just joy, excitement, and possibility. Bring markers, draw the forms you dream of (see Chapter 4 for examples), make up your own terms, create hope and silliness through color.

2. **Choose a scribe to guide the process.**

   - Who is most excited about co-creating?
   - Who has the most time and flexibility?

   In any/all of these cases, set expectations up front that there will be a lot of back and forth with drafts, and everyone's voice will be heard.

3. **Create a process for the back and forth while shaping and editing the agreement or map.**

   - Cowriting on a shared document
   - Sharing the draft one after another in an email circle where each person edits and passes it to the next

4. **Make final revisions.**

   - Allow the drafter to work with the edits to create a second draft and the process repeats.
   - Call a meeting to work through comments and edits, and do a next round if needed (and a next, and a next . . .).

   TIP

   If you're getting stuck on points or endlessly debating language, ask yourself these questions:

   - Why do I need to be right about this or get my way versus compromising with this person or people I love?
   - Am I afraid of disappearing into the needs of the group?

REMEMBER

- Is something happening right now with how I'm being respected (or not) by my partner(s)?

During the drafting and revising process, enjoy yourself:

- You're stepping outside of a very scripted social and relational system that most people never question.

- You can be exactly who you are and say what you want.

- Get excited about seeing your partners' contributions. You've chosen them because they're amazing people with big hearts.

5. **Celebrate your finished work.**

- Make or go out for a meal.

- Sit together and create a final affirmation ritual.

- Put it in a place of honor in your wallet or in your home(s).

- Have sex. Poly-processing-triumph-sex should be as good as make-up sex! Make it so.

6. **Own the document.**

Refer to it on a regular basis. Show respect and appreciation for what you've done together by using it. Update the agreement as you need to.

After you hit your stride as a co-creator with your partners, this skill will serve you for poly eons.

Putting Together Forms That Work

Forms that work attend to the specific needs of each poly constellation. This section illustrates how different agreements serve different needs.

REMEMBER

Having or asking for a lot of rules isn't the same as feeling secure or being trustworthy. Conversely, feeling secure and fully trusting your partners opens up a world of possibility for everyone.

Polyamory doesn't always require endless processing (a term for deliberative problem-solving). You can refer to the chapters in Part 2 to consider how communication styles, setting boundaries, and understanding your attachment story can help reduce what Jack calls potential drama in his commentary (that follows).

Building strong relational skills and building success within your partnerships around sustaining boundaries, honoring agreements, and showing consistent respect — even the most difficult and contradictory feelings — all adds up over time. Accordingly, polycules may find less and less need to process as trust and love grows and grows.

I think what I'm most proud of has been my ability to manage the potential drama around having a primary partnership and adding a lot of sex and intimacy with other people on top of that. I have always wanted both of those things, but I very much don't want a ton of processing and emotional labor, and I have been able to do that. Of course, I'm a man primarily relating to other men, and I don't think that the societal baggage about open relationships is as weighty as it is for women and some nonbinary people. —Jack

Creating the path to joy through form

You don't need to know what forms you're dreaming of to start your poly journey, but being able to articulate some of your hopes and ideas to potential partners is a great start. These sections look at some of the forms the book's contributors aspire to and have tried with their partners.

You'll be making your relationship agreements when you're at your best —when the sex is great, the horizon is full of possibility, and generosity abounds. But you're making them to cover you and your partners at your worst, when agreements and hearts have been broken, when people are leaving or fighting over kids and assets. Accordingly, clarity is king.

Make agreements that will hold everyone in the group well, so that you don't have to take the breakup or relationship shift to a courtroom, where most of the judges and other functionaries you'll meet take a very dim view of polyamory. You not only don't want to put yourself and your partners or children through the horror of court battles over custody or assets, but you also don't want to possibly create case law that will be used against the entire poly community for decades.

TIP

Think expansively and lovingly when making all your agreements and try to put in fail-safes or backstops that can prevent formal legal battles. And remember that agreements shift over time. You're creating a template that you can reference and come back to, over and over.

Poly relational forms: Drawing your aspirations

On the path to creating the polyamorous family they want, nonbinary polyamorist Aredvi drew this hypothetical polycule:

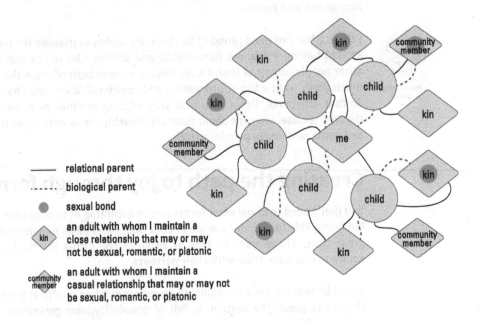

- —— relational parent
- ----- biological parent
- ● sexual bond
- ◆ kin — an adult with whom I maintain a close relationship that may or may not be sexual, romantic, or platonic
- ◆ community member — an adult with whom I maintain a casual relationship that may or may not be sexual, romantic, or platonic

As you can see, one of Aredvi's top priorities is to parent up to five children. They imagine doing this in a multi-partner polycule that has many people engaged in parenting — at least 11 — with a smaller subset of these people connecting to Aredvi as romantic or sexual partners. As a communally or group-oriented rather than partner-oriented poly person, Aredvi has placed themselves at the center of their polycule.

When I look at this form, I get excited about all of the possibilities, and I wonder how various life stages will shape and reshape it. I also think about what kind of agreements might be needed. Formal or informal parenting agreements might be crafted. Whether these agreements would need to be formal or legal depend on Aredvi and who they choose as family. Many poly people go into parenting in particular with clear legal agreements (like marriage, for example), whereas others decide that informal commitments witnessed by a community of loved ones carry more weight and meaning.

Here are some examples of the types of agreements that Aredvi's polycule may consider:

>> **Co-created documents about parenting values, responsibilities, and hard limits:** Getting these documents notarized adds weight to them should you ever need to resolve a conflict in a court system.

>> **Economic security agreements around sharing income, assets, and expenses:** These kinds of agreements are especially important if there are significant resource inequities in the group or if one member eschews waged work to take on child-rearing work full or nearly full time.

>> **Partnership agreements such as marriage, civil union, or domestic partnership:** These formal legal agreements often confer employment, state, and private benefits.

>> **Agreements about sexual intimacy and commitments with intimate partners, lovers, and passing fancies:** These agreements take care to honor people's desires and bottom-line emotional limits.

>> **Agreements about safer sex and pregnancy prevention or management:** These agreements carefully manage risk and outline steps in the case of trust breaches, mistakes, or health emergencies.

LEGAL AGREEMENTS AND POLY LIFE

Legal theory and policy advocacy for polyamorous people and their families in the United States is in its early stages of development. Legal rights for poly families are undermined by *Reynold's v. United States*, an 1878 decision that outlawed polygamy, as it was commonly practiced among Mormons in the 1800s. This case established the legal standard that an individual can't marry more than one person. To date, only three Massachusetts cities recognized multi-person domestic partnerships: Arlington, Cambridge, and Somerville. And four in the nation prohibit discrimination based on family structure: Berkeley, Oakland, Cambridge, and Somerville.

Today, groups like the Polyamory Legal Advocacy Coalition (PLAC) and the Chosen Family Law Center are forging important ground for equitable policies and nondiscrimination legislation for polyamorous people and their chosen ones.

Poly relational forms: Overlapping and adjacent maps

In contrast to Aredvi's polyamorous family map where children and parenting relationships are a big consideration, Rob's polycule map describes himself and his partners only.

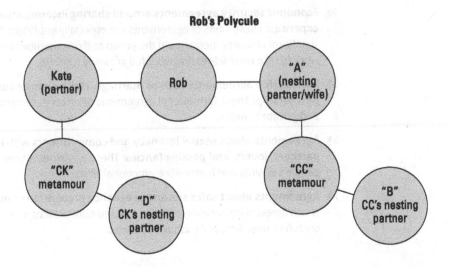

Rob's Polycule

Although Rob has a son, he doesn't include him when he draws his polycule, in part because his polycule emerged from an established marriage. Members of his polycule connect with and adore his son, but Rob and his partner Angel are solely responsible for raising him. You can see from his drawing that when he considers the things he's balancing in his polyamorous life, he's specifically focused on the forms he's creating with his partners and his partners' partners, around their romantic and sexual commitments.

POLYAMORY STORY

I'm married to my wife, Angel. We have a son. I also have Kate as a partner. Angel is also in a long-term relationship with a man who has another partner. I would describe Angel's other partner as poly-adjacent as he dates my wife and they are committed, but he isn't interested in dating anyone else, nor does he identify as poly. My wife identifies as *polyfidelitous* (sexually exclusive with her chosen poly partners) and is only in a relationship with me and her other partner. Kate has another partner. I also have friends who are more than friends, but there's a different level of emotional intimacy there.

Additionally, though I'm not necessarily *dating* anyone in a second polycule, Kate and I consider ourselves part of another polycule where we're very close friends with everyone involved. This second polycule feels more like a chosen family.

We socialize together, three of us play in a band together, have engaged in other forms of exploration (for example, kink), and support each other. This second polycule feels more a configuration of people with very similar, radical values around chosen family, the spectrum of relationships, and so forth. —Rob

Rob has also mapped out his and Kate's polycule. Here, you can see that a number of people in the polycule are important to Rob and Kate, but there's no sexual connection, so he has these members floating in the encircled area, adjacent to him and Kate.

Rob and Kate's Chosen Family Polycule

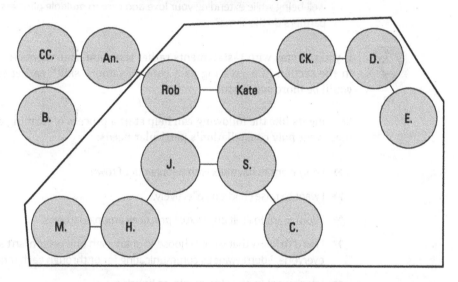

In terms of agreements, we did have initial limiting agreements early on, but those were primarily based around communicating about nights out, having a curfew on dates, and not having sex on the first date. We tried not to talk about veto power because we had read enough early on to feel that this concept was problematic. We did initially have a rule against public displays of affection when co-mingling with partners, but this didn't last too long. We wrote things down about rules and tried to update them as we went. We decided that after I had two serious partners (at separate times) who had issues with my wife's partner (and eventually her for a variety of reasons), that *kitchen table polyamory* (a poly form where partners are all familiar with each other and can hang out informally) wasn't going to take place, so many of the rules now are boundaries around contact sadly. I believe we also had a rule about age gap as well, but that hasn't been a real issue to this point. —Rob

Working with the unique needs of your poly constellation

When you're creating the poly formations that work for you, your essential agreements will all hinge upon the unique and specific needs of your partners. Most conversation will circle around the who, what, when, and where questions of connecting intimately with others. You can search up and consult countless possible checklists to help you find your way. All of your considerations, large and small, essentially boil down to this:

> What do you need to maintain your self-respect and physical and emotional well-being while extending your love and care to multiple partners, while your partners do the same?

TIP

If you can stay with I-statements rather than you-statements (see the guidelines in the section "Co-creating as a core polyamory skill" earlier in this chapter), you'll be more successful.

Statements like the following can help start a process of forming agreements that meet your poly constellation's particular needs:

>> I only want to have sex with people out of town.

>> I want to raise children collectively.

>> I don't want to limit any sexual practices among partners.

>> I need to know that what I choose to share with one person isn't shared with everyone; I don't want us communicating for or through each other.

>> I don't want to mix kids, assets, or housing.

>> I need simplicity and minimal processing.

>> I want to have a lot of sex and experimentation.

>> I want to be fully engaged with each partner when I am with them, no intrusions of others.

>> I can manage people flowing in and out, but I want two core partners.

>> I need two nights a week with my primary partner that is all mine.

>> I don't want to know what my partners are doing with others, and I don't want to report on my activities.

>> I want many romantic partners, but I don't want to have sex with anyone.

>> I don't want to be out about being poly.

>> I don't want to have *barrier sex* (condoms, dental dams, gloves) among the core partners; instead, I want consistent birth control practices and sexually transmitted infections (STI) testing.

>> I only want to have sex with one person in the group and then a mix of romantic and platonic intimate connections.

Think ahead about game-changing events that might occur, such as the following:

>> Home ownership or loss of housing or job loss

>> Pregnancies, both wanted and unwanted

>> Parental needs and death

>> Child needs and crises

>> Prevention of and care for partners with STIs

>> Accommodations and care for partners who fall ill or become disabled

TIP

Talking through what-ifs about big life changes and unforeseen events can tell you a lot about how your polycule might operate in good times and bad.

Calendaring — Tracking your activities

Calendaring is the process of co-creating a schedule for your poly life, most often centered upon dating, sex, parenting responsibilities, and social events. Your calendar, or how you're spending your one wild and precious life (Mary Oliver reference, consult the search engine of your choice), speaks volumes about your values and how you're living polyamory.

Do you have a primary relationship? The calendar should reflect this. Are you in a *nonhierarchal* poly relationship (one where no one is primary)? If so, your calendar will confirm this.

Of course, organizing your life around your values and your priorities isn't always possible. Few people have endless resources. You might have children. You might have significant financial commitments and constraints that impact where, how, and with whom you spend our time. Additionally, relationships have seasons — ebbs and flows. Your calendar will reflect these tensions and seasons.

Consider a few favorite calendaring practices when you're making yours:

>> **Create a shared calendar for everyone in the polycule.** As events and dates get added, everyone can see them. By doing so, you're literally practicing your full transparency values.

>> **Have some fun with the calendar.** Color-code polycule meetings, group dinners, one-on-one dates, overnights, sexcapades, and the like. Seeing and comparing the ratio of process-y meetings to sexy events, and group gatherings to intimate time can be helpful.

>> **Create a monthly or bimonthly meeting.** Talk through all the responsibilities that each of you are juggling and get a shared sense of where the free time is on the calendar. Dole out fun and sexy time so that everyone gets some of their biggest wants and needs met.

>> **If you have a creative person in your poly constellation, let them lead you in an art project.** Experimenting with humor, music, new calendaring forms, and engaging visuals.

There's a lot of *uggghhh*ing in the poly community about calendaring, but making sure that you're individually and collectively investing your time so that it aligns with your values and priorities can be a clarifying and even liberating exercise.

Love is infinite, but time is short. Take care of yourself and your partners with thoughtful, co-creative calendaring.

I balance my desire to spend time with all of my lovers and partners with my capacity to be with everyone through capacious scheduling. I once saw a meme floating around on social media that said poly people have a scheduling kink and there's definitely some truth to that! For me, scheduling helps build anticipation rather than anxiety in relation to spending quality time with partners and lovers alike. —Kamilah

Realizing That Nobody Gets Everything They Want

There's no doubt that a core myth about polyamory is that everyone's needs get met and that there are no sacrifices.

In the following sections, you can wade through a lot of contradictory ideas and tensions embedded in polyamory. A hard truth you may come to — after the endorphin rush of opening yourself to more than one lover subsides — is that even with more partners, you may still have to sacrifice some of your wants and needs to sustain your poly relationships.

REMEMBER

More people to love also equals more people to make compromises with. Here are some practices that you can incorporate to become better at compromising and taking good care of you and your partners:

>> Trust that you can get what you need — without winning every point.

>> Listen deeply. When I'm anxious and when I start to think I'm losing something important, I try to stop talking and listen more actively.

>> Pivot from your point of view to your partner's. What is your partner trying to take care of right now as you disagree? Can you help them get what they need?

>> Let go of the need to be right. I often ask myself when I feel like we can't get to the other side of a disagreement: Would I rather win this point, or would I rather we all end this conflict and go cuddle up and be close?

Recognizing the difference between poly euphoria and poly dystopia

Poly euphoria happens when co-created agreements meet most of everyone's needs and are followed, whereas *poly dystopia* happens when you live in a maze of endless rules, constant processing, surveillance, and breaches of trust.

Over the years, I've worked with a lot of clients who have a hard time recognizing what they already know. They come into a coaching session reporting that they're confused or trying to figure something out when it's clear to me that they aren't confused at all, and they already have their answer. They just don't like their answer, so to postpone their grief about the hard truth that they're holding, they employ me as a coach.

And my work then is to reflect back to them the knowledge they continue to deny: Their polycule is in chaos. People are breaking agreements and harming each other. My clients are usually hanging on for dear life in a storm of bad behavior, deflection of responsibility, and pain. They don't want to break up with one or all of their partners. They spend a lot of time trying to convince me and by association themselves that everything is fine. This situation is workable. They have a plan to fix it.

These next sections can help you uncover and accept what you may or may not know as you try to move through and beyond the chaos and denial of poly dystopias.

As a coach, I've devised some simple assessment questions for clients in this situation. When all is chaos, simple and direct questions can help to cut through. A great way to assess whether your agreements are working for you is how they function. This exercise is for when times get tough. These simple questions quickly cut to the core of the functionality of your poly life:

>> Is everyone in the polycule able to pursue their pleasure?

>> Are sacrifices and compromise resting more heavily on one person, or are they shared?

>> Is love really making more love — or is it creating a terrible tangle of pain, rules making, and interminable discussion?

>> Are breaches and conflict more common than connection and care?

In the midst of agonizing denial about the functionality of their poly constellations, my distressed clients often point to the complexity of polyamory, but the litmus test for your mission statements, agreements, poly forms, and functionality is startlingly simple:

>> Do they work?

>> Are you generally happy? Or are you more often drained by conflict?

The answers to your functionality assessment may be hard to accept when you're caught in the whirl of a compelling, taxing set of relationships, but the truth is, many polycules operate with relative ease and very little drama. Agreements get made without rancor and blowups, people keep to them, and trust grows. Over time, these agreements get even more flexible, or fall away altogether, because the people in the poly constellation have demonstrated their trustworthiness so consistently. People feel seen, heard, and cared for. Love is indeed — very inconspicuously — making more love.

Agreements are co-created; rules are imposed. If you feel like you're living in a surveillance state of ever-more unfolding, complex rules, you may need to reconsider whether this mix of partners is workable for you.

Over-negotiation isn't always or often about negotiation, sometimes it's about incompatibility. —JD

Having safer sex with multiple partners

I can't think of any one area as most important in the realm of honoring agreements in a poly constellation, but adhering to commitments on safer sex and pregnancy prevention have got to be near the very top of the list.

REMEMBER

All sex involves risk — emotional, social, and physical. *Safer sex* happens when all these risks are put on the table for you to consider in deciding what actions or intimacies meet your needs and also take the best care of you. Safer sex often involves the use of barriers, for example, to prevent pregnancy or the spread of sexually transmitted infections (STIs).

Having sex with multiple lovers means that each person in the polycule's sexual health is linked to each other. You can tell your lover that they're your number one priority all day long, but leaving them vulnerable to an unwanted pregnancy or to contracting a health condition that they may have to manage for decades shows them no love.

Here are some best practices for navigating safer sex and pregnancy prevention in your poly constellation. Many of these, I learned from Emmett Patterson, a longtime sexual health advocate and collaborator at Building Healthy Online Communities (BHOC):

>> **Assess the well-being of your polycule by asking the following:**

- How is everyone's sexual health? Do any members have ongoing, transmissible conditions?

- If so, what are best practices the group might establish for preventing transmission?

- Among people who can get pregnant, what do they need from their sex partners?

- Does everyone in the group have health insurance and access to STI and pregnancy prevention tools and care?

>> **Educate everyone in the polycule about pregnancy prevention and these needs in the group by considering the following:**

- People who can get pregnant might talk about what their plans are for pregnancy over the lifespan and what their course of action would be should they get pregnant in the group.

- The polycule can create individual and collective responsibility plans around pregnancy.

- The people in the polycule who can get pregnant would need to lead this discussion.

>> **Educate everyone about any sexually transmissible conditions in the group by doing the following:**

- Take on education as a team — encourage group learning and team discussion.

- Don't isolate, overburden, or stigmatize any member.

- Discuss, don't whisper or shame; put everything on the table.

>> **Consider what sexual activities risk transmission of any kind of STI by doing the following:**

- Learn about functional risk levels versus disinformation and scare tactics around STIs.

- Discuss what kinds of activities people might be willing to take off the table as prevention.

- Discuss what people aren't willing to sacrifice for maximal prevention.

- Discuss the circulating impacts of undertaking risks.

- Think about how to minimize risk and maximize pleasure together.

- Strategize about how to contain and address risks while pursuing pleasure individually and collectively.

>> **Commit to a collective prevention and testing scheme that's workable and accessible to all by doing the following:**

- Consider whether you need a written agreement.

- If so, write it down. Written agreements in high stakes situations literally — but also symbolically — cement commitment.

When in doubt, lean into practices of mutual respect, care, and shared pleasure, while leaning away from judgment, rules, and punishment.

TIP

WARNING

Transparency is crucial when navigating safer sex and pregnancy prevention. If someone in the group is afraid of being judged or shamed for disclosing a condition or a worry or a desire, you've created an environment that puts them, and the whole group, at risk.

Coming through on your commitments

True pleasure is being able to count on each other. Let me repeat myself: Showing up for each other creates more trust, more joy, more pleasure. In this section, I provide more information about what you can do to grow trust and joy in your polycules by coming through on your commitments.

Coming through on commitments creates possibility; and breaking agreements creates pain, chaos, more processing, and more dreck. More love creates more love only when love is a verb. Love is action, not a series of poetic declarations or convoluted promises.

TIP

Sex and relationship coach Asha Leong posits that a core basic in polyamory is simply a commitment to: "Tell the truth as you know it, as you know it."

When partners have dug themselves into a hole around fear-based or obsessive actions and breaching commitments, there's often a convoluted set of conversations about honesty. What is it? *What does honesty really mean?* Most often, this kind of deflective speech-making grows in the gap between when a partner has come to understand or act on something and the time it has taken them to inform their partners. Having clear guidelines about honesty and information flows can help contain this kind of chaos.

Sometimes, you can be in denial about what you know because when you come upon a big truth, it can be hard. You may have to change something foundational in your relationship or life. But the instruction in Asha's guideline is clear: After you know the hard thing, and you've given yourself a minute to digest it; tell your partners.

Coming through on your commitments to being honest means you're being accountable to your partners. These days, a lot of people throw the word accountability around like they know what it means, but often, they don't. My favorite teacher on accountability, the activist Shannon Perez-Darby lays this out with such clarity: "Accountability means taking responsibility for your choices and the impact of those choices."

When breaches of trust happen in relationships, accountability isn't something you can exact from another person (see Chapter 13 for more on this). Accountability is something you engage in — as follows:

>> You take responsibility for making a choice that broke a commitment.

>> You take in the harm your breach of trust has caused.

>> You accept full responsibility for the harm caused by your actions.

>> You apologize.

>> You take steps to learn what led to you break the commitment.

>> You consider what harms in your formative story might have driven some of this hurtful behavior, not as a way to excuse yourself, but as a starting place for getting help in stopping the behavior.

>> You get help — from a close group of friends, professionals, or a support group — not from the person you've impacted with this behavior.

>> You make appropriate amends. Sometimes this means ending a relationship with care. Sometimes it means giving someone space. *Most often, this means committing to changing your behavior.*

REMEMBER

Be the poly partner you need by modeling accountability. Come through on your commitments, even when doing so is hard and even when breaking them would be so easy. In a world where so much is uncertain, and out of your control, your behavior is one thing you have complete power over.

Your actions — your small, daily acts of love, your imperfect acts of repair, and your big swings at changing the world through your talents, your aspirations, and what you're committing to in your life — are so meaningful.

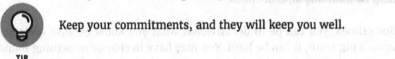

TIP

Keep your commitments, and they will keep you well.

Chapter **10**

Opening an Existing Monogamous Relationship

Y ou're likely reading this chapter because you or someone you care about is thinking about opening an existing monogamous relationship. And by *opening*, I mean considering a fleeting encounter or significant romantic or sexual relationship while in a partnership that was established as a couple, a closed system. In this chapter, you can find resources, activities, and stories to support your research and decision-making process as you consider whether opening up your relationship is right for you.

Probably the most important thing in this moment is to be honest with yourself, even if you can't tell anyone else that you're considering polyamory. Be clear with yourself about what's motivating your process of inquiry or discovery and what you fear most. The number one thing you can do to ensure a good outcome is to tell yourself the truth.

It's okay if you're reading this chapter because you're at the end of your rope in your relationship, or because you have a crush on someone and you don't want to leave your partner and blow up your life. It's okay if you're reading this chapter because your partner is insisting on opening up your relationship and you want nothing to do with polyamory. Any and all of it is fine. Just respect where you are and go from there.

Making the Decision to Open Your Relationship

Opening a relationship that was designed to be sexually exclusive isn't for the faint of heart. Often, one partner wants an open relationship more than the other. Sometimes, the discussion about opening up comes in the aftermath of lies or infidelity. Although opening a relationship after trust has been broken isn't ideal, it's not impossible to make it work. If you're struggling to reestablish trust as you embark on an opening process, see Chapter 13 for in-depth discussion about healing from trust breaches.

No matter how you've arrived at this point of questioning — in whatever tender and searching state you find yourself — welcome. You have a lot to consider when figuring out whether an open or polyamorous relationship is right for you. The following sections provide some information and tools to support your decision-making.

Weighing the key considerations

Every couple has different key considerations to weigh in deciding whether to open their relationship. Crossing the line in the sand defined by monogamy or marriage — that of sexual exclusivity for the duration of your relationship — can feel seismic. And indeed, many people find several adjacent things in life changing after they open their relationship — from how and with whom you socialize, to who you bring to family gatherings.

TIP

Rather than taking on or projecting a wholesale life revision in this one decision, boil it down to what matters right now, between you and your partner. To do this, you can try the next two activities to figure out what makes sense for right now. You might also want to refer to Chapter 3, which has activities to help you think about whether polyamory is right for you.

Figuring out the "why"

Each person in the partnership should undertake this exercise privately. If you each do the assessment, after you complete your process, you can decide when or whether to share your answers. The important thing is to focus on yourself and to answer the questions as though you'll never share them.

ACTIVITY

Give yourself some private space so you can tune out any competing influences or concerns, like the needs of your partners, parents, or friends:

>> What are the ways you're most alive in your partnership right now? What parts of you and your dreams and passions are best supported here?

>> What parts of you are hidden or suppressed (they can be sexual, social, professional, artistic, emotional, and so on)?

>> When did you give up on or start hiding these parts of you?

>> When you think specifically about your sexual life in your partnership, how are you most alive and true to yourself?

>> What are your favorite and most satisfying ways of being sexual and/or intimate with your partner or lover?

>> When you think about your sexual life in your partnership, how are you hiding? What have you suppressed out of fear of judgment or fear of scaring off or repulsing your partner?

>> What haven't you said to your partner that really needs saying if you're going to open the relationship with integrity and care?

>> On a scale of 1–10, with 10 being the most extreme, how frustrated or depressed are you by the sacrifices you've made in abandoning or suppressing this or these parts of yourself?

>> On a scale of 1–10, with 10 being the most likely, how likely is it that you'll leave or need to break up if you *don't* open the relationship?

>> On a scale of 1–10, with 10 being the most likely, how likely is it that you or your partner will leave or break up if you *do* open the relationship?

>> What do you think opening or bringing a new intimate partner into the relationship will solve?

TIP

This reflection exercise is full of emotionally taxing questions, so take your time. I worked with a couple that took months to complete their assessments and still longer to decide to share them. The key is to get honest. Why is polyamory an attractive idea to you right now? What has been missing in your life that has brought you to this point? You can start and stop and come back to this activity later to finish it. Let your answers rest on you. Let them give you clues about what your next right step might be.

Some couples finish their inventories and decide that it's time to get professional help (like a therapist) so they can share what they've written in an environment where it can be best heard. Some feel confident that they have the tools to be vulnerable and share important truths that their partner might not know, so they can work through these issues together.

Taking a readiness inventory: Are you strong, supportive communicators?

If you aren't sure whether you and your partner are capable of sharing your inventories and hearing each other, this activity may help you gain a sense of your readiness. Part 2 looks at relational skills and your capacity to process conflicts. Those chapters may help you figure out whether you're ready to share and engage on these sensitive topics.

ACTIVITY

As you prepare to share your answers from the previous assessment, these questions can help you evaluate your readiness as affirming communicators. Take your time and score your relationship here:

>> **Communicating constructively:** Score 1–5 with 1 being that you experience repeating, fraught, and unresolved conflicts and 5 being that you're excellent at getting to resolution. Ask yourself:

- What is conflict like between us?

- Do we resolve differences reasonably?

- Are our conflicts cyclical and intense and never ending?

>> **Fighting fairly:** Determine whether you can resolve conflict without shaming, blaming, shouting at, or hurting each other. Score 1–5 with 1 being you or your partner at times or often inflict serious emotional or even physical harm and 5 being that no one resorts to any (or almost none) of the listed harmful fighting behaviors.

>> **Owning your part:** Score 1–5 with 1 if one or both of you believes that you *never have a part* in the difficulty, it's all on the other person; and 5 for if both of you are largely self-referencing when you have arguments.

- Can each person take responsibility for their contribution to the current conflict? That earns a 5 score.

- Can you see and own what part you are playing in the difficulty? If it's only you (or your partner), that earns a 3.

>> **Staying cool:** Determine whether you can stay kind and supportive to each other even when you're angry or upset. Score 1–5 with 1 being you both

absolutely can't do this and 5 being you're both able to be reasonably supportive even when upset.

>> **Finding support:** Assess whether you have good people to confide in about the relationship who don't trash your partner or have an agenda for the relationship. Score 1–5 with 1 being neither of you have anyone like this and 5 being you both do.

If you find that your capacity is low after taking this inventory — in the 5–12 range — I suggest finding resources on building accountable, nonviolent communication strategies (refer to Appendix B on surviving abuse).

GASLIGHTING AND OTHER FORMS OF INTIMATE PARTNER VIOLENCE (IPV)

One in three women in the United States will experience intimate partner violence (IPV) in her lifetime. In the 2023 National LGBTQ+ Women's Community Survey, 47 percent of respondents reported surviving IPV, with bisexual, pansexual, queer, genderfluid, and transgender respondents reporting even higher levels of exposure.

Gaslighting, or a concerted campaign to deceive a partner over time in an effort to undermine their sanity or belief in themselves, is the most common form of emotional abuse reported by survivors, across the board. Second to gaslighting is the disruption of friendship networks or imposing social isolation.

These two forms of emotional abuse are so common that they're often underestimated in terms of their destructive impact. If you find your confidence in yourself undermined in your relationship, if you can't answer a lot of the inventories in this and other chapters because it's so painful to see where you are in your relationship, if you're exhausted by arguments that shame and blame you, if you can't see your friends without an argument, if your world has shrunk down to a tiny, cramped space inside your partner's judgment of you, then you are in trouble.

Your partner may have a passionate attachment to you, but they don't know how to be loving. They're hurting you — and you deserve all the kindness, care, and emotional safety in the world. You don't have to do or be anything to earn this, because generous care and emotional support are your right for just being imperfectly you. Everyone deserves that foundation. If you're struggling or suffering, see Appendix B for places to get help.

Considering important dos and don'ts

In this section you can browse through some common challenges and caveats in opening your relationship, while also taking in some best practices or dos and don'ts.

Do take responsibility for your power as a couple if you're seeking a third

If you're seeking a partner or partners as a couple, understand that your existing relationship creates a foundational power dynamic. You two have figured out a lot about how to communicate. You have a shared agenda in looking for a partner or partners. You have an established base from which to pursue other attachments. You need to consider how to balance that power and not overwhelm or exploit these advantages with new partners.

REMEMBER

Balancing power means that you're up front about what you're looking for and what you're offering new partners. You take care with communicating directly. Transparency and respect, as always, are critical.

Couple privilege is a term that gets tossed around in poly community. Here's what it means:

>> If you're starting to date, can one person in your couple enact a *veto* (unilaterally decide that it's over)? If so, inform your dates of this decision-making structure in your relationship.

>> What unspoken history between you and your partner is operating as you pursue this new partner — perhaps a history of infidelity between you?

>> How will you balance the existing, shared store of knowledge and communication shorthand between you, while informing a new partner to the best of your abilities about what you two are able to offer?

>> How will you balance the social legitimacy and the primacy of "the couple" with showing respect to a new partner, privately and publicly?

There's no cookie-cutter answer to these questions: Keep them in your sights as you reach out to new lovers and consider how to build transparency, mutual respect, and full consent.

Don't talk yourself out of it

If you've made your way to nearly opening up your relationship, no doubt there are a lot of overwhelming messages flying around in your head. Some might sound like these common monogamy-only messages:

> Marriage means sacrifice. Polyamory is immature and selfish. You don't have a right to your pleasure. You're abandoning your vows.

Ask yourself these questions:

» Are these voices or beliefs yours or someone else's?

» Marriage or partnership involves compromise, but how much?

» Do you really owe a civil or church-based institution the level of self-denial you've been carrying?

If you've made vows with or promises to your partner, then the two of you can decide how to live out those promises, together.

Do expect the unexpected

You can plan all the plans you want together, but you can't control outcomes. You might have very clear ideas about how opening up your relationship will go for you, what you're capable of, and where your limits are — and a year from now, all these ideas may be obsolete. The actual experience of opening up to new intimacies and new parts of yourself, while your partner does the same, isn't entirely predictable.

Don't catastrophize

If all goes well, some wonderful things will happen. You may make some new intimate connections that open up your world, bring immeasurable joy, and strengthen your primary relationship. Undoubtedly, though, mistakes will be made. Miscommunication, hurts, and missteps will happen. That's okay. You're human. So's your partner. You're in this together.

WARNING

Don't make a catastrophe out of a misstep. Take responsibility, apologize, work it out, and keep going.

STARTING TO SEE SOMEONE NEW IS A LOT

When one partner starts dating somebody, that's a big moment. The time that you're dedicating to this new person is always an issue. Later in my poly life, I got good at describing how it is for me when I meet a new person, but early on it was harder to figure out. Now, I always try to share this with my partners so that they can understand my process and not be afraid of it.

These days, when I see my lover taking on a new lover and they're super excited, I'm like, *Oh my god, I can't wait to see them.* I get so excited and happy for them. And I know that they're in there, right in that newness, and that it's everything. That's when you're so curious about each other. Everything is wonderful, and you're just excited to learn everything about them and to have other people get to see that excitement.

I think a lot of times people try to hide that excitement from their partners; they're afraid that if they really show it, then partners will be like, *Oh, no! This is not what I signed up for.* So, I think that has to really be incorporated into the conversations because the newness intensity will always happen. You'll always be excited about a new person. And you'll always spend more time with that person in the beginning, and then it kind of levels out. —**Ignacio**

Knowing What to Do: One Wants To, the Other Doesn't

Probably the most common request I get as a sex coach is to help monogamous couples with asymmetrical needs. Often, one partner's libido is significantly more turbo-charged than the other's. Sometimes, one person is interested in kink activities — like role-playing or power play — and the other isn't. Another very common difference couples report is that one partner experiences themselves as fundamentally polyamorous and the other as fundamentally monogamous (see the nearby sidebar).

Managing asymmetrical needs for sexual exclusivity

The fact that you and your partner aren't a perfectly matched set around your desires or your relationship preferences makes sense. Very few couples align on everything that matters to them. Couples that stay happy and connected over the long haul often:

>> Are aligned around core things that matter *the most* to them — things that may or may not be about desire — they could pertain to things like parenting, politics, or the flow of your social and material lives.

>> Are able to adapt or be flexible about core needs their partner has that are outside their interests or comfort zones. And again, these things may or may not pertain to desire — like traveling, spending lots of time with friends or family, or having a passion that demands a lot of time.

Being in relationship means being in a constant state of compromise. Despite all the rom-com hype about finding *the one*, few people in long-term, monogamous partnerships find yourselves in a situation where you don't have to give up on significant wants in order to stay together.

The promise of polyamory for such couples is that:

>> You might have to give up fewer of your core needs or wants.

>> You might be able to experience or stretch into parts of yourself that have been hidden or buried in your relationship.

>> You might find another partner who enjoys things your partner hates or can't be a part of.

>> You might be able to drop resentments and stop having the same old fight with your partner over the things that you can't get from them.

By adding these new pleasures and possibilities into the mix, you might be able to bring a lighter, renewed, or more joyful self home to your relationship with your primary partner.

All these exciting changes are possible when opening a relationship, but certainly not a given or a guarantee. Opening up with care, transparency, and full consent is critical to the success of the endeavor. And it's often easier said than done. I discuss these three components here.

Opening with care

Opening *with care* means the following:

>> You co-create agreements at the start — rather than, say, come home from an office event and tell your partner you made out with a coworker. (See Chapter 9 for ideas about co-creating agreements.)

>> You make sure *both of you* are getting some of your core unaddressed needs met.

>> You don't run off or disappear into a new crush.

>> You keep your agreements — as opposed to saying: "I know we said condoms only, but she's on the pill.".

Being transparent

Transparency means very simply: *no secrets*. Consider these points:

>> You aren't hiding a crush or a hidden agenda as you create agreements.

>> You aren't agreeing to boundaries you know you'll violate because you just want to get to a yes with your partner so you can start this experiment.

>> If you're lying to yourself about what you're up to in opening your relationship, stop. Tell yourself what you're holding on to and then tell your partner. All cards are on the table. Period.

>> If it's not safe to tell your partner the truth, get help. *Safety first.*

>> If you think being transparent is impossible in the agreement-making part of opening your relationship, it's unlikely that you're going to be able to manage what comes after opening the relationship.

Committing to full, affirmative consent

Here's what full, *affirmative consent* means:

>> Telling about past abuses of trust.

>> Talking as much about yourself and what your intentions and hopes are as possible.

>> Rejecting coercive control. No one person in the relationship is held hostage to a relational demand, such as a partner's housing being put to risk if they don't agree to open the relationship.

FUNDAMENTALS: I'M MONOGAMOUS (OR POLYAMOROUS) IT'S JUST WHO I AM

When I work with couples who have *asymmetrical needs* around their relationship forms — that is, one person states that they're patently monogamous and the other reports that they are fundamentally polyamorous — I ask them to dig deeper with this series of questions:

- How did you discover that this way of being was a core or essential part of your social and intimate makeup?

- Have you had bad experiences with the opposing relationship form — monogamy or polyamory?

- Did a parent implant this fundamental sense of yourself through either imperative (I'll disown you if . . .) or bad behavior, such as a damaging monogamous commitment or series of infidelities?

Sometimes, you might experience a way of being as essential or given to you, but it has been conditioned in a dramatic or coercive context without your even noticing it. Digging through your attachment story (see Chapter 7) can provide clues about this.

There's no doubt that monogamous conditioning is omnipresent and unrelenting (see Chapter 2). And there's also no doubt that polyamory offers potential relief from the many sacrifices that long-term monogamy demands.

My question for partners who present this asymmetry as a fundamental dilemma is:

Is it more important for you to live out this part of you — this *fundamental way of relating* — or is it more important for you to stay with your partner?

What's more important to you in terms of living the life you want to live and taking the best care of yourself? My clients hate this question. It often feels impossible to answer because it's so either/or, but that's the nature of fundamentals. If this relational way of being is indeed essential to you, and the opposite is essential to your partner, then you have to decide between these two things.

If monogamy or polyamory *isn't quite a fundamental* — that is to say, if you can modify your ideas or practices around this deeply held way of being and have some wiggle room around this — then there's often a third way (refer to the section "Finding a third way") — a possible way forward together.

Finding a third way

I worked with two clients over nearly three years on the asymmetries in their monogamous marriage. G. had a more robust libido than K. He wanted to open their eight-year relationship. K. had a stressful job working with survivors of sexual assault that impacted both her libido and her trust issues. These two people had deep love for each other and a vibrant community of friends and extended family that supported their relationship. G.'s family of origin could be critical and difficult, and K. was a great support to him. K.'s work was often emotionally draining, and G. loved surprising her with spontaneous getaways and fun events. I often thought in session: *These two people adore each other*.

So, I did a lot of investigating with them around a possible third way. K. reported that she was fundamentally monogamous, but I wondered if she might be capable of a stretch — by trying out some *monogamish* activities (sexual activities with others that reserve emotional intimacy exclusively in the primary partnership). G. longed for a second partner, but I wondered if he might be satisfied with something less relationship-oriented, like kissing or playing with others. I proposed possible activities with them:

>> What if they went to parties and K. selected someone for G. to kiss?

>> What if K. pursued a crush that she could connect to first, and G. could just observe this period without pursuing anyone himself?

>> What if they tried to pick someone up together at a party or event and K. was in charge of what happened or didn't happen?

All these activities were designed to put K. in the driver's seat, which seemed like it might be helpful because one of her big fears about opening the relationship was that it might spin out of control and that G. would develop big feelings instead of remaining emotionally monogamous with her.

Over many months, we drew up desire profiles of the couple, affirmed their relationship, laughed about their various foibles and adventures, and improved their communication skills, but K. made no foray into any of the possible third way activities. My heart sank in this period as their coach because what I've often observed is that a partner will say — this person, and our relationship is my top priority — but then they won't move into any new or comfort-zone stretching activities that might preserve it.

G. and K.'s relationship had been monogamous for eight years when they came to me, despite G. letting K. know that he had engaged in mostly polyamorous relationships when they started dating. K. acknowledged this when they met and noted that polyamory wasn't something she could see doing in the early attachment phase of their relationship. To preserve his relationship with K., G. denied feelings, opportunities, crushes, and intimate connections with others for many years. And then when G. finally raised the issue of polyamory at the eight-year mark, K. experienced G.'s desire to open the relationship as a betrayal. K. believed that G. felt she wasn't enough, rather than that he had a legitimate desire to operate more expansively socially and intimately.

So, after three years of our work together, K. and G. broke up.

It was G. who eventually decided he could no longer live with this level of self-denial, and they broke up soon after. As a coach, letting go of my own attachment to their wonderful connection and to stop wondering what more I could have done to help them create a third way together was difficult.

Finding good love is an amazing, wonderful thing. Preserving and sustaining it — hard work no matter what form your relationship takes.

ACTIVITY

This third way investigation is a great exercise for any couple who wants to open their relationship, because even if you're both interested in opening up, you're often not quite on the same page about the who, what, when, and where of it. Work through these questions:

>> What could be a fun, low-stakes beginning activity to start to open the relationship? Pick things that you know could work for your partner.

- Cruising at a bar, event, or online. Solo or together — for some, picking out potential dates for each other or a third is hot and fun.

- Helping each other create or edit an online profile.

- Defining an ideal first date or first try and the other person supporting you in figuring out how to pursue this ideal.

- Creating a pick-up or make-out scenario together where the person who is most anxious about opening the relationship is in charge.

- If you both want to know very little about each other's exploration, helping to create the time and space for your partner to pursue their interests outside of your view.

>> What could you let go of in terms of your need to either control or accelerate this process that would take great care of your partner?

- Creating a series of compromise scenarios that addresses your bottom-line needs and meets some of theirs.

- Initiating fun and playful discussion about possible dates, moving away from the grinding arguments you've been in.

- Initiating a dinner with poly friends or another couple that's in an open relationship to either get support or cruise them.

>> Do we both need to have other lovers?

- Understanding that having asymmetrical needs sometimes means that one person needs a lover and the other needs deeper intimacy with their friends, or needs more childcare so they have time to themselves, or is able to finally make music or get an art studio.

- Choosing a monogamous/polyamorous third way solution can be extremely relieving and exciting, while often drawing skepticism from people outside of your relationship.

REMEMBER

The point is to meet both of your core needs, not to do the same thing. What others think doesn't matter. What matters is what the two of you think.

TIP

When you're creating third way options, be generous with your partner. You may find yourself holding more power in the moment, but that may not always be true across the long span of your relationship. I've observed many people come to regret their failure to own and mediate the impacts of their power after it has shifted in their relationship over time.

Finding a third way is an exercise in sharing power, so that everyone gets their fair share of the goodies — even if the content differs considerably.

THE LOVE PARADOX: YOU'RE ENOUGH AND NO ONE PERSON IS ENOUGH

A crushing paradox that goes against all fantasy happily-ever-after endings is:

- You're perfect just the way you are — *fully enough*.

- And no one person can meet all of a loved one's needs; the love of a singular being is *never enough*.

This seems so simple and obvious, but all the mythologies about love in popular culture steer you in the opposite direction on both counts.

- The beauty and fashion industries (among others) hinge on selling you the idea that you'll never be enough, and you must continue to purchase your way to improvement for the entire length of your not-enough life.

- The romance, relationship, and marriage industries hinge on selling you the mythology of a singular soulmate, that perfect needle-in-a-haystack person who will meet all of your social, sexual, and familial needs.

Total bunk, on both ends. You can be entirely enough, perfect in your imperfections, a wonder, and a gift — and still not meet any one person's needs, soulmate or not. In fact, no one is meant to do this. To live a life of meaning, you need to address your own needs and build your well-being in community — among friends, family, loved ones, coworkers, like-minded collaborators, people you admire, advocates, artists, writers, musicians, sports teams, spiritual community, nature, and the list goes on.

No one person is going to *complete you* or take total care of you. And you aren't solely capable of satisfying all the complex needs of anyone else.

Why didn't we all learn *that* in kindergarten?

Escaping tolyamory

Advice columnist Dan Savage is famous for coining absolutely spot-on sex terms, and this one is arguably his best: *Tolyamory*, a combination of tolerance and polyamory, referring to the state of pretending that you don't know that your monogamous partner is having emotional, intimate, and/or sexual relationships with others — so that you can preserve your marriage or partnership.

Some sex coaches believe that tolyamory is in fact the most commonly practiced form of polyamory, and if we included it in the polyamory canon — which I don't — they may be right.

It's a commentary on the omnipresent imposition of marriage and monogamy that more people would prefer to deny their partner's participation in hidden relationships than address the constraints of monogamy and its impacts on their partnership and well-being.

The preponderance of tolyamory, then, is significantly shaped by the social conditions a lot of couples find themselves in these days:

>> Familial pressures to stay monogamous, even if only in appearance

>> Fiscal pressures around how prohibitively expensive it is to create two households if the truths hidden by tolyamory were revealed

>> The exhaustion of daily demands in the current structure of society —
working too much, having low job security, and parenting in isolation,
among them

>> Social pressure to be a success, to appear as though you're handling it all, and
living in the picture-perfect couple or family

Escaping the status quo and the often emotionally deadening space of tolyamory
means having to step up and talk to your partner about what's really going on
with you and what you — and they — need.

If tolyamory really is about a desire to preserve your relationship, then there are
other, better, and more enlivening ways to do this.

Trying Out Polyamory: Set HOT Goals

If you've ever worked in a nonprofit or corporate setting, you've likely heard of
SMART goals, which stands for goals that are Strategic, Measurable, Achievable,
Realistic, and Timely. The idea behind starting with a SMART goal in a big campaign, for example, is that picking something small and winnable helps grow
team spirit and confidence. It helps you build momentum toward a larger goal
that might seem impossible at the outset of the project.

In service of gaining confidence by creating attainable early benchmarks, I've
created HOT goals for the couples I coach who are attempting to open a previously monogamous relationship. The following sections examine what HOT goals
refer to and how you can use them in your relationship when you're considering
polyamory.

Getting a feel for HOT goals

Here are key elements of HOT goals:

>> **Honor where you are at.** Honoring where you are means you're accepting all
the fears and frustrations that got you here by being extremely gentle with
each other and reassuring. This may seem obvious, but don't expect your
partner to stop carrying the fear and resentments they've been carrying or to
somehow transform into somebody else because you've decided to open
the relationship.

>> **Offer possibility.** Offering possibility means being smart about what you're
attempting as you open the relationship. Don't take the biggest swing right

out of the gate. Don't offer something you aren't ready for. Stretching yourself beyond your emotional capacity on your first foray at opening up is likely to create hurt and shut things down quickly.

>> **Try it on.** You did it! You got to this place of experimentation by coming through for each other and taking a risk. Now your big job is to extend yourself and be generous with your partner. And see what happens!

Honoring (and not burning) your primary relationship

If you want to preserve the euphoria and protect the new discoveries that opening your relationship is bringing you, take excellent care of your primary partner. Don't just tell them you love them, *show them*. Be attentive and generous. Moving into new experiences and new love can be intoxicating. But it all goes better for everyone if you do more than just chase that high. Make sure you honor your primary relationship.

For a great example of what not to do — when I was doing sex education in my early 30s, I was extremely excited to present a workshop on *Dom/sub dynamics* (relationships where one person takes control and the other turns control over to them) with a Dom that I was passionate about. Our relationship was new, and I talked a lot about the workshop with my partner F. I was very enthusiastic about them attending. Our primary relationship didn't have this dynamic, and I wanted to share my experience of it with her. I could see as I talked about it that F. had reservations, but I persisted; in retrospect, I can see that my *New Relationship Energy* (early dating bliss that can be obsessive) was clouding my judgment. Eventually, F. agreed to attend.

And it was a disaster. F. was unprepared for both my thrill at talking about Dom/sub dynamics and my public attachment to my new lover. While she presented a strong supportive front at the event, the pain and hurt she experienced took months of talking through to mend. At first, I was defensive and pushed all the difficulty back on F. She had agreed to come to the workshop. I remember I said: "I'm not a mind-reader." But eventually, I could own that I really didn't listen attentively when we had our discussion. I had such a strong agenda. F. didn't take very good care of herself because she wanted to please me, and I didn't take very good care of F. because I was thinking only of my euphoric new sub life.

Going after your HOT goals

As you're pursuing your HOT goals, and perhaps racing around in the early excitement of opening up your relationship, remember:

>> Don't mess up. The opening risks really matter. Honor them.

>> Slow things down if it all starts to feel like a lot, but don't stop. Ease into the change, affirm each other, and try not to shut down out of fear.

>> Assess whether you're acting like a partner (supporting, affirming) or like a parent (defining, constraining) with your beloved. *Be a partner*.

POLYAMORY STORY

MAKING ROOM FOR MISTAKES

What people don't account for as they open their relationships is carving out a nice big hole for all the mistakes that they're going to make. They need to go into it saying: We will fail. We will get on each other's nerves; we will make a mistake because that's absolutely true. Because that's how you learn. And we think that we can bypass that by creating all these rules. And then as soon as somebody breaks one, it's like: you're horrible. You didn't follow the rules. I told you this already. So, *your fault*. And that's just cancel culture. It's *carceral* (cancel and carceral culture are built on polarized blame, punishment, and discarding people). We're putting in these dire consequences. We told you the rules. You didn't follow it, you fed it up! Rather than: this is hard, this is an imperfect process, and we're going to fumble together.

Let's assume this is a learning process and how to come back from it. So, it's literally saying yeah, we're gonna f–up. And what do we have that's holding us together? What is the glue you know?

Is it our communication? Is it our values? Or the fact that we've come through other hard things together and we believe in us?

But I think we lie to ourselves, right? Because we find this idea of opening things up and it's like, *amazing*. Yes, this is great. Of course it makes sense. Yes, multiple lovers. Yes, this and that. And then you say okay, it'll be good. Let's just put all the rules down and we'll be fine. And that's not how it works. It's great to have those rules to fall back on to reassess, but I think that we have to honestly say to ourselves, "This is a new adventure. And we don't know exactly how it's going to go." —**Ignacio**

So many couples destroy the possibilities for polyamory by just being dismissive and self-centered when they're crushing on their first new date or interest. Many others take all the heat and the fun out if it by trying to control for every possibility. It's okay if things are little messy. Let yourself feel everything you're feeling and try not to have big conversations when you're either exhausted or activated. Try, be kind, be patient. Try again.

Success Creates More Success

Couples who make successful first forays into polyamory together — those who listen attentively to each other, resolve conflict well, create reasonable parameters, and then stick to them — are in a strong position to build from a place of success in their polyamory exploration. You're ready to get into the building mode, which the following sections explore.

Building trust and joy

When you've achieved your first HOT goal, convene. Review. Congratulate. Have celebration sex! Discuss what's next, and whether you want to expand on your vision or try something else.

REMEMBER

There's no rush, even if you're experiencing quite a rush of feelings. Bask in your success, appreciate each other, and appreciate the new energy that being open to others is circulating back into the relationship.

I find this effect to be among the least anticipated and appreciated in the process — that wild joy that success at opening up the relationship circulates back to the relationship. Relief! Freedom! More love!

POLYAMORY STORY

YOU CAN'T MAKE RULES FOR OTHER PEOPLE'S BEHAVIOR, BUT YOU CAN COMMIT

Seven years into our relationship my sweet love organized a threesome between us and a close friend of his. It was everything I dreamed of. Hot, fun, novel. That experience opened something in me, and it felt like I could never go back. We decided to try non-monogamy.

(continued)

(continued)

That first year was a disaster. We fumbled in every way I see so many people who were previously monogamous do. We had too many rules. Rules trying to control for jealousy, commitment, the primacy of our relationships. The rules failed. You can't make rules for other people's behavior. Through time and lots of practice we landed on a rhythm that works. We threw out the rules in service of commitments. We have financial commitments, we own a home together, we co-parent dogs. We love each other deeply, and I'm committed to a lifelong practice of showing up for this love. These commitments aren't rules we have to follow but practices that we return to again and again.

In the ten years since going all-in on non-monogamy we've both had multiple other serious, committed relationships. We've transformed the ways we talked about our practices and moved from using the term non-monogamy in favor of polyamory. We've "come out" as polyamorous to our friends and family. If, at the beginning, I'd known how hard the path to get here would be, I'm not sure I would have done it, but I'm so glad I did. The journey has been transformative. It's widened my relationships, helped me learn to better understand myself, and made space for lots of hot sex. It's also brought my partner and I even closer together. We are the most honest, transparent, and clear about our love and commitment as we have ever been. —**Shannon**

Expanding your exploration

If you feel confident that your poly exploration is going well, you may want to try out more things that you've identified in your list of wants and needs (see Chapter 3 for many additional activities that help you identify your interests and Chapter 6 to figure out your hard limits). Chapter 4 presents a number of different model polycules to appreciate and consider. There are literally endless possibilities for expanding on poly possibility, and only you and your partner know what will work for you.

REMEMBER

As long as love, honesty, and respect are the drivers of your discovery process, you're on the right path.

Chapter **11**

Coming Out Polyamorous

You don't have to come out to live an empowered poly life. Let me say that again for the people in the back: You can live a full polyamorous life without being public about that choice beyond the privacy of your polycule.

While the power of claiming your identity and living openly is undeniable, you're the only person who knows what's going to work. You can weigh the stressors and supports in your life, the pros and cons of coming out, and make decisions that take the best care of you and your beloveds.

TIP

Secrets make you sick. Privacy can make room for you to be more of who you are. So, an important question is what's the difference between secrets and privacy:

» A secret is often forced upon you by someone with power over you. Secrets leave you queasy, worried, fretting, or afraid.

» Privacy is something you set up and secure for yourself: "I can decide when and where to tell my story. I can take care of myself and my loved ones." Privacy feels like you are the boss of your life.

This chapter helps you consider what coming out means, to think through to what degree you're ready to come out – to yourself, to your family, to a potential date, to your rugby team, to coworkers, or whoever — and to help you build the support you need to make your best coming out choices.

Deciding Who to Talk to or Tell

Coming out is a process, not an event. You come out first to yourself, and then take a lifelong journey of sharing your truth and your desires with others in a zillion different situations as you decide how to live.

Monogamy is a default standard in society. Nearly everyone assumes you are monogamous unless you tell them otherwise. How important is it for a cab driver, your child's teacher, your landlord, or your boss to know?

In some of these cases, coming out might mean you're claiming your true self and your partners in public, and it can build joy and self-esteem. In others, it might mean that you're exposing yourself to someone with the power to shape your life or your future prospects, and it can bring fear and trepidation. The following sections help you sift through the risks and rewards of coming out poly.

POLYAMORY STORY

I never understood monogamy beyond it being about possession. I haven't lost friends or family and I don't hide it, but I think a lot of people take me less seriously as a person when they find out I'm poly. They think my life isn't fulfilled without possession of a person. —Mija

Starting with yourself

The most important person to come out to about being polyamorous is you. If being poly is fundamentally who you are and how you want to pursue love and make family, then the most important person to tell is you.

Here are some questions to ask yourself about who you are (there are many more in Chapter 3):

>> Have you often had crushes or been in love with more than one person at the same time?

>> Do you feel like love makes more love?

>> Has limiting your love to one person felt strange, confining, or like you were living a lie?

These questions can help you figure out how you want to pursue love:

>> Have you often imagined yourself living in a threesome or among a group of lovers?

>> Has collective living or loving been an attractive idea?

>> Have you felt like you had to hide all these feelings to fit into monogamous relationships?

REMEMBER

Being true to yourself isn't overrated. Living your life as an open book among family, friends, and colleagues is enlivening. You spend less time worrying, sifting, and creating a narrative for others. You spend more time stretching into all the amazing possible ways to be you.

When you come out to yourself, you're opening a door inside you that can now lead outward: to new ways of being, and a new dynamic, vibrant life.

POLYAMORY STORY

While in monogamous relationships, I'd often find myself desiring others. Ninety-nine percent of the time, I did nothing to pursue these feelings. I'd just acknowledge them and wonder if something was wrong with me. The idea of profound love, true commitment, and a sense of security kept drawing me in. I was unfamiliar with polyamory, but I had heard about players, cheaters, and the unconventional. I didn't consider myself a player or a cheater, and I didn't think I fit into the unconventional category. My understanding of polyamory developed over time, through my personal experiences and curiosities. —**Ignacio**

Telling your crushes

The second most important people to come out to are your crushes, the subjects of your lust, love, and family story. In the section "Getting out there: How to come out" later in this chapter I describe how to tell your crushes — and others — about what you're discovering about yourself. There, you can find a lot of handy exercises to explore fun, engaging ways to share your formative ideas and hopes for and with your poly connections.

Sharing with others

When considering coming out to everyone else, ask yourself how important the people are and how will coming out to them enrich your life. Only you know. Read the section "Building Community: The Joy of Coming Out" later in this chapter for more help in figuring out who, how, and when you might want to come out, but here I examine some of the possibilities around who.

COMING OUT POLYAMOROUS: PARALLELS TO LGBTQ+ COMING OUT

The fight for LGBTQ+ rights has flourished over the past 50 years or so by catalyzing a massive global movement for coming out, and in doing so, widely sharing the vitality and humanity of LGBTQ+ people. Still, not all LGBTQ+ people in this period have chosen to come out, and yet many have still embraced their identities, loved their partners, and lived full lives.

In many countries being LGBTQ+ is still illegal. In more supportive territories, the United States included, some legal protections may be on the books, but depending on what region you live in and how you identify, coming out can expose LGBTQ+ people to violence and impoverishment.

I'm sad to say that coming out polyamorous today can also draw discrimination and abuse. As polyamory grows across generations and cultures — as more people come out and mount campaigns for acceptance and equity in partnership and family policy — more social and legal space is being created for coming out safely, without stigma and economic repercussions.

Like LGBTQ+ people around the globe, polyamorous people don't benefit from the legal recognition and widespread social and religious support enjoyed by our monogamous peers.

Consider the 2023 U.S.-based National LGBTQ+ Women's Community Survey, where 5,002 respondents were asked the question: How often do you tell people that you are LGBTQ+? They listed these categories of people as those whom they *always tell*, in descending order:

>> Close friends (80 percent)

>> Family (52 percent)

>> Healthcare providers (48 percent)

>> Work colleagues (32 percent)

>> Schoolmates and teachers (24 percent)

>> Religious/spiritual community members (21 percent)

The follow-up questions to survey respondents who told no one about their LGBTQ+ identity was: If you don't tell people, what are some of your reasons? Here were the common responses:

>> To protect personal privacy (27 percent)

>> To avoid social stigma (23 percent)

>> To preserve and protect relationships (18 percent)

If you use LGBTQ+ coming out as a stand-in for polyamory, this question provides some notable parallels. Participants in this survey considering any kind of coming out that might draw social or economic backlash most often turned to their closest friends first.

This is a great first strategy, but you can see from this very large group of LGBTQ+ women, coming out to close friends isn't a universal top choice. Sometimes the people that you've grown up with or that you've become close to due to a shared experience or passion aren't your best choices when coming out polyamorous.

If you're very close, you likely already know where your friends stand on polyamory or on relationships in general from the hours spent talking about your lives over drinks, shuttling your kids around, or volunteering at your church. As your lives unfold, what you need from close friends can change, and adjustments to your friend groups arise. Coming out polyamorous is the kind of seismic disclosure that might call for such adjustments.

TIP

If you can't come out to your closest friends about being polyamorous, you may need to find some new friends (check out the section "Pod mapping" later in this chapter.)

POLYAMORY STORY

One time I was out with a group of friends at a bar, and one of them asked me about my relationship. My other friend who was there said "Oh you mean that fake relationship they're in? Cuz you know they're gonna cruise someone from this bar tonight." Everyone just kind of laughed and we moved on, but internally I felt really hurt and very unseen. It caused me to distance myself from this friend almost immediately, I stopped hanging out, replied to texts less and less, until we just stopped talking. —**Bishop**

Considering Other People to Tell

After you come out to yourself, you may be ready to tell others in your life. When deciding who to tell, think about who is most likely to provide the best support. These are the people in your life who are great listeners and want the best for you. The following sections may help you identify who some of those people might be.

Chatting with your family

In the section "Sharing with others" earlier in this chapter, I discuss the National LGBTQ+ Women's Community Survey. Number two on the list of most trusted resources when coming out was *family* at 52 percent. If this question had been asked 25 years ago, before LGBTQ+ life became more open and before significant gains in legal rights, family would certainly have registered much lower on the list. LGBTQ+ people who came out in the '80s and '90s, for example, were routinely disowned.

In many ways, the movement to gain acceptance for polyamorous people and their partnerships is at 1990's LGBTQ+ benchmarks, especially for polyamorous heterosexual people coming out in their families.

WARNING

As a survivor of disownment in the mid-80s for coming out as a lesbian, I can only say this: Proceed with caution. You know your family and you know what you are risking in coming out. Weigh the pros and cons carefully if you meet any of the following familial conditions:

>> Have aggressively hostile family members that could threaten custody of your children or even threaten you with physical harm

>> Rely on your parents or other family members for financial support

>> Find that familial connections are crucial to your survival given other hostile conditions you face (like racism or ableism)

>> Know that close relationships with family members provide love and care that's essential to your mental health

REMEMBER

If any of these describe your situation, ask yourself whether family members really need to know. Assess whether it's better for you to manage some of the difficult or depleting aspects of keeping your romantic and intimate life private, otherwise known as closeting your poly life.

The closet can be exhausting for the person shielding themselves and their polycule from their family. You can struggle with low self-esteem and depression. You may have thoughts like "Why can't my family love me for who I am?" or "How can my family supposedly love me and not know me?"

Another cost of living under the radar as polyamorous in your family of origin is that it typically creates internal tensions and pain within the poly constellation, often around the elevation of one member as the acknowledged partner and the silencing or the pretend-friending of one or more members in order to appease family-of-origin prejudices.

Polycules can do a lot for each other in these scenarios:

>> Accept that the cost of the closet is worth it for whatever it delivers to you and your poly family — materially or emotionally — if you're navigating family prejudice or violence.

>> Co-create and affirm whatever closet/outness strategy you're practicing as a unit and then own it.

>> Find creative ways to celebrate invisibilized members who carry the weight of separation or loneliness around traditional holidays or other important milestones.

>> Minimize and rotate who carries the weight of these family of origin disruptions.

>> Take spectacular care of each other as you navigate a polyamory-hostile world.

Opening up to healthcare pros

Healthcare providers ranked close to family in the always-come-out-to category in the LGBTQ+ women's survey at 48 percent. Being open with your healthcare providers about being polyamorous — for example, needing to report that you have more than one sexual partner — may be crucial in some healthcare situations to access appropriate health testing and care.

But does a healthcare practitioner need to know you're polyamorous when you get checked for a sinus infection? A mammogram? An annual physical? All for you to decide. In general, healthcare practitioners provide better care when they know your story and how family demands and supports figure into your health.

FAMILY DISOWNMENT HAS LIFELONG COSTS

Although 7 percent of women between the ages of 18 and 93 in the National LGBTQ+ Women's Community Survey report being disowned for their LGBTQ+ identity, another 4 percent also report being disowned for having different values or holding different social and political views from their parents.

Polyamorous life certainly fits squarely under the different social view category. Disownment isn't a small thing — being cut off by your parents is associated with higher levels of homelessness, depression, addiction, and lower incomes across the lifespan.

Telling classmates, teachers, or coworkers

Schoolmates and/or teachers and coworkers are people that LGBTQ+ women's survey respondents *always came out to* only 24 to 32 percent of the time. This answer ran counter to my sense of how out and proud so many LGBTQ+ people appear at work and at school these days. But many respondents reported discrimination on the job and in learning environments. What is observed in general doesn't always translate into real life, especially among those who live in regions with hostile social and legal climates.

Again, these survey results are a helpful proxy for polyamorous people considering coming out. You may use this data to pose questions on your coming out journey:

>> What are the real vulnerabilities you face in coming out given your current family, school, or work situations?

>> What is a concrete risk and what feels like internalized sexphobia or shame?

REMEMBER

Sexphobia describes the current state of sex in popular culture: relentlessly projected at us, while intensely judged and condemned. On the one hand, sex sells everything from whiskey to vacuum cleaners. On the other, many people, and especially women, girls, LGBTQ+, and BIPOC people face public shaming and cancellation for prioritizing the pursuit of their desire, on their own terms.

Pondering telling religious community

That survey respondents' religious community members rank so low as people they *always come out to* (21 percent) should give you pause. Many people depend on their religious communities for the spiritual and day-to-day foundations of their lives. Very few mainstream religious traditions — those that have built churches, synagogues, temples, and mosques — affirm polyamorous families or relationships. Most have strict policies against sexual activity outside of procreation, monogamy, and marriage. Many define the enthusiastic pursuit of sexual pleasure as sin.

WARNING

Proceed with caution around risking your spiritual home or community by coming out polyamorous there.

TIP

And if you live in a more open spiritual community, stretch into that freedom. Pagan communities, some expansive offshoots of the major religions, and many self-organized spiritual spaces are more affirming of polyamory.

Building Community: The Joy of Coming Out

Coming out poly is about connection, community, and often, release. Letting go of your reservations — having navigated your safety needs — can be wildly freeing and joyful. Coming out can help you carve out the space for expansive poly possibility. Here, you can sift through questions about who, how, where, and when to come out. You can also assess whether you have enough support in your life to come out, and if not, how to build a poly-positive pod of confidantes and supportive activities.

Figuring out the who

Building the polyamorous life you want starts with building the community you want. At the outset of your coming out considerations, focus first on the who:

>> Who do I want to tell?

>> Who am I excited to tell?

>> Who matters to me?

>> How might coming out create an opportunity to be closer?

When I think about the people who have been the most supportive to me about polyamory, they didn't come from a particular place; they represent a range of genders and sexualities; they have very different spiritual lives and practices. But all of them share some key traits that you may consider in finding your poly-positive supporters:

>> People who love adventures

>> People who are great listeners

>> People with questions rather than answers

>> People whose only agenda for me is my happiness

>> People who believe in my ability to create a life that suits me

Generally, my closest poly-positive supporters have lived outside of the box in some aspect of their lives, but not everyone. One of my closest confidantes is a Catholic nun (on second thought, that's a pretty out of the box choice . . .). She doesn't always understand what I'm doing in my intimate and familial life, but she supports me wholeheartedly.

TIP

Another thing to consider when you're deciding who you want to share your excitement about polyamory with is finding people who are already in polyamorous relationships and the community. Consider the following:

>> Who in your life is the most poly-proficient and can help you get started?

>> Who might help connect you to other polyamorous people and community?

Pod mapping

You can use *pod mapping*, a tool created by Mia Mingus and the Bay Area Transformative Justice Collective (BATJC) to help assess your support system as you consider coming out.

Designed to help BATJC members get through times of crisis by diagramming a pod of supporters, this handy map became a go-to resource for people experiencing health or family crises or those trying to escape violent situations.

I've adapted this tool (see Figure 11-1) and used it for many years to assess whether I have the right balance of close friends and socializing, daily love connections, trained health professionals, and joy spaces in my life. My pod map is the core scaffolding of my health and vitality. When I experience big changes, and people drop off the map, I know I need to recruit someone new into the mix or build in a new practice to shore me up.

TIP

While preparing to come out, you may want to draw up your current pod map and see who's there. These types of questions can get you started:

>> Who are you closest to in your life right now?

>> Who takes care of you?

>> What practices are in place that support your joy and connection?

>> What teams or fandoms or health or art practices rejuvenate and enliven your days?

To create your own map, follow these steps:

1. **Place yourself at the center of your pod map.**

2. **Fill in the names of people you trust the most in the six dark-lined circles around you.**

These are the people you can count on to be in your corner, no matter what. You may not have six people, and the map helps you think about whether you need more confidantes and supporters to grow your polyamorous life.

3. **Add the names of other people you rely on in the dotted circles.**

The dotted circles represent people who know you less intimately than your group of six, but they bring fun, energy, support, and laughter to your days. My crushes are sometimes in the dotted circles. Wonderful people I see only a few times a year or colleagues whose work really supports mine are dotted-circle people.

4. **On the outside, in the larger circles, pencil in professionals, resources, or practices that you can rely on to round out your life.**

I have my spectacular massage therapist and life coach in one of the big four outer circles; seeing my favorite bands on tour as much as possible inhabits another; traveling to Ireland periodically to visit my cousins in a third; and my weekly recovery group meeting in the fourth.

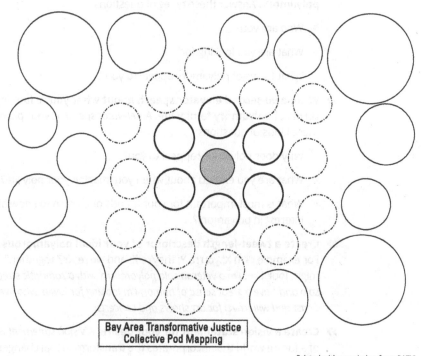

FIGURE 11-1: My pod map.

Bay Area Transformative Justice
Collective Pod Mapping

Printed with permission from BATJC

If you create a pod that has a lot of empty spaces in it, or a pod filled with people who are draining or judging you every day, then that's good information to have. Maybe it's not the right time to come out. Maybe it's time to build your support pod so you can come out polyamorous into an accepting and affirming community.

Getting out there: How to come out

As I mention in my book, *Great Sex: Mapping Your Desire*, when you're sharing information about your desire with friends or potential crushes, I encourage readers to be playful. Sexphobia can create heavy burdens or fears when you're trying to share personal and intimate information.

TIP

But you don't have to accept this overarching sex-negativity. You can decide how and when it's best for you to start getting out there and testing the polyamorous waters. Here are some of my favorite suggestions on how to come out:

>> **Write a four-line personal profile based on your newfound interest in polyamory.** Answer these types of questions:

- Who are you?

- What are you looking for?

- What forms of polyamory appeal to you?

>> **Write a 90-second elevator speech about what you're looking for in terms of polyamory family life.** An *elevator speech* is your pitch. Answer these kinds of questions:

- Why does polyamory appeal to you?

- What are you excited about when you imagine your poly life?

- What is most important for your friends or a crush to know about your interest in polyamory?

>> **Create a tweet-length descriptor of your ideal polyamorous partnership.** For example, "I'm X; you're Y; they're Z; and we're XYZ together." In my case, it might look like: *I'm a veteran solo polyamorist with a romantic streak; you're also solo and have a great sense of humor; I'm looking for lovers who live on the East Coast and will travel for art shows and concerts.*

>> **Create a vision statement for your desire.** A *vision statement* is a description of a future world that incorporates the transformational changes you aspire to. If you were fully living into your polyamorous aspirations, what would your life — socially, sexually, and in the day-to-day flows of family — look like?

>> **Create a polyamory organizational chart.** It shows the kind of forms you're interested in (I discuss many different forms in Chapter 4).

These exercises are designed to get you to start to brainstorm and distill your thinking about polyamory and to place yourself at the center of your coming out process.

TIP

The material you generate here can help you open a conversation with a possible poly supporter, friend, or crush. Pull out that organizational chart, or share your new profile description, and start a free-flowing conversation. Find people who are delighted by your creative daring and ask them to create a counterpart to your discovery process so that you can start to find commonalities and exchange insights.

Planning when and where to come out

Selecting the right time and location to come out can greatly improve your outcomes. Here are some suggestions on when and where:

>> **In the great outdoors:** Spending time outside, taking a walk, getting some fresh air, or sitting in a quiet area are great places to have the chat. For example, "I asked you here because you're a person I trust, and I've discovered something important about myself that I want to share."

>> **During a coffee date:** Choosing to have this conversation while enjoying a cup of coffee or tea is a great idea. Select a table that's outside or not smashed up against others for a little privacy. Go during an off hour when the cafe may not be as busy. Sit facing each other. Ah, coffee. "Let me get your favorite."

>> **After an activity:** Going after spending time together doing something you both enjoy is another great option. Afterward you can share your exciting news in a quiet location.

>> **Over video or phone:** Coming out in person — the physical proximity, the ability to read body language, the option to hug, affirm, or comfort each other — is best.

However, meeting in person isn't always possible — for example, you live several hours apart — and in-person may not be the best for you as a communicator (see Chapter 5 for info and discussion about communication styles). If you can't have the conversation in person, then the best-to-worst options are as follows:

• **Video:** Zoom, Skype, Facetime, or other video messaging options allow you to make eye contact, read each other's body language, have an intimate conversation, and read tone and intent well.

• **Phone:** The phone is your second best not-in-person option. The phone lets your confidante hear your voice. They can tell when you're excited or taking a deep breath. You can take in when they're laughing or working hard to listen.

- **Text:** I don't recommend using text for high stakes conversations. People tend to talk in shorthand when texting. Tone is especially difficult to read: Is this person being sarcastic? Dismissive? People can also disappear mid-conversation. Texting has too many avenues for misinterpretation and misunderstanding.

- **Snail mail or email:** I put these two options last because people seem to be using them less and less, especially snail mail. But writing a well-thought-out note about your process of learning about yourself, how you're thinking about the polyamorous life you want, and why you're confiding in this important person in your life can be a wonderful exercise.

Coming out letters also give the sender some physical space from the receiver, if that's what they need.

Don't ever hit send on an email when your blood pressure is up, your heart is beating fast, or you're mad at the person! Feel free to write all the letters you want in that kind of emotional space to work through your issues so you can get to a place that feels centered and true. But in the end, you want to send a note that's measured — firmly grounded and abundantly who you are.

Avoiding hot-button places

Starting a coming out conversation at a major holiday dinner or in bed at the end of a long frantic day of work and/or managing kids is a recipe for disaster. And yet, in my practice as a sex coach, I can count up many, many coming out conversations of all kinds that have happened in these two, very high stakes locales.

Here are places to steer clear of when having a coming out chat:

>> **During holiday dinners:** Just no. Even when this goes well, which is almost never, there's so much extra that hangs around the edges and impacts family interactions for years.

>> **In bed:** Partners often spill heavy relationship truths at 11 p.m. after an exhausting day in the place where they have had some of their most vulnerable, intimate moments together. Crush confessions, coming outs, breaches of trust, major relationship changes —all these announcements need to be made in the light of day. Respect the bed.

>> **In the car:** What is it about the car? If you're a parent, you know: So many big conversations happen in the car. I'm not a fan of the car for coming out

reveals because you can't make eye contact with the driver, and if you can, you want to make and keep eye contact in high stakes exchanges. Also, you're trapped together if things start to go wrong.

Nonetheless, a lot of coming out conversations happen on drives. If you're going to do this, choose your confidante wisely. Consider the impact on the driver. Hydrate, snack, and choose a pleasant route.

Finding Polyamorous Friends: Going the Long Road Together

Discovering polyamorous friends is crucial for sustaining your poly life. Of course, not everyone needs friends or can risk finding poly friends. But the good news is that you can create community in online spaces, groups, and meet-ups even when you're relatively isolated in a hostile community or when you're navigating risks of social or economic retaliation (check out Appendix A for some resources).

In my young life as a lesbian, every time I had a breakup or a difficulty in my relationships, my family of origin would pounce on this as evidence of the sickness and unsustainability of lesbian life. And they weren't alone. Many of my so-called friends would seize on the opportunity of my vulnerability to draw me into their agenda for my life. This heightened my distress and gave them more ammunition in their battle to rid me of queerness.

As you approach polyamorous life, here are a couple of ways you can create solidarity and reciprocity with the pod you build:

>> **Choose friends because you're interested in them, not because they can do something for you or provide entree into a community.** Find people you want to build conversation and possibility with — people you want to support, as they support you, as you share resources, joy, and hardships over many years.

>> **Mind and tend to your pod.** There's so much uncertainty in today's world. Here's one thing that's entirely in your hands: your commitment to growing reciprocal, expansive, and joyful love here, among your friends. The universe often feels so big and full of dangers. You can't fix it all, but you can carry each other through.

4

Dealing with Common Challenges

Understand that polyamory means connecting with more lovers or partners and all the life challenges that come with *more*.

Discover the universality of jealousy and how to identify and cope with it.

Consider how to address breaches of trust and broken agreements and see how others have healed and moved forward.

Hear from parents who are polyamorous about how they navigate multiple relationships and thorny questions.

Weigh how life changes might impact you as a poly person, whether your shifting libido, geographic changes due to work or family needs, disability, aging, or breakups.

Chapter **12**

Coping with Jealousy

amed couples therapist Esther Perel has said that jealousy is both erotic breath and erotic rage. It does seem like jealousy is as natural as breathing, and the tone and tenor of that breath is a venomous, possessive anger.

In this chapter, you can hear from polyamorists who don't believe that jealousy is natural, but instead a learned behavior embedded in a society built on scarcity and competition. Nonetheless, jealousy is often a constant in people's social and sexual lives. Here, you can also find advice about how to think critically about jealousy in your life and unlearn behaviors that are working against you as you pursue your polyamorous dreams and desires. You can also consider what resources you might need in order to let go of jealousy and embrace more expansive ways of being as you pursue love and partnership.

Realizing That Everyone Gets Jealous

Feeling and coping with jealousy is a near-universal experience. Everyone gets jealous of others — whether of your high-achieving siblings, brilliant coworkers, that college pal who posts their world travels, or people who show interest in your lover. The following sections help you drop whatever judgment you have about you or your partner's jealous feelings and instead adopt a position of curiosity about them. You might ask yourself:

>> In general, what are your jealous feelings trying to tell you?

>> What are your partner's jealous feelings communicating about them?

>> What could jealousy be revealing about what's working or not working in your relationship?

>> Does your jealousy align with your values about relationships?

>> What can you learn from the jealousy you are dealing with right now?

POLYAMORY STORY

My first instinct is always to be like, *Oh, I'm not jealous. I'm just not a jealous type.* I feel jealousy if somebody gets a raise or a promotion over me, that I can feel. But when it comes to like — are you looking at a person too long? Or did you talk to them too much? That often just doesn't register as jealousy for me, especially in the moment. If I go back and try to analyze what happened, jealousy sometimes pulls up on the register for me, but I think it's the discernment of whether it's actually jealousy or insecurity. Those two often go really closely for me, hand in hand. —**Rox**

Jealousy is a scarcity response

Today's culture projects and generates scarcity at every corner. Capitalism as an organizing structure literally runs on scarcity and competition. Even as a child, your social life was steeped in competitive contests — from your sports teams to your grades in elementary school. Nearly everyone is formed inside a system that tells you that competition is good, and if you want to have a good life, you must compete to land at the top of the heap.

Despite the terrible impacts of voracious competition and endless growth on the planet, competition and the scarcity mind-set are still seen as wholly good and even natural.

Jealousy, then, is a crucial part of this system. If only one country or scholar or lover can be the best, the smartest, and the worthiest, then all others are losers, and you can't find yourself at the bottom of that pile. The consequences are dire — from not getting into that top college, to failing to obtain that dream job, to living a penniless, lonely life.

Jealousy is your internal alarm system to threats against the lover you must acquire to win the partner-scarcity game. Accordingly, people grow into their romantic and relational life fueled with anxiety about not being enough, and ultimately, losing and being left behind.

I call this activity "What Would It Mean to Be Enough?" That we aren't enough is such a fundamental teaching in U.S. culture and society. Here are some reflection questions for you:

>> What is your first memory of feeling like you weren't enough — too big or too small, not smart, cute, funny, strong, or hot enough?

>> How old are you? Who is telling you this?

>> What kind of impact did this have?

>> What is your most humiliating memory of being not enough?

>> How do you think this impacts you today?

>> Are the messengers or catalysts in these scenarios trustworthy?

>> Have the messengers in these scenarios harmed you in other ways?

>> How or why are you giving them power?

>> What if you could stop believing these lies?

>> What might life be like in a world where you are enough?

Keep these notes with you as you move through this chapter.

Monogamy culture reinforces jealousy

Monogamy and marriage fit neatly into the overarching competitive system of society because they align to push you to choose one person early in your lifetime, or you'll lose out. All the good partners will be taken if you don't get yourself into a position to be an attractive partner — physically, socially, materially. Time is *so short* to prove that you're the best catch.

And as you race to position yourself as worthy and attractive, you're also inundated with messages about the scarcity of appropriate, available partners. Your parents might be telling you not to wait too long, or that you're too picky, and that all the best candidates will be chosen or spoken for by the time you decide on someone. Your friends might be getting married, and as you look over that relationship fence, the grass is definitely greener over there, on the married side — even, unbelievably, when you think that some of these matches are a very bad idea!

Monogamy culture tells you that good people are disappearing every day, and you'll likely end up alone if you don't figure it out now.

Getting out of this mind-set is no small thing. It's scary. Depending on the expectations of your family of origin and your friendship circle, it may be driving a significant percentage of conversation and activity especially while you're in your 20s and 30s.

What would it be like to get off of this competition and scarcity train? What if love were abundant and to be shared? What if you could love your partner and also love others, and they could do the same? And how might *not competing for love* reveal the problematic outcomes of competition and extraction all over our society, and the planet? (See Chapter 4 for lots of examples of polycules formed outside of this one-and-only-for-life ideal.)

TIP

If you look at it this way, unwinding jealousy has the potential to free you from so many constraining systems and practices in your life.

POLYAMORY STORY

We came back from this big bi week of a national swinger's conference. James doesn't like exercising. I love exercising. I just do. I always have. But we've been home a week, and he's like: "You know what? People thought I was hot. They found me hot, and I want to be even hotter. I'm going to try to go to the gym twice a week; will you help me? Can we go together?" My dream of ten years just happened! I don't care what he looks like. I mean — he's *adorable.* For me it's my fear: *Please, don't die. Please be strong to have great sex with me for a long, long time.* But he's like a peacock, you know, that's his personality! So, I'm like, oh my god, he's doing it! This is my dream! **—Elizabeth**

THE ELEPHANT IN THE ROOM: THE TICKING FERTILITY CLOCK

A huge driver of manufactured scarcity and fear around love is the loud ticking of the fertility clock for people who want to give birth to children. Advancements in assisted reproductive technologies have expanded the window of opportunity for some, but many of these tools are not medically or financially accessible. And finding suitable partners to parent with has long driven jealous competition and even panic in dating and social spheres, from one's 20s into the 40s.

This is perhaps one of the biggest barriers to letting go of the monogamy imperative and scarcity thinking — being unable to imagine raising children in a polyamorous context. But there are countless ways to do this, some of them outlined in Chapter 4, which looks at different poly family configurations. The bottom line: You have more options than monogamous marriage to raise healthy, joyful, well-adjusted children. Rejecting the monogamy-marriage-children-by-mid-30s imperative can be an enormous relief — around the intensity of competition for partners and the anguish of jealousy in your life. As soon as you do this, you may realize a million other ways how this confining fundamentalism may be driving your choices — about friends, work, schooling, leisure, laughter, art, sociality, and pleasure.

There's more than one way to create the partnerships and family of your dreams. You just need to allow yourself the space to *actually dream a little* to find your way.

Polyamory culture can stigmatize jealousy

Monogamy culture isn't the only culture that has a problem with jealousy. In polyamory circles, jealousy can be stigmatized as uncool or immature. The story goes: If you're a true polyamorist, you don't experience jealousy, *which is utter nonsense!*

You don't suddenly live outside of this overwhelming monogamy-centric, scarcity culture when you start considering polyamory. All the envies and jealousies of your upbringing, the excruciating formative romances of your teens, and your early dating history combine in your life as you find yourself at this point of curiosity or exploration. Just because you don't *want* to be jealous doesn't mean that you won't be. And aspiring to move beyond jealousy and possessiveness in your dating and partnering life doesn't mean this is where you are today.

TIP

Feeling jealous as you explore polyamorous connections is utterly common and perfectly okay. Things will go a lot better if you can own and report on your jealousy to your loved ones, rather that deny it and act out from that fear-generated place of scarcity and unworthiness.

Getting to the Root of Your Jealousy

This section helps you dig deeper into your jealousy story. Even though the experience of jealousy may be universal, it's also personal, and your unique formative experiences of competition, scarcity, and feeling less-than are likely at play as you navigate jealousy.

Uncovering your jealousy story origins

Your *jealousy story* is embedded in a larger story of competition and scarcity in your family and community. While I'm sure you can remember intense feelings of jealousy from your childhood, these feelings emerged inside your family system of scarcity. Chapter 8's activities on looking at your family's history of trauma may also help you think about this.

TIP

The important thing when thinking about how jealousy functions in your life is not to think about it as singular or isolated to the situation you find yourself in. As you consider how you want to respond to your jealous feelings, don't be hard on yourself. Be curious. Find out more about your larger story. Think about this excavation as digging up contextual clues to your reactivity. Consider it as an exercise in identifying the resources you might need to relieve your jealousy or move away from scarcity thinking and toward your partner when you feel threatened or jealous.

ACTIVITY

Your *family story* is the context for your jealousy story, but it doesn't end there. You get to decide how you want to deal with jealousy in your life and your relationships. To further help you, use this checklist:

>> What messages existed in the family you grew up in around jealousy?

>> How did your parents or caregivers talk about other families or neighbors in terms of material envy, judgment of their choices, and so on?

>> How might family migration or displacement relate to your fear of not having or being enough — the violence, material scarcity, and social vulnerability your ancestors experienced?

>> Did your parents talk about your looks, or virginity, or marriage prospects as social capital — as a means of securing your or the whole family's material well-being or safety?

>> Did your parents negatively compare you to your siblings, cousins, or friends' children, in terms of looks or accomplishments?

>> Did you parents express judgment about other marriages in your family and in their friendship circle?

>> How did your parents handle their own jealousy with each other?

>> Were there lies or blowups about jealousy and infidelity?

As you sift through the material you've generated here, you can start to determine how your family history around jealousy has impacted your experiences of jealousy and the way you talk about or hide your jealousy.

Discovering your jealousy triggers

As you think through the broader context of your jealousy story, another step toward taking on your jealousy is discovering your *triggers* — what sets you off around threatened. Working toward letting go of controlling or possessive thoughts and behaviors starts with discovering when and under what circumstances you are likely to be activated around your jealousy.

Knowing when you're most vulnerable

This exercise can help you sift through the circumstances that leave you most at risk for jealous reactivity. Go through these steps:

ACTIVITY

1. **Ask yourself this question: When are you most vulnerable to jealousy?**

Early in a relationship?

When your partner announces a new crush?

When you're overextended at work or as a parent?

When you haven't had a vacation in more than a year?

When your partner cancels your date night?

When you're getting all the drudgery while your partner has fun?

After you've broken up with another lover?

When you're not feeling well physically?

When your depression is weighing you down?

When your partner is overworking?

When your partner goes on a date after an unresolved fight?

The possibilities are endless. Dig a little and think about the history of jealous blowups in your current and past relationships.

2. **List your biggest fights or explosions around jealousy.**

Look to see if a pattern emerges or any certain trends around your vulnerability. Determine whether you can ask your partner to say or do something to head off the kind of distress you've encountered previously.

If you can, identify what has worked in terms of taking care of yourself and your jealousy in the past. What's a tried-and-true method to care for you during jealous episodes?

The material you've gained from answering these two questions can form a foundation for noticing when you're vulnerable, so you can back away from reactive jealousy. It can be a guidepost to figuring out how to ask for help and reassurance.

I've had terrible, consuming, jealous periods in my life. When I look back on them, I have a lot of compassion for struggling Jaime. I didn't think I was worthy of my partners —mostly, I thought I wasn't as physically attractive as them, and I could see threats to my relationships at every corner.

When I observe myself in pictures from these events, I could just weep. Because:

» I'm beautiful. I'm absolutely fine. I'm in whatever league I was certain I'd never gain entry to.

» I remember that even though I'm smiling in these pictures, I'm actually having a terrible time. I'm ridden with anxiety. Often after these parties I'd have a horrible fight with my partner over some actual or imagined slight.

In some cases, my lovers were having their own struggles with self-hate and powerlessness and were deflecting their own pain by feeding my insecurities. In others, my partner was honestly bewildered by my perceptions and behavior, and these fights corroded their trust and interest in me.

REMEMBER

Patriarchy is a truly hellish, draining system of control for women and femmes especially, but for everyone. Looking at these pictures, I can see that it had me by the throat in my 20s and 30s. What might my life be like today if I had been present to my own glorious strengths and beauty in these relationships? What if I had been able to be present with my partner at these events and meet others not as competition or threats, but as possible friends or collaborators or lovers?

Jealousy lives inside the terror of scarcity, and it also shrinks possibility at every corner. It *creates scarcity by shutting everyone out*. It's one thing to have an intellectual critique of the systems that make you hate yourself — patriarchy, white supremacy, ableism, ageism — it's quite another to actually purge their effects from the ways you regard yourself and interact with your loved ones.

But if I can do it (much of the time), I hold out hope that you can do it, too. You can commit to resisting these systems, to recovering yourself, and to growing in a community of loved ones who can see you and reflect back your brilliance and amazingness.

Being a jealousy detective

Here's another great exercise to help you excavate your history of not being enough, and support your healing from scarcity thinking:

1. **Gather up pictures of yourself with your partners or sweethearts from high school, from your 20s, 30s, 40s, 50s, 60s, 70s, and so on.**

   Look at yourself in these photos. Shower yourself with love and approval. Take in how beautiful you are. Try to go back and remember how jealousy showed up at this particular event or in this relationship. Ask

   - What were you afraid of?
   - How did you think about yourself then?
   - Was your partner fueling your insecurities?
   - What was driving your jealous feelings?

2. **Take notes across these relationships and decades:**

   - What repeating patterns do you see?
   - Under what circumstances does jealousy come up for you?
   - What effect does jealousy have on you and your relationships?

3. **Free-write a love letter to yourself.**

   A *free-write* is a stream-of-consciousness exercise. Don't edit what you write. Don't stop. Just look at the pictures. Review your notes from questions 1 and 2 and write.

   Give yourself what you couldn't give yourself then. Celebrate your strengths. Comfort yourself.

4. **After you finish the love letter, put it away and come back to it in a day or two and then ask yourself:**

   How can you attend to or unwind your jealousy so that it doesn't create conflict and distance in your relationships?

Figuring out how to take care of yourself

Jealousy actually *feels* terrible. The stress of jealousy on your body is significant. It generates stress reactions akin to trauma reactions, where cortisol and adrenaline are released, and your system is compromised (Figure 12-1 shows how your body responds to jealousy stress).

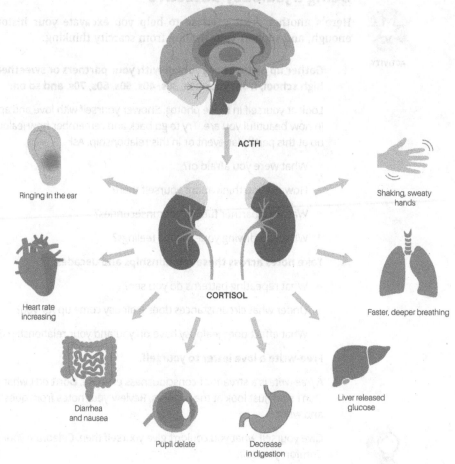

STRESS RESPONSE

ACTH

Ringing in the ear

Shaking, sweaty
hands

Heart rate
increasing

Faster, deeper breathing

CORTISOL

Liver released
glucose

Diarrhea
and nausea

Pupil delate

Decrease
in digestion

FIGURE 12-1:
Jealousy stress
response.

pikovit/Adobe Stock Photos

ACTIVITY

What steps can you take to help yourself *physically* when you find yourself in a
jealous spin or rage? Here's a three-pronged practice to help you when you're in
the grip of jealousy:

1. Notice the activation of your jealousy.

You likely already know that your body lights up when you're jealous. Your
heart starts to beat faster, your blood pressure may rise. Start to recognize
your specific signs of jealous reactivity. Do the following:

- **Measure how your body responds.** Your heart rate, posture, emotional
  state, breathing, eyesight, hearing

- **Track the physical impacts of jealousy**. Doing so helps you to take care
  of yourself when they start to take hold.

2. **Walk yourself back.**

When jealousy starts to escalate in your body, note what you need to do to walk yourself back, physically, or what you need to talk yourself down.

You may want to do a range of activities, including

- Breathing — to deescalate, to move yourself back to a peaceful, less agitated state
- Calling your best friend
- Writing down what you're thinking or feeling and then putting it all away somewhere safe, for later
- Telling your partner you need a minute
- Stepping out into the fresh air and taking a walk

Try to assign your scarcity thinking to whatever spiritual center you rely on in your life (such as God, an ancestor, or the ocean). Let go. You can't control your partner, but you can take active steps to support your own agitated system. You can improve your situation. You can find relief.

3. **Tell yourself that you're enough.**

Do it, even if you don't believe it. Create a mantra for yourself and whisper it to yourself. Recite a poem you love to yourself. If you're still mired in self-hate, *fake it 'til you make it.*

Looking at pictures of younger Jaime often helped me *fake it 'til I made it* around believing that I'm enough. Because younger Jaime is so much more beautiful and engaged than my self-critical, beleaguered brain understood back then. My self-esteem at the time was much less developed, and yet there I am, *making my life anyway.* Seeing how wrong I was about past-Jaime helps me realize how wrong harried-Jaime might be about me in the present. I'm an unreliable evaluator at nearly every juncture. So, in any given moment, I can assume my negative assessment of me is just flat-out wrong. I'm enough. I'm more than enough. I'm writing *Polyamory For Dummies*! I'm living my dream.

REMEMBER

What you're trying to do here is create a practice of care and support around your jealousy rather than denial and judgment. Tracking the escalation of jealousy-driven adrenaline and stress hormones in your body and working to counter them by soothing and caring for yourself can go a long way toward finding release and relief. At minimum, such awareness can help you create the kind of space you need to stop lashing out or creating distance in your relationship.

WARNING

Reactivity around jealousy creates the very thing your jealousy is terrified of — a distant, resentful partner, rather than an intimate partner who can hold and soothe you through your most vulnerable moments.

Monogamy culture sends the message that your worth is based on finding and holding onto love. But if I can find worth and value in myself, I can deal with my jealousy better. I once threw a "Make Something Your Partner Doesn't Like Party," and it was one of the best parties I ever threw because people got to share something they enjoy with other people and their partners didn't have to feel bad about not wanting to eat it. One woman made mac and cheese because her husband hated it! I made beets because my primary partner hated them. It was so great to have a reason to make and enjoy something outside of my relationship with my partner. Sometimes addressing jealousy is just about remembering and appreciating all the different things you are. —**Robin**

If you're feeling tortured by jealousy — if it feels constant or nagging or intrusive in your daily life, you may be in trouble — in terms of your mental and physical health. If so, seek help (refer to Appendix B for resources).

IF YOU'RE IN YOUR PARTNER'S PHONE, THERE'S NO GOOD NEWS

During one particularly gruesome period of jealousy and obsession with a partner, I started surveilling them. We shared a computer and sometimes they left various private modes of communication open by mistake. They didn't always have a password on their phone. We had an open relationship, but I was certain they were involved in various kinds of relationships that were off limits per our agreements.

This was a truly terrible time in my life. We had moved to a new state, and I had no intimate friends locally. My new employer was abusive. We were in a much less diverse community — our mixed-race, queer family was visibly strange in the environment, drawing unwanted and even hostile attention. The kids were young, and parenting demands were high. Looking back on this time, it makes sense to me that I came to overrely on my partner and to imagine threats to my sense of security.

And what was on their computer or in their phone? It doesn't matter. After you're breaking your partner's trust and invading their privacy, the relationship is mortally wounded. The substance of what you find is beside the point. Unless you're capable of coming clean and making radical changes, this kind of trust breach is very, very hard to come back from.

Creating Support Versus Judgment

Probably the biggest mistake you can make around dealing with jealousy is to ascend to a place of superiority and judgment about how uncool or unpoly-like it is for your partner to feel jealous or struggle with jealousy.

REMEMBER

Let me say it again: Don't shame your partner for their jealousy. And don't be hard on yourself for having jealous feelings. You live in a universe that indoctrinates you with scarcity fear, monogamy imperatives, and self-reproach. Don't add fuel to that dumpster fire.

Consider what it would be like to create an environment where you expect jealousy to arise in your poly relationships, and you welcome it as information about how well you are communicating and taking care of each other. The following sections explore this idea.

Good polyamorous people experience jealousy

Some people really do have a stronger inclination toward polyamory and experience very little jealousy. Consider the following from Elizabeth:

POLYAMORY STORY

I haven't been in a monogamous relationship since I was 20 years old. I lived with a group of women in college. We read *The Ethical Slut*, and my friends were like — Oh, that's interesting. But for me, it was: *Oh my god, this is who I am. I'm never going back!* It was kind of two pronged. First of all, I would fantasize when I was dating people about them dating somebody else too. It felt so oppressive to me to have this person that needed me *all the time*. When I read *The Ethical Slut*, I thought: oh my god, what if he could have another girlfriend that wanted to do this thing (that I really don't like doing) with him? I mean — that *is* the dream I'm living now!

Many people aren't like Elizabeth and don't think about themselves as naturally or constitutionally poly. You may have had to fight your way toward this part of yourself by weeding through a lot of negative conditioning and demands in your formative and adult experiences. Nonetheless, like Elizabeth, you can be *a good poly person*. Because you can face and survive managing your jealousy.

REMEMBER

Two of the keys to freedom from jealousy and self-reproach are simple:

>> Drop the self-judgment and perfectionism.

>> Drop the judgments of your partner.

WARNING

Telling people they suck at being poly is the worst way to deal with jealousy. If someone is doing this to you, they're out of line. If you're doing this to someone, you're out of line.

TIP

Use the resources in this chapter and in Appendix B to stop destructive behaviors around jealousy and figure out how to get the support you need.

Supporting your jealous partners

The best route toward dealing with jealousy is to *go toward the very hard thing* rather than to deny, deflect, or retreat. If your partner is in deep distress, it's likely to activate your scarcity fear: *She is trying to take this away from me! She never supports me!* And if you're the one in jealousy distress, you may be picking fights over something else or accusing your partner of things they haven't done to cover up what you think of as your problematic jealous feelings that your partner would be judgmental about.

TIP

Instead of jumping into denial, deflection, or blame, move toward your jealous self or toward your jealous partner with compassion.

ACTIVITY

This activity lets you investigate what's going on in your relationship. Instead of being judgmental or defensive, you and your partner can choose to be curious together instead. Here are a number of statements that show openness and interest in what's happening for your partner:

>> Oh honey, tell me more about this. I thought you were excited about my new lover.

>> I'm so glad you told me you're feeling this way. Thank you for trusting me.

>> I'm so sorry you've been carrying these feelings by yourself; it must have been really hard.

>> Do you know what set these feelings off? Was there some particular action that I took, or didn't take?

>> When did things start feeling off for you? Can you remember what was going on?

>> What do you need right now? How can I support you?

>> Let's just take a breath together. I know we can figure this out.

>> You're really doing a great job identifying what's going on for you lately. Your hard work is paying off.

>> I'm impressed that you've been able to share this. How can we work on it together?

SUPPORT BUT DON'T ENABLE

Supporting a partner when they have jealous feelings can be helpful and even grow intimacy in your relationships. Buying into or capitulating to jealous and controlling behavior is something else entirely. If a partner is finding fault with every poly connection you make, working to constrain your friendships and generally making your life smaller and more difficult via constant accusations of disloyalty or cheating, you may be in an abusive situation. Controlling partners will wear you down and exhaust you with blaming, shaming, and name-calling. In these cases, jealousy has become a toxic partner in your relationship, and you're in danger. Seek help (see Appendix B).

The core practices that underly all of these statements:

> **DON'T:** Judge, Escalate, Egg-On, Ridicule = **JEER**
>
> **DON'T JEER** at your partner for their emotional state.
>
> **DO:** Reassure, Embrace, Affirm, De-escalate = **READ**
>
> **DO READ** your partner's emotional state and respond with care.

Finding ways through together

Taking on jealousy as a team project is a great way to avoid stigmatizing your partner or deflecting and denying that jealousy is even an issue. Addressing jealousy as a *we* instead of a *you* greatly improves your likelihood of success.

This activity allows you to deconstruct jealousy together. Follow these steps:

ACTIVITY

1. **Identify the things that trigger each of you.**

   Pinpoint what happens in your bodies so you can start to name these triggers and help each other address when jealousy is operating.

   At the same time, start to build a practice of breathing together when you feel one or the other of you getting activated.

TIP

2. **Create a supportive shared catch phrase to use when you notice jealousy starting to take over the conversation.**

   Here are some examples:

   - Hey, I'm here for you. We're in this together.
   - It seems like you're being overtaken by the green monster — Roar!
   - Is today a kill-all-my-darlings day?

TIP

Use humor. Break up the intensity by reminding each other that you've created a strategy together.

3. Agree on supportive action to counter jealousy.

Determine what you can do for each other when one of you is experiencing a jealous episode. See if you can agree to do something that you love together. Is there a song, a dance, a snack, an ice-cream parlor, a walk, a hobby, a sport, or a goofy activity that can de-escalate the jealousy and bring you two together?

If one partner has identified specific triggers, create specific practices to counter those activating events (such as what follows).

4. Phone a friend.

Work together to identify excellent, resourceful friends to text or call when you're activated around jealousy. In the heat of activation, you can support each other by saying something like: "Maybe Angelique can support you right now. Do you want to reach out to them?"

Understanding Compersion: More Love Grows More Love

Before I moved into polyamorous relationships and community, the idea of *compersion* — the feeling of expansive love and enjoyment one experiences while observing your beloved being loved or sexually attended to by another lover — seemed like something in a sci-fi fantasy world. Sure, there were societies where everyone loved each other without jealousy and where constellations of lovers wanted their beloveds to experience as much pleasure as possible. *They were just on the moon.* And not even a moon close by, but one so many galaxies away, its winking light could barely be seen.

Well, this may be hard to believe if you've only lived in monogamous social worlds, among monogamous and married couples. But you don't need to move to the moon to find compersion. In fact, polyamorous socializing and communities have experienced so much growth in the past decade or so that finding polyamorous-identified people — in social groups, at events, or on apps specifically designed for polyamorous people and other social and sexual adventurers — is much, much easier.

BRING IT HOME HOT

We've joked about it for a long time, but besides safer sex, the only rule we have is *Bring it home hot*, and we put that in our wedding vows. And people ask: what does that mean? When we had a two-year-old, it was: You better be ready to get up at 8 a.m. after your out-until-3 a.m. date. Because I'm not here for doing this by myself.

At this stage, we've been together 15 years, and I'm not a particularly romantic person, but travel and going on our annual trip to the sex resort and things like that are important. I need my cup filled up in that way, because James spends time with his girlfriend at kinky events. So, they definitely have their things, right? And so instead of being jealous, it's just better to be like, *I want sex in fancy hotels too!* So, it's about paying attention to the equity of the hot, sexy times. **—Elizabeth**

Compersive people, practices, and relationships all turn in a social world accessible to you, all you need to do is reach for it. In the next sections, you can get a peek into some of the practices in this expansive dating and partnership universe and see how you can find joy in each other's joy.

Looking closer: Compersion is an abundance response

Because jealousy is a learned behavior, you can unlearn it. Jealousy thrives on scarcity terror, and compersion is an abundance response. Rather than seeing everyone as competition or a threat, the compersive framework is curious and interested in bringing more pleasure and possibility into the sexual or family system. People who are compersive get excited when their partners have crushes, and they wonder what new parts of their lovers might come to life in this new relationship. They also wonder what kind of sexy experiences might bend back around into their relationship with their lover because they're in a space of opening up, of discovery.

Even though jealousy can seem as natural as the air you breathe, compersion is often described as strange or fantastical. *No one is happy seeing their lover with someone else.* Except many people are. It may not have been a first response. Compersive people may have needed to learn about their jealousy first. They may have needed to develop a community of friends enjoying compersion to start to be able to imagine themselves experiencing it.

Like all feelings, compersion is complex. It's not just one thing but a combination of things. You may feel scared and anxious as you observe your partner hold hands with or have joy during your introductory coffee hour with their new lover. You might not be ready to see your partner kiss a new love. Conversely, you might be wildly excited to see your partner's joy with their new crush and even turned on. You might decide you want to be closer to this new person. Or you might decide you're thrilled for your partner, but you don't want to observe them on their dates. All these responses are perfectly valid ways of experiencing compersion.

Chapter 6 on boundaries can help you figure out what your best path toward experiencing and sustaining compersion might be. It's not a one-size fits all proposition. And it's not a fixed experience. Where I'm at with compersion changes with each of my lovers and with the trajectory of my personal growth and healing. In my 20s and 30s, I felt particularly tender and possessive when I was falling in love with my partners — those early stages of attachment were very activating around my jealousy. And then, as we grew trust and intimacy, my fearfulness would fall away, and I often had profound experiences of compersion that opened up many other avenues of joy in our life together. In my 60s, compersion is so natural that it's sometimes hard to believe how painful jealousy was for younger Jaime. But the evidence of it — in a handful of broken relationships and long-term, painstaking healing processes — is undeniable.

If, as author and healer Prentis Hemphill has stated — "Boundaries are the distance at which I can love you and me simultaneously" — you might think about compersion as possible for you at the proper distance. For some, this means never knowing anything specific about the other sources of your partner's joy; for others, it means knowing as much as possible, and even creating close relationships with your partner's intimates.

Nurturing abundance through trust and responsiveness

You may wonder how you can nurture an abundance response and minimize jealousy and scarcity reactions. The simple path to disarming jealousy is to be consistent with your boundaries — both keeping yours and respecting your partner's and by being generous and caring with your partners, in sweet easy times as well as during hard periods of discord and disagreement. As you come through for your partners over time, you're likely to observe their controlling and fearful responses fall away. More trust and responsiveness brings more air and possibility into any relational system.

If you hope for more, give more. Be that trustworthy lover you long for.

Finding joy in others' joy

The Buddhists have a term for finding joy in others' joy — *Mudita*. When a parent watches a child grow, mastering their challenges and enjoying their lives, this is a quintessential experience of Mudita. And sympathetic joy, the joy you feel when your bestie falls in love or gets that job they've long wanted is another joy that circulates in the universe where compersion lies. If you're a person who easily experiences these adjunct compersive feelings, then compersion may not be too great a leap for you in your dating and sexual life. If, however, you tend to feel jealous or self-denigrating in any of these scenarios, you'll need more support to get your compersion on.

TIP

Whether you're more or less naturally compersive, it will help if you can find new places in your life to grow a practice of finding joy in others' joy. Look to activities that foster collaboration as opposed to competition; identify projects that draw in expansive communities beyond the people and ways you grew up; look for institutions that are built on sharing, collaboration, and team spirit versus those that hold up a charismatic leader or are organized around a star system.

Find spaces that nurture Mudita and sympathetic joy, so that your compersive tendencies have a place to sprout and flourish.

POLYAMORY STORY

FINDING YOUR DISNEYLAND

I'm the big extrovert between the two of us, but by the end of the week at this sex resort, I had really had my fill and I said: "I'm going to bed at 10 p.m., and I don't even want to have breakfast with other people tomorrow." And the usually introverted James wasn't ready to leave. And I thought, *Oh, that's amazing!* He said: "But we have to see so-and-so." And he had been up every night all week to 3 a.m. and I was like: "*Honey, your slutty side!* You need to give that part of yourself the love it needs. Because I have never seen you engage with people socially like this, except for when we were at Disneyland." Literally, James found his Disneyland! **—Elizabeth**

The Buddhists have a term for finding joy in others' joy — Mudita. When a parent watches a child grow, mastering the challenges and enjoying their lives, this is a quintessential experience of Mudita. And sympathetic joy, the joy you feel when your bestie falls in love or gets that job that they've long wanted is another joy that circulates in the universe where compersion lies. If you're a person who easily experiences these ajunct compersive feelings, then compersion may not be too great a leap for you in your dating and sexual life. If, however, you tend to feel jealous or self-denigrating in any of these situations, you'll need more support to get your compersion on.

Whether you're more or less naturally compersive, it will help if you can find new places in your life to grow a practice of finding joy in others' joy. Look to activities that foster collaboration as opposed to competition; identify projects that draw in expansive communities beyond the people and ways you grew up; look for institutions that are built on sharing, collaboration, and community spirit versus those that hold up a charismatic leader or are organized around a star system.

Find spaces that nurture kindred and sympathetic joy, so that your compersive tendencies have a place to sprout and flourish.

FINDING YOUR DISNEYLAND

IN THIS CHAPTER

» **Dealing with an affair**

» **Determining whether recovery and reconciliation is even possible**

» **Making changes to agreements after broken trust**

» **Understanding the core elements of a recovery process**

» **Recognizing that only you know the right pathway forward for you**

Chapter **13**

Recovering from Broken Trust

T
oday's culture is steeped in casual deception. Advertisers exhort you to buy (useless) things that will save your life. Or take off pounds. Or gain some skill you absolutely must have to survive in this competitive world. It seems like not such a big leap that your intimate life may also be awash in misrepresentations and sometimes whole campaigns of dishonesty in an attempt to hold you in place in some way, or to diminish your power.

This chapter explores the context for dishonesty in your relationships and helps you think about how you've healed or need to heal from past or present breaches of trust. You can also make connections between your history of surviving broken trust and your interest in and fears about polyamory.

Taking Time to Recover

An important consideration in deciding how to address a breach of trust is to give yourself time. Even though your relationship, and your life, may feel like it's in a state of desperate emergency, attending to this incredibly painful and disruptive event doesn't mean it all needs to get solved in the next ten minutes.

And trying to get to resolution when speaking from a place of deep pain and betrayal almost never goes well. The following sections provide some help in thinking about the best next steps when you've had a breach of trust in your relationship — whether it was prior to your consideration of polyamory or after you created parameters for your poly exploration.

Helping you take time — A checklist

When you realize that you've been lied to or your partner has crossed a clear boundary, you may literally stop breathing. Being blindsided by a lie or series of lies can have cascading physical consequences. As always, everything is better with a breath or two. The emotional pain can create energetic devastation and even physical illness. Pay attention to what you're feeling. Allow yourself to take a time-out and recoup your energy.

TIP

De-escalating your own sense of panic or distress can take time and support. Here are my go-to support activities in times of a trust breach that may work for you:

>> Text, talk, and be with your closest friends.

>> Play your favorite soothing music or a survival anthem.

>> Eat good food. Determine whether a loved one can cook for you, or whether cooking for yourself might soothe you.

>> Change your venue. Ask yourself whether you need to get out of the apartment? Out of town?

>> Spend some time doing your favorite physical activity. Maybe you enjoy a team or individual sport. Maybe you like dancing. Maybe heading to the gym or to the hills for a hike will take great care of you. Moving your body in joyful or connecting ways can be a great support.

>> Get your fan life on. Go to a concert. Go see your team fight to win. Go be with other fans.

>> Take in some art. Go see a favorite play, an exhibit, a performance. Remind yourself of the bigger you beyond this really tough moment.

> » Consider bodywork. Bodywork, including massage, can help when a sense of betrayal is lodged deep. Look for a *trauma-informed practitioner* (a therapist, teacher, or bodyworker who has training in trauma).

> » Hydrate and rest. Let me repeat: Hydrate and rest.

Telling your story

When I've been lied to or betrayed by a lover or a partner, I need to tell the story. Over and over again. It's like my brain is trying to make sense of something it doesn't quite believe yet. I go through the events of finding out or receiving the disclosure. I put together timelines that led to the events. I re-create the story of the relationship with this new information inserted into the false narrative and dig around in all of the dishonesty that has brought me to this moment.

If you have worn out one friend telling them the story, choose another friend. Call an old pal who went through something else with you. Go to a support group. Walk around your neighborhood or in nature and tell yourself the story in your head again. Get out your journal and write. Tell your therapist.

The only way to heal and to plot the right course forward for yourself is to really hear this story. And to hear it, you need to tell it because if you're like me — when I really love someone — I can deflect and deny and minimize what's happened to me. I can try so hard to see my lover's side of it that I can lose myself. Telling your story over and over again helps you hear it, shakes loose your denial, and clears a path to the next right step.

One of my favorite pieces of advice from a former AA sponsor is this: You can't will yourself to clarity. Clarity comes.

Telling your story over and over again is a clarifying practice.

Sifting through each person's needs

When a breach of trust has happened, you and your partner(s) may have wildly differing needs. And that's okay. It's important to find a way to accommodate each of you, while holding to your boundaries (see Chapter 6). How can you do this, especially if one person wants to talk through everything immediately and another needs time and space?

First off, this is a near-universal problem, so don't be disheartened. You may think of the immediate aftermath of discovering a trust breach as triage in the emergency room. The nurses figure out right away what the most life-threatening situations are and address those first. Can't breathe? Let's get you a breathing tube. Bleeding profusely? Staunch that wound.

Speaking truth about the broken trust

Your broken trust triage statements may look something like this:

>> I can't talk to you right now.

>> I need to know exactly what happened right now.

>> I need (you) to find another place to stay.

>> I can't talk about this or work on this if you're seeing this person.

>> I'm going to scream if we talk right now, and I refuse to do this.

>> I need you to hold me and comfort me while I cry.

>> I really want to have make-up sex, but I think it's better if you don't touch me right now.

>> I need to cry and scream, and I can't do that with you here.

>> I can't hear an apology; you're just upset that you've been caught.

The person who has broken trust might have triage statements like these:

>> I need you to stay.

>> It's over with the other person, I need you to believe me.

>> I need to know you won't leave me.

>> I don't want to hurt you, and I want to keep seeing this person.

>> I love you the most, but I can't do what you want.

>> I have to go see them, but I'll be back.

REMEMBER

You may notice that I've only offered I-statements here. *I-statements* are simple declarations (like those listed above) that lay out your truth and keep the focus on your feelings and experience. I always add the caveat: "I think you're a jerk" isn't an I-statement.

I-statements are the way to go during a trust breach, but in my experience, it can be very hard to get to them. Being lied to or betrayed is the greatest generator of you-statements in the universe. "You need to stop seeing him. You screwed up big-time. You're the biggest liar that has ever lied."

If you can hold to I-statements in your triage moment, you'll feel better about yourself, and the decision-making will go better. But if you do a bit of finger-pointing — you-ing — don't feel bad about yourself. Think about what you want here. Do you want to be self-righteous and just blow everything up? Then have at it. Sometimes a blowup is just part of the way through.

Determining what you need to do

To determine next steps after a trust breach, you might want to create an emergency plan to de-escalate the situation. Then, you can start to figure out what you need and whether mending this breach and moving forward is even possible. Here's a simple guide for an emergency plan:

1. **Think about and create your specific needs and triage statements.**

Figure out how to get some space to breathe and to take in this new information.

2. **Make a short-term agreement.**

Here's what pieces of it may look like:

- I won't leave you and neither of us will see other lovers till we talk.

- We'll talk on Friday, after I've seen my therapist.

- We can get a mediator or therapist for our next conversation.

- I'm staying at my sister's this week while you stay here. Next week you'll need to find somewhere to stay while I come back.

- I'll try to think well of you while we're figuring this out.

- Any more lies or breaches in this period and I'm done.

3. **Take a time-out and tell the story to yourself and as many loved ones and supportive professionals as you need.**

Through it all, remember to take spectacular care of yourself.

Figuring out whether recovery is possible

Assessing whether recovery is possible, and whether a mended relationship of any kind, in any form is sustainable — may take some time. Things can't go back to the way they were prior to the breach. This experience will change you and the way forward, as it should. The question is what's possible.

SOMETIMES, THE LITTLE THINGS ADD UP

When we talk about trust being broken in a relationship most people assume infidelity of some sort is the source, but in my experience, it's what your partners do *not* do that leads to breaches in trust.

In a previous poly configuration, I had a partner who had another partner, but at the time was my only partner. It was kind of like a V shape with me and their other partner being on the top ends of the V, and not connected to each other.

A few years into the relationship, my partner and their other partner were taking a trip abroad. This trip was something they both had been really excited for, and I was really excited for them to take it.

But I got very sick while they were on the trip, and I asked my partner to spend some time talking with me and comforting me, but when we finally got on the phone, after five minutes they told me they had to go because their other partner had ordered food and the food was there. It felt like a really weird slap to the face.

And although this seems small, what it revealed to me was that this was a part of a greater pattern they had displayed throughout our relationship. And once I realized that, the feelings of trust I had for this person quickly began to dissolve. —**Bishop**

A mistake some couples or polycules make is rushing to apology and forgiveness rather than taking the time to poke around a bit in what has happened, how you feel, and what you need. Apologies and forgiveness declarations can be shortcuts when people are experiencing unbearable feelings and situations. People may also jump to an instant list of corrections or fixes. All because you don't want to stay in these feelings. Or you don't want to have to really talk about the problems that underlie the breach of trust — like you've been checking out with overwork, or your partner is having an emotional affair with a friend, or you're completely unavailable because of the caregiving you've being doing for your parents.

Sometimes structural changes in your relationship that pull your attention away from your partner or exhaust you aren't fixable. You have an infant to care for, or your partner has a parent who is dying, or you just got fired. If you're with someone over time, life unfolds, and life is demanding and messy. Inside of all of that messiness are unmet needs for both you and your partners — and if one of you has breached an agreement to get those needs met — it can be difficult to consider whether you can ever trust them again.

Taking an inventory of possibilities is important to navigate the road to recovery. Here are a few questions to ask yourself about whether recovery is possible:

>> Is the person who has breached trust really taking responsibility for their actions?

  - If yes, how are they doing this?

  - What actions or changes are in place that demonstrate taking responsibility? Will these actually give you the space to heal and create a constructive way forward?

  - If no, if they are deflecting, and blaming you or others, or minimizing what has happened, do you think they're capable of owning their part eventually?

  - What indications do you have that your partner is capable of building a path toward owning their actions and making a real amends?

>> Do you have the capacity to forgive and reestablish trust — do you think it's possible to learn from this, let go, and move forward with your partner?

  - If yes, what are the conditions and actions that will make regaining trust possible?

  - If no, do you want to build that capacity?

  - What do you need in your life and your day-to-day connection to your partner to build on your capacity to trust?

You might not know the answers to these questions in the immediate aftermath of discovering a trust breach, and that's okay. Take your time. Get support. These questions can be a guide as you move out of emergency mode and into considering your options and devising a plan for the way forward.

A partner who has been unable to communicate honestly and be rigorous about assessing their own behaviors and shortcomings in a monogamous relationship is unlikely to do better in an open or polyamorous relationship. In this case, love might not make more love — instead, adding more people to the mix is likely to sow more chaos, deception, and pain.

Investigating the nature of the dishonesty for clues going forward

Sorting out what kind of lies are happening in your situation — its sources, its functions, its impacts — may be helpful. Lies aren't justifiable, but many lies can be explained by looking at a lover's childhood burdens, or trauma history, or patterns in past relationships. Having an explanation doesn't mean you need to excuse the lie or forgive the person breaching your trust. It's just helpful context for you as you consider what this means to you, your partner, and your relationship.

Being lied to makes me feel unmoored or a little lost, especially since I survived a childhood full of both casual and consequential lies that were meant to protect me or uphold the status quo. All kinds of things were presented to me as absolute truths — from Santa Claus to daily lies like swearing would make my tongue turn black, or my grandmother was happy in that nursing home, or school segregation was better for everyone. It makes sense then that I was both desensitized to and unprepared for being lied to by my lovers.

ACTIVITY

This activity allows you to be a dishonesty detective and examine the lies you are dealing with more closely. Core questions to ask yourself or your partner include the following:

» How is this lie connected to lies that my partner survived as a child?

» How does this lie echo lies that I survived as a child?

» How is this lie connected to survival mechanisms that my partner developed to take care of themselves when they were young and powerless?

» What was the function of this lie? What did it hide?

» Is this lie singular or part of a series or campaign of lies?

» Is my partner ashamed of themselves on a fundamental level?

» How does their shame mirror some of my shame — and does this amplify my sense of emergency right now?

» Did our original agreements about our relationship hide or mask needs that my partner was ashamed to share?

» How might this information help me figure out my next steps in recovering and taking care of myself?

As you recover from a trust breach, you may want to think about how or whether lies permeated your childhood and your educational process as both a child and an adult. The devastation you might feel at having someone abuse your trust might be very current, and it also might be amplified by abuses of trust in your past, either in romantic or in formative familial relationships.

TIP

Sorting out the past from the present is important work in order to stay present and assess what your next best action step is in recovering from a breach of trust.

NO ONE IS PERFECTLY TRUSTWORTHY

Thirteen years into our relationship, my boyfriend lied to me. We had some agreements about safer sex in our open relationship, and he broke our agreements and lied about it. We had come through a lot by then — he had gotten sober about five years before that. And I could see why he did it — he had a very controlling parent, especially around his sexuality, and he grew up feeling very hemmed in emotionally and sexually. He had to keep a lot of secrets just to be himself. This kind of sneaking around wasn't about me — it was just his trauma surfacing.

I knew what he did wasn't meant to hurt me and what he did really didn't endanger me or my health. In fact, if he had asked me, I would have easily agreed to changing our safer sex guidelines. I think when he did it, he was in denial about it breaking my trust — like he wasn't even aware he was lying. But being lied to really hurt me and undermined our relationship.

When people lie to me, I feel like they're trying to control my reality. And I resented being put in the position of his controlling parents in his internal story, because that's the last thing I am or want to be. I let him know that lying was a deal-breaker for me and that he needed to figure out why he had lied and make a meaningful apology, or I was done.

And he did this. Which was wonderful, but what really struck me during the whole crisis was that I was not in crisis. I was so much less emotionally activated than I expected. And that was because in the whole of our life together — my boyfriend is wonderful. He's extremely trustworthy. He works so hard on his emotional growth, and he's generous and loving with me.

And this was a mistake. This mistake came out of work he still needs to do. It hurt me, but it wasn't about me, and I could see this clearly. Our forgiveness work of many years really held us in this period: I love imperfect him and he loves imperfect me. And I can take care of myself and still believe in him when issues arise, because he takes responsibility for himself and he takes action to do better.

The deal is there are no guarantees. There is no perfect love out there. There is no "the one." There's just each of us struggling to act according to our values, and deeply caring for each other as best we can, as we grow. —**Dean**

Adjusting Agreements As Needed

Rethinking and adjusting working agreements in your relationship after a breach of trust is reasonable (you can find help on creating poly family agreements in Chapter 9). What is this breach telling you about the life you have constructed with your partner(s)? What kind of longing or compulsion does your lover describe as a catalyst for crossing a boundary you both or collectively put into place? The following sections help as you consider what kinds of adjustments you might make to stay on a path together, what to do if you want different things, and whether to get outside help if you need it.

Considering adjustments

ACTIVITY

This adjustment exercise can help you look at your current agreements and consider whether you and your partner(s) need to make an adjustment. Another good place in the book to look to for help is in Chapter 6, which lays out consequences in the case of a breach of boundaries. I suggest looking at the following inventory after you're out of crisis and are in a place of being able to talk with your partner without high activation, or fight-or-flight level of energy. Ask your partner(s) these questions:

>> Do we have a partnership or family mission statement (see Chapter 9)? Does it need adjustment? Do we need to create a new one?

>> What relationship agreement has been broken? Is this an agreement we want to keep in place, or has this crisis revealed a change that needs to be made?

>> What do you wish we had thought about that we missed when we made our initial agreements?

>> What need were you trying to get met when you broke our agreement? What do you think about this need now? How are you going to take care of yourself moving forward?

>> What's a bottom-line need or boundary that is immovable for you? What deal-breakers remain?

Realizing that everyone doesn't need the same thing

When trust has been breached, it's important for each person to sort out and identify what they need to recover. Different people need different things. That seems simplistic and obvious, but when an imbalance of power happens like an abuse of trust, there can be a rush to equalize things. Partners may attempt to make remedies by requiring the same actions or recovery strategies for each affected person. Remember that differences can be tricky to manage during a crisis, and these differences are often a strength in relationships and may be part of the core attraction that brought you and this person together.

TIP

As long as you all respect and commit to taking responsibility for deceptive behavior, needing different things in a recovery process isn't a bad thing.

Closing ranks — don't tell your friends

A really hard thing for couples or polycules when there has been a breach of trust is the shame and fear that comes up around it and a desire to close ranks and keep the crisis to yourself or yourselves. That's reasonable because when emotions are high or when your emotional and material security feels threatened, you tend to go into a heightened, protective mode.

But in most cases, you'll need the opposite to heal, recover, and make good decisions. You'll need the affirming love and belief of your closest people, the reflections of others who have survived affairs or other trust breaches, and the strong arms of your confidantes to hold you in your pain.

You may fear that people will hate your partner and decide you're an idiot for staying with them and trying to work things out, or that other people's judgments and agendas will make it hard for you to listen to yourself and what you need. And you may be right. You know your friendship circle (see pod mapping in Chapter 11). If you don't have two to three people in your life who can truly be there for you in a time of crisis, then perhaps this trust breach is revealing a piece of this picture that's a contributing factor to this shattering moment.

REMEMBER

Over-reliance on your partner(s) can put tremendous pressure on your relationship. If you or your partner(s) don't have a vibrant network of loved ones, your relationship might be overworked and exhausted as it attempts to meet an impossible set of needs — best friend, lover, parent, provider, intellectual peer, playmate . . . the list goes on. Your recovery will go better if and when you have the supportive community you deserve.

Seeking equity in care rather than symmetry

Rather than attempting to do exactly the same things when recovering from a breach of trust, partners would do well to seek equity in care. *Equity in care* means that effort goes into ensuring that each person impacted has the space and resources to recover and heal.

One of you might need a new therapist or support group. Another might need weekly massages. One might need time away from the kids to cry or get in touch with feelings that are too overwhelming to deal with in the mix of their day-to-day responsibilities. Another might need to spend time with friends or family. Is one person absolutely overwhelmed with grief while others are doing relatively well? What is the intervention that will bring each impacted person up to a comparable state of wellness or capacity to manage this crisis?

Getting outside help if things are volatile or you get stuck

Getting stuck when you're trying to recover from being lied to by a lover is a common experience. Everything in your life as you know it is suddenly called into question. What else don't you know about? What's real and what's fake? What does love even mean when someone you love has trampled on the most sacred thing you can give them — your trust?

In several parts of this book, I discuss the importance of true friends in sifting out what you need and what paths you want to pursue, and this is one of those critical times or situations to reach into your network of loved ones to stay unstuck and commit to your healing. Friends who have some experience with polyamory can be especially helpful right now.

But sometimes, friendship networks don't have the deep bench of skills you need during a time of crisis like this. If so, peer counseling, grief support, massage, or talk therapy can all provide the kind of relief, respite from obsessive or negative thinking, and even bodily comfort you deserve. (Chapter 7 goes into more detail.)

Don't wait until you're mired in depression or find yourself in volatile circular arguments with your partner. Let people who care for you know you're suffering. Let trained professionals ease some of your burden.

TIP

Injecting some air into your systems of communication and interaction while you're recovering from a trust breach is especially important. You have to keep moving. Getting the support you need is crucial to that movement.

Recovery Is Possible

Against all odds and the intensity of your belief that everything is ruined and nothing ever will be the same, your relationship can recover. Nothing ever will be the same though. That part is true. In the aftermath of a breach of trust, you'll need to re-create many things: your ideas about yourself, your relationship with your partner or partners, and your pathway forward. The following sections provide concrete tools for moving forward, into a place of rebuilding. I've used these — and my clients and friends have used these — to foster sometimes inconceivable reconnection and repair. Whether you have been the creator of, or the person impacted by a breach of trust, these tools can help you recover and move forward.

Making a great apology

Probably the single most important determinant on that way forward is whether the person who has broken trust is able to make a sincere apology.

Activist and writer Mia Mingus has created an excellent set of guidelines for making a great apology. If you can start here as a couple or polycule, you have a lot in your favor in the recovery column. If you or your partner don't have the capacity to make an apology on these terms, get help. Seek friends or counseling resources that can help you get there. As a coach, I have watched couples who have survived deep, disturbing betrayals come back from these abuses of trust — and a sincere, unreserved apology was the foundation of that recovery, every time.

TIP

Follow these key steps to apologize:

1. **Say you're sorry.**

   Simple. No equivocations. And "I'm sorry you feel hurt" isn't an apology. "I'm sorry I hurt you by telling you lies over many months." That's an authentic apology.

2. **Name the hurt.**

   Say what you did, plainly. "I told you lies over and over and made you think you were jealous or creating problems because I was trying to cover my tracks." No back-door discussion of your partner's issues, such as "I know this was hard on you because you're insecure."

3. **Name the impact.**

   Describe what effect your behavior had on the person you've hurt. "I know over time this made you question yourself and it nearly drove you crazy." Or "I know that you can't trust me now and that I will have to work to regain your trust."

4. Take responsibility by naming your actions.

Own what you've done; you alone are responsible for your actions. "I know I could have told you about my loneliness or my attraction to X, but I chose to hide those feelings and to start an affair instead."

In my mind, this step is one of the most crucial parts of the apology to get right. Often, people who have broken a partner's trust will say something like: "Things were messed up in the relationship for a long time." Or "Relationships are dynamic. I didn't get here on my own." Which may well be true. But the decision to break trust and deceive — responsibility for that rests solely upon the person taking that action. Making a true apology rests on your willingness to own your behavior, 100 percent, without reservations or footnotes.

5. Commit to stopping the behavior and not doing it again.

This is a big step. Many people find themselves apologetic when a breach of trust has happened, but changing behavior so that you're a more trustworthy partner is serious work. In a monogamous relationship, committing to stopping a behavior most often means that a partner ends an affair and usually all contact with the person.

In a polyamorous situation, committing to change can often be more complex. The breach may be about breaking an agreement like creating a more intimate relationship with a new partner than you initially agreed on or failing to sustain safer sex practices. In these cases, it might not mean ending the relationship with the person in question but adjusting practices or agreements. Accordingly, stopping the behavior means to stop telling lies and to recommit to adhering to your agreements but not necessarily removing the person from the poly constellation.

When trust has been broken, figuring out the best way forward in a complex polycule can be challenging. The important thing is to listen to the person or people whose trust has been betrayed around what their needs are going forward. And to adjust your agreements and act accordingly.

Apology + honesty + consistency + time = rebuilding trust

Although a great apology is a crucial first step forward, it's just one step in a longer process. A core part of a long-term amends process is for the person who has betrayed trust to *sustain their commitment to honesty over time* and to consistently show up emotionally for the person or people they have harmed.

TIP

A sincere apology *plus* a commitment to honesty *plus* consistency *plus* time is the recipe for rebuilding trust. It's not rocket science; it's a very clear path. But that doesn't mean it's easily done.

WARNING

Reconciliation and trust-building is a big job. When you have hurt someone, witnessing the impacts of your abuse of trust, over and over, is hard. It's easier to check out — to maybe stay late at work a lot or to renovate a room in the house instead of sitting through painful dinners where your partner cries or is depressed.

SOMETIMES, MORE THAN ONE APOLOGY IS IN ORDER

I didn't cheat but . . .

You aren't responsible for your partner's cheating or bad behavior. You're only responsible for yours. Is there anything this crisis has revealed to you about your behavior and what you might want to atone for? Is there some lesson in here for you to take in and use to make whatever you create after this breach with your partner better, stronger, more honest, less fraught?

In Shannon Perez-Darby's landmark essay, *The Secret Joy of Accountability*, she notes that when she was surviving an abusive partner, she didn't like some of her behaviors. She realizes she was trying to do her best in a terrible situation, but:

> "It's easier to tell you what he did and harder to tell you what I did. It's harder to tell you about the times I lied to him. It's harder to tell you about the panic attacks or moments when I just couldn't fight anymore. I'm afraid that if I tell you the whole story, the extent of the devastation will, paradoxically, get lost. I'm afraid I'll tell the wrong story. I'm afraid that I can never explain just what it was like; that if I do a bad job of sharing my whole truth, then it'll be like I'm lying, and all of this healing work will have been for nothing. I'm afraid my story isn't the story you want to hear. I'm afraid to say that my healing means taking responsibility for the fucked-up things I did because then I'm not the survivor everyone wants me to be. . .

> "In the course of surviving, I cried a lot. In the course of surviving, I lied, manipulated, invaded my partner's privacy. In the course of surviving, I hurt and put in harm's way my friends, my communities, my partner, myself. In the course of surviving, I hurt my family connections. In the course of surviving, I drank."

As counterintuitive as it may seem to offer an apology in the face of having been so clearly wronged, my advice to you is this: If you also have an apology to make, take the opportunity. You won't regret it.

TIP

And even though every person in the partnership or polycule should take great care of themselves during the recovery process, if you have breached an agreement, showing up for your partner(s) emotionally in the aftermath will be a crucial step on the path to mending your relationship.

Forgiving and letting go

Only you can decide if you can forgive and let go around a partner's abuse of your trust. Only you know what a healthy next step is for you. If you have a partner who is making a sincere apology and is undertaking a consistent amends process, you have an opportunity to rebuild trust. The question is — do you want to take it?

TIP

A truth underneath the truth of how hard it is to forgive a partner who has lied to you is that it shakes the very foundation of your faith in yourself.

How could you not have known? How could you have put your trust in this person? How could this person who has seen you at your most vulnerable cast aside that sacred offering by deceiving you? Often the path to forgiveness of your lover starts with forgiving yourself. And that can be very hard to do, especially if you're deflecting your anger at yourself by aiming it exclusively at your partner.

I don't want to be overly simplistic or fake-optimistic about this. Or campaign for forgiveness as though it's appropriate in every situation — *because forgiveness truly isn't appropriate in many situations.*

But forgiving a partner who has abused your trust can be an incredible gift *to yourself* under the right circumstances. As Shannon Perez-Darby suggests in her fearless self-inventory (see the nearby sidebar) — it's easier to create a polarized, flattened story of your situation when you've been harmed than to delve into the complexities of trying and failing to be the best version of yourself as you attempt to love your partners and be vulnerable.

Forgiving your partners as they fail you, as they perhaps show you the worst side of themselves, demonstrates a kind of faith you may desperately hope others will extend to you as you make your imperfect, blundering way through life and love.

Forgiveness is a gift for the worthy. And by that I mean, those who are willing to go the hard way with you and those who are willing to be just as fearless about their self-inventory as you are about yours. You don't owe anyone your forgiveness. You get to decide who you share your intimate life with and what your bottom-line needs are. You can decide to forgive; you can decide to walk away. Nobody else has to like it or understand your decision. How you organize your intimate and sexual life and investments is entirely, solely, up to you.

FORGIVENESS LIGHTENS YOUR LOAD

About seven years into our relationship, my boyfriend got sober. And rather than relief, I found myself feeling resentful about all the times his drinking had impacted me. In the midst of all the drinking, I just stuffed it all down — I had to get through it, and I had learned how to do this from living with an alcoholic parent. When he got sober — all the resentment just bubbled up. I needed help moving forward.

Our couples' therapist asked me to tell my boyfriend about the times he had hurt me through his drinking, and what I was still holding onto. Then, he was instructed to repeat them back to me. Hearing him say it, while he was actually looking at me — I finally felt heard. It felt like he could take in what I'd been through, and how his actions impacted me, and that he was making a real apology.

During his drinking, when something bad happened, he often acted like it was the first time, like he didn't remember the pattern. It was infuriating. It was relieving to finally have him hear about and acknowledge all that had gone on, to see him care about it deeply.

These sessions helped me feel increasing compassion for him. I could see how painful it was for him to take in what he'd done. This process — of me telling him a story or a hurt that I'm holding onto and him mirroring it back — has been useful for years now. We can draw on it whenever we need it, outside of therapy.

I think this work gave me the first honest experience of forgiveness in my life. Very few people actually ever get this — with estrangements in our families or with breakups. I don't feel burdened by this history anymore. It's not this big weight between us. And the repair that we have done together — it's extraordinary.

And I think maybe the biggest gift is that I know how to take care of myself now. I'm not afraid that he's going to relapse, or that some terrible breach is going to happen — because even it did, I have more trust in myself. **—Dean**

Chapter **14**

Parenting While Poly

W hen considering polyamory, many people find the idea of parenting within a family unit of multiple lovers to be a deal-breaker. That makes sense because as a parent, your job is to be protective of your children, and the world in general is hostile to polyamory. In fact, it's so hostile that I anonymize all contributors' offerings in this chapter to protect these parents, and their kids, who are sharing the gift of their experience.

For poly contemplators who are already parents, the idea of adding new adults to the familial picture can be daunting or scary. Many people grew up in monogamous households where breakups and new romantic partners for one parent created painful and sometimes abusive situations. Others have struggled in their existing parenting partnerships — working hard to align their parenting values and practices with their partner. The idea of starting all over again by adding another parenting partner — ach! And then, there are the parenting soloists — those parents who are accustomed to having all the control around parenting practices and who may be distressed just thinking about the compromises that a prospective new parent might pose.

People exploring polyamory who aren't yet parents but considering parenthood may find the idea of creating a parenting-centered or parenting-aspirant polycule overwhelming. Finding one person whose romantic, sexual, *and* parenting mojo matches yours is hard enough, let alone multiple partners. Not to worry. I take up these important topics, one question at a time in this chapter.

Making Clear Agreements

Like all aspects of life as a polyamorous person, happiness and functionality rest on the clarity of your co-created agreements, including poly family agreements that pertain to parenting values, caregiving, and roles. Chapter 9 has many tips and exercises to help you create a broad range of poly family agreements, and you can fold your parenting concerns into those. Wherever you are on your parenting journey, you can ground yourself in your values and needs about parenting and work from there. The following sections walk you through some key issues and concerns.

Remembering that lovers aren't co-parents

All lovers aren't meant to be co-parents. When monogamous people begin to organize their family lives, whether a lover is excited to parent, or possesses the requisite skills, is often a deal-breaking or deal-making consideration. A gift of polyamory is that you can separate your needs for a lover or emotional and romantic partner from your needs for a co-parent.

Everyone in my polycule loves and appreciates my kids; many have close relationships with them. Some have lived with me and my kids at different points, but almost none of them have interacted with my children as a parental authority over the past 25 years.

One of the things I understood about myself early on as a parent is that I wanted to maintain maximum control over parental decisions. I didn't want to compromise my vision for raising my kids, and I didn't want to haggle over my daily practices with anyone else. At the same time, I very much wanted to have a lot of different people in the mix showing my children love and presenting examples of all kinds of ways to move in the world. Parenting as a *solo polyamorous person* (a person at the center of their poly constellation, with a variety of intimate and love connections rather than a "partner") gave me the best possible route for achieving this.

ACTIVITY

Here are some of the questions you might ask yourself as you consider parenting as a poly person:

>> What are your bottom lines as a parent? In other words, what absolutely can't happen here? In my case, these things pertained to physical punishment, yelling, and using shunning and shaming as parental tools.

>> What's your vision for the tone, tenor, and vibe of your family home? Is it highly structured? Is it chaotic? Are there lots of people flowing through? Is it formal? Do people drop in all the time? Are there sleepovers?

>> What happens when you or your partners don't live up to your vision or your promises to your children and each other around care and guidance?

>> What strengths do you and your partners bring to the table?

>> What complexities or conditions — physical, mental, historical —are you and your partners carrying into your life as parents?

>> What happens when you can't solve things? What's your conflict resolution or crisis plan? How will you make amends and heal?

Talking these questions through with a potential parenting partner gives you a lot of information about your alignments and differences and whether co-parenting should even be on the table.

POLYAMORY STORY

In terms of poly and parenting I chose my lovers carefully. I chose lovers who either were parents themselves or who delighted in children. I think in general, though, I made a choice to have my children meet and get to know my lovers, while not involving my lovers in my parenting, as in *yes, that's mommy's special friend.* —W.

Understanding that co-parenting is a significant commitment

I can't think of a more significant decision in my life than choosing to parent. This singular commitment changed all my other commitments and created crucial pathways for my social, professional, and familial life. I often tell my first child that the leap of faith I took to have him created all of the other amazing leaps of faith that followed.

TIP

Think carefully about who you want to bring into your parenting life. You can raise wonderful children many different ways, despite societal mores and myths suggesting that there's only one way. The crucial thing is to be able to provide a baseline of material and emotional security for your child, and for yourself, so that you can actually have the space to enjoy your children and to show up as your best (or at least better) self with them.

That doesn't mean you have to be rich or you have to be married. It doesn't mean any of the things that mainstream culture tells you. You know what it means in your life to have enough material, social, and emotional security to function, and to have the space to grow. Secure your parenting life by building this for yourself, and then extending that world to your child.

In my case, I came to understand my deep need to be fully in charge of the daily work of parenting my kids, without compromise. And in the case of the village of loved ones I built around them — people flowed in and out in the ways they wanted to, bringing so much energy, differing worldviews, cultural traditions, resources, expertise, hobbies, and passions.

The villagers in my polycule have literally saved me and my children over and over again: going on vacation with the kids, providing short-term accommodation when we had a housing crisis, getting one of them interested in reading, amping up another's interest in a second language, finding us a family therapist, paying off a student loan. When people comment on how hard it must be to be a single parent, I let them know. I'm a solo parent by choice, but my kids have grown up in a mighty village.

And even though my villagers have largely not functioned as co-parents, they do possess a lot of characteristics that I think are important in potential co-parents. They are

>> Generous and open, not controlling or judgmental.

>> See children as fully formed people, not a possession or clay to mold.

>> Are interested in what the kids have to say.

>> Respect me as a parent and support me rather than see me as deficient or needing them to improve the parenting situation or my kids.

>> Have lives that they love already. My kids aren't there to fill some kind of unmet need for them.

All these characteristics align with my parenting values. The question for you is, *what are yours*? The activity in the preceding section can help you create your own list of preferred co-parenting characteristics so that you can consider whether any of your lovers fit your needs around co-parenting.

You can also consult Chapter 9 and look at two example polycules, one that centers parental aspirations in their connections and one that has a clear separation between his lovers and his life as a parent. Chapter 4 also presents different poly family forms, some created by parents. There are so many different possible parenting paths to consider.

I UNDERESTIMATED HOW VULNERABLE I WAS

I had one of those breakups you look back on and you're just like: God, I had all the support in the world, but I just couldn't leave this person. Z was 2 or 3 years old. And I think I underestimated how vulnerable I was as a solo parent, as a new solo parent.

And I put up with some sh** I never thought I would put up with in a million years, things like safer sex violations, things like boundary violations. And this person was trying to step up and take care of Z and was taking care of Z for a 12-hour period once a week — the pickup from daycare. Do the evening sleep and drop off at daycare the next morning. And they had an incident where they lost their temper and they hit Z and there was no coming back from it. I know it wasn't intentional or premeditated. I know they love Z. And I was just: *Oh, right. I'm done.* —**B.B.**

Creating a village committed to your kids

An unsung, major benefit of parenting in poly life is the possibility of creating a dedicated village of multiple friends and lovers to take up the nurturing of your children. Although so much criticism of polyamory centers on a judgmental view of the alleged chaos that multiple partners and potentially multiple parents present, not nearly enough ink and breath is spent on the miracle of multiple adults committed to your child's well-being, even if they aren't acting in a formal parental role.

REMEMBER

Having many hearts and eyes on your children can be a great blessing. That's especially true if partners follow your lead around defining what's in your child's best interest and affirm you as a parent. The old adage, many hands make light work, is especially relevant. My not-parent lovers have done everything from set up the nursery to help organize the college graduation party, and so, so many things in between.

TIP

Center yourself in your needs as a parent and trust yourself to grow the structure that will serve you best. And importantly — commit to healing from whatever needs addressing in terms of healing from your family-of-origin story. You can figure this out.

MOVING FROM SOLO PARENTING INTO CO-PARENTING

I'm solo poly and have never lived with a partner. And when P. hit 6, he started to ask, "What about a dad?" He already. knew his donor. There's never been any secret about that. And he started to ask whether G. could be his dad, not just his donor.

And when G. and I were planning to have a baby — we had known each other in Queer Asian Pacific-Islander-identified movement work for a decade by then — we had a weekly project-baby meeting where we would just talk about doctor's appointments, costs, feelings, you know, all the things. So, we started to have meetings again, talking about, what does it mean for G. to not be a donor but be a dad? And after about a year of talks, we made it official when we were all on vacation together. It'll be two years in August, and G. has stepped into P.'s life more as a dad. And we were clear going into it that this was going to mean being on some sort of continuum, from fabulous gay uncle to 100 percent all-in full-on parent, right?

We agreed we would see what would evolve, letting P. kind of drive that bus. And so just last month, G. changed his base from San Francisco to our house on the East Coast. So, he's still very much a global traveler, but he's now based here in my house instead. Wow. You know, he had an apartment in the Castro with all the gay boys and gave it up to come here and live the poly family life with us. So, wow! Grateful. —L.L.

Dealing with Conflicts in Parenting Styles

In this section, you can consider different ways poly people parent and how they've navigated conflicts with their lovers and co-parents. Refer to Chapters 4 and 9 to see several poly parents navigating differences with primary partners and also considering complex poly parenting scenarios.

You might look at the variety of options there and think: *wow, a lot of potential for conflict!* Or: *won't this be confusing for the kids?* But confusion and conflicts in parenting scenarios tend to emerge on these three basic fronts: differing values, lack of clarity around roles, and living together.

Prioritizing your values as a parent

Literally any poly family form will work for you if you're foregrounding and living your parenting values. When you're caught up in new love, everything seems possible. And indeed, a new lover may create expansive possibilities for you as a parent. But you have to stick to your parenting beliefs and needs and tell the truth, even if it derails the love train a bit.

In my case, I chose to live with my daughter's dad for a period, which was difficult for both them and me. They're a germaphobe, and I track dirt all over the house without even noticing it. They love structure, and I hate it. My life as a parent is like a Jackson Pollock painting — let's throw some more paint up there and marvel at the flows. I also had been a solo parent for years by the time we had our daughter. While I adored my parenting partner as a lover, I really hated struggling with them around the different ways we parented in our singular household. Eventually, we both came to see that we would be better parents living apart.

I don't have a lot of regrets in life, but I wish I had thought more carefully about our obvious differences before we established our household together. We actually are wonderful parents when we aren't living under the same roof, and far from being confused, our daughter has thrived in two homes with vibrant and distinct worlds that spin around her.

My passion for my daughter's dad clouded my judgment at the time, and my romantic ideals about living together took over. Eventually dismantling that household was painful, and when I look back on it, I wish I could have saved us that pain. But hindsight is 20/20. If I could do it all over again, would I give up the amazing memories we have of her infancy and toddlerhood in that house? Probably not.

TIP

As you create your poly life and commitments, you grow, you learn, you love your partners desperately, you try. And when you do this as a parent, the stakes are incredibly high.

Prioritizing your child's well-being

When it comes to conflicting parenting values and practices, you have to get clear with yourself what you believe are bottom lines around your child's well-being. Knowing what your parenting values are is crucial to getting through conflicts and conversations. Knowing where you have wiggle room and where you don't will serve you in any parenting relationship configuration.

Some conflicts can be ironed out. For example, one of you thinks the children should be more involved in sports and the other prioritizes time at the library. But others strike at more fundamental parental territories. For example, one parent thinks that children should fear you a little bit, so that they respond to your rules and limits, and the other believes that fear-driven kids hide themselves and stop trusting their parents, or that making your child fear you is abuse in and of itself.

In a case like this, you may need to take the conflict to therapy to find resolution.

Accepting that not all partners are meant to parent

A mistake I see poly partners make is to try to fit their square-peg lover into their decidedly circular poly parenting universes. You may have a very expansive, romantic idea about the way you want your family to look and for parenting to unfold with your children. However, the lover or lovers you've chosen might be entirely unsuited to this vision.

The good news is, you have much more flexibility in this situation than a monogamous parent who's in love with an incompatible parenting partner.

Your lover is your lover for a good reason (I hope). You don't need them to fit your parenting ideals. In fact, having a lover who doesn't connect in any way with your parenting and family life may be wonderful. Instead they might create a kind of alternative universe for you, building sexy and fantastical worlds — beyond parenting — that feel absolutely unattainable when you're mired in laundry, school lunch planning, and carpools.

After a decade of being together, J. has only just met my children. And our connection is really great. I feel like I can lean in there more, which means: *let's make more sexy time happen.* We've had so much loving and caring and building of connection with him and his partner over the course of the pandemic. Now, I feel like — let's go back to sexy time, which is, maybe we need to do something that's away from the house and away from dogs and really like, lean back in. —Z.

Telling or Not Telling the Kids

Coming out poly can be a big or a very small deal depending on your family values, where you live, and whether your family security is vulnerable socially or economically. In my case, my kids knew me as a queer activist and a sex educator from a very young age, and I can't pinpoint the day I told them that I'm polyamorous. It was in the air, and when they reached high school, conversation about it became less theoretical and more attached to people in my life whom they already knew and had loved for years.

As you think about whether you want to tell your kids that you are poly, think about the following key considerations to ensure a good outcome.

Recognizing what information is age appropriate

My golden rule has always been to just be myself with my children, to talk about my values, and then to answer direct questions about my story and my relationships as they arise. I definitely kept my multiple lovers private when they were in elementary school because I didn't want them to carry this knowledge inside of such a conservative monogamous society.

TIP

My sex educator self has always prioritized age-appropriate information, honesty, and safety. Kids are carrying a lot of anxiety these days — for themselves and for the planet. I want our family unit to relieve them of those burdens and to create a soft landing, not add to them. So, coming out has been embedded in a foundational context of care.

POLYAMORY STORY

The key thing is to be clear about what's developmentally appropriate. I remember the weekend that we all got together, we went to a community event. Before, we had brunch, with our new lover T.'s roommates. And so it was like, T., J., and F. all live together, and these are new friends. So the kids got it — me and your Mommy have new friends. And just like my children's friends, some friends stay over, and some friends don't. And that's developmentally appropriate, because it's actually never been the kids' business what happens once everyone goes to bed. They came to know more about the relationship in the context of — there's always been this sense of this clan around you, and this is just another manifestation of that. —Z.

Protecting yourself and your kids from others' judgments

It's highly likely that your child will hear judgmental, terrible reactions to their disclosure that their parents are polyamorous. You can prepare them by letting them know that not everyone believes that people can love more than one person at the same time. You can have an expansive conversation about how love functions in your family and other families and how love grows more love in so many different contexts that they experience. This is the fun part of the protective conversation — helping them connect to the wonder and the amazingness of the love that's in your family and attached to friends who they may now just be learning are your partners.

And the important second half of this conversation is helping them do a scan of their environment — friends, school, sports teams, social clubs, church community, and so on — so that they can start to assess likely reactions and what they might have to deal with.

Here's a great set of questions to create an environmental scan with your child:

>> Does your child want to share this news with their friends? Discuss the difference between secrets and privacy. *Secrets* are generally shame-driven and hurt. *Privacy* is about keeping information to ourselves from a place of strength and self-care.

>> Who's likely to be the most supportive friend when learning this news about the family? If your child wants to come out to their friends, disclosing in the order of strongest supporters first can be a good strategy.

>> Even though they might not know what their best friend thinks about polyamory, they do have a lot of other information about that best friend in terms of their family structure, religious traditions, values, and how that family deals with various social issues.

>> Although they might not be able to anticipate how their friend group might react, their friends have a history of responding to other confidences and disclosures in the group. How did those conversations go? What are the parallels here?

>> If this disclosure gets all over school, are they prepared for it? *Are you as parents prepared for it?* What does that mean? Is there any conversation your kids would like to have with supportive teachers or counselors before they tell their friends? Is there a conversation your child would like you to initiate?

>> Is there any reason to worry about job security if this disclosure starts to spin out into wider view in your community?

If the answer to this final question is yes, I suggest a full stop on any consideration around coming out to your kids. Even if your child tells only their BFF, there's simply no controlling the story after that.

My kids were really proud of having two moms. And then when L. came in, the way we talked about it with the kids and in the community was *we're all together.* And in some ways, it's not important for you to know what we're actually doing together, right? It's just, we're together. And I think there was a tremendous amount of judgment that I got, and not just from straight folk. In fact, a lot of queer women were like, *This must be horrible for your children.* —Z.

Giving your kids credit — They often know even when you don't tell

I coached a couple who decided not to come out to their kids. Their sexual life together had been private, so why would their polyamorous sexual practices with others be any different? And then, over time, their emotionally intelligent middle-school-age daughters started asking them about their respective lovers. Why was Jazz around so much? And why did Dad laugh so loud at everything Amira said? While the family had a robust group of friends that circulated through their lives, the children had zeroed in on their lovers because they could feel the enlivening love between these friends and their parents, and they were curious.

This happens fairly often, especially in families that talk about feelings a lot or discuss friendship issues with their children when called upon to help them solve problems. What to do when your kids have figured everything out, despite your best efforts to keep your relationships private?

This couple decided to deflect these questions while their girls were in their preteen years, eventually shifting their strategy and coming out to their children when they were in high school. By then, their daughters had a close group of supportive friends and had developed positive relationships with their parents' respective partners as family friends.

EVERYTHING WE'VE BEEN TAUGHT IS WRONG

Everything we were taught about parenting was wrong. People saying, for example — don't bring your lovers around your children. And I don't believe in that. I just don't. It's based on a monogamous kind of structure, that you don't bring anyone around until *you're sure they are the one,* because your kids will get confused.

No. This isn't confusing at all. You're showing the building blocks of relationships. You're teaching your children how you navigate different relationships and what connection is about. It's outside of that *finding the one* project.

I prioritize openness, honesty, and answering questions. I work on being open to all the questions that my kid — and now my grandkid — may have. When my daughter was young, I talked about it with her as options. You get to choose what you want. There's monogamy, polyamory, non-monogamy. I'm sure there's a bunch of other stuff we haven't even made up yet, but there are choices to be made, and you have the ability to navigate all these things. You can have different experiences and experiment. I've always talked to her about that, even when she was a little — saying, you know, even if you're monogamous, even if you want to get married — because little kids are just indoctrinated into that model. I'd say, "Of course you can do that." *And* "I really encourage you to get out there and enjoy life — experiment." **—N.**

Emphasizing parental presence

When talking with your children about polyamory, the most important thing to emphasize is *parental presence* (this means be there for the sensitive or challenging moments) — answer questions honestly, make eye contact, listen, affirm their reality, help them reflect and problem-solve. In a word (or two): show up. You are there to support your child's emotional and familial security.

Many parents start this conversation as a hypothetical chat, after their children have brought up learning about polyamory in the abstract, or perhaps when one of their friends is struggling because they've learned that their parents are polyamorous.

Your child might say to you, "Dad! Can you believe this? Marny's Mom and Dad have girlfriends and boyfriends!"

TIP

And your best course of action here is to be curious. Just listen to your child's experience of this. Ask questions. Marny might be having a terrible time with this news. Your child might have very fixed ideas about relationships based on the dominant model. If you listen well, you'll get a lot of information about the starting place you'll have if and when you decide to come out to your child about your own polyamorous life.

In the moment, figure out what your child needs: Comfort? Reassurance? You can express faith in this family and let them know you believe in everyone's right to love as they need to, while caring for their children. But first and foremost, make sure they're learning that you're there, as always, to take care of them. In doing so, you can ask good questions about how they might want to support their friend.

WARNING

If you find yourself *activated* or struggling with fear, breathe. Listen. Save your opinions for later. After you step away from the conversation, get the support of your partner(s) and try to figure out how to address your child's distress when you are in a less volatile state. As much as you can, be there for your child, as they try to figure out what they need.

And, if you're in the process of coming out to your child or children, parental presence is even more important. Whatever disclosures you're making, they need to know first and foremost what impact your poly life will have on them: Does this change your household? Does this change who will relate to them as a parent? What kind of choices do they still have, and what choices have you made for them? See Chapter 11 for more on this, but here's a series of short hypothetical responses should your child experience distress when you come out:

>> Daddy and I still love each other. We're a still a couple — or still married — and will always be your parents. That will never change.

>> Malik is going to move into the house in September, but he isn't your parent. He's your <insert fun term here.> (One family I know chose the term *wizard.*)

>> All of your usual routines aren't going to change.

>> What questions do you have for us?

>> What do you need right now?

TIP

One of my children is the asker of a thousand questions and the other is the deserter of high stakes conversations. One wants to know everything on the spot and the other retreats to their room and then eventually asks questions from the back seat of the car in the grocery store parking lot. Parent the processer-type you have in front of you, not the one you wish you had.

Considering social risks and impacts

As a parent, you're the arbiter of social risks for your children. You can minimize them by thinking about these key risk factors for them:

>> How old are they?

- Any disclosure that is remotely adjacent to a conversation about sex in an elementary school setting can create a lot of reactivity and backlash and even bring state authorities to your doorstep.

- The middle school era can be a hormonal mess around anything and everything dating and relationship-related. Tread carefully.

>> Are their friends loyal and not gossipy? Do their friends have conservative parents who could cut them off if they come out to them?

>> What are worst-case scenarios for your child and for the family if this information gets widely shared?

>> Is your child likely to be able to hold their own if a bunch of mean kids at school come after them?

>> Is your child's school administration likely to be competent around addressing this if there's some kind of backlash? Or will it likely ignore poly-negative bullying or make things worse?

>> Are your children different? Do you have one kid who waves away peer disagreements and one very-attuned-to-what-others-think-of-me child? How can you attend to these differences?

Think about impacts on your kids and their existing support system as you consider whether now is the right time to come out.

I also had my eye on the reality that my kids were developing their sexuality. And I think my life offered them a view of all kinds of relationships. They knew I was polyamorous and at different points, they thought most of my friends were probably my lovers. Then they realized that some weren't. It made them ask a lot of questions — who and what are lovers? How do you decide? And, we had so many great conversations about love. And now, I have one adult kid who's very, I would say, pansexual and polyamorous. And then another, who's like, super heterosexual and monogamous. And I think they are both just super clear about who they are. —M.L.

Being out and open isn't the same risk for every family

After you come out to your kids as polyamorous, you can't take it back, and they're now holding information that could be harmful to them socially, or to the family. Depending on what state you live in, what kind of legal and policing systems are in place, and what kind of social power and vulnerabilities your family holds, coming out poly can be like putting a weapon in your child's hand that they don't know how to control.

Coming out polyamorous isn't the same risk for every family in every locality (refer to Chapter 11 for more details). Although no law prohibits having more than one partner or lover, only a few localities legally support or protect multiple partner families.

Poly parents have had their custody challenged by hostile family members. Polyamorous families have had neighbors call child protective services on them. Poly families have endured anti-poly job loss. Nosy landlords have tried to oust or raise fees on their poly renters.

You know what risks your family is carrying in terms of average, daily discrimination and violence. Being visible about polyamory adds a layer of vulnerability. Be sure you fully understand your family's vulnerabilities before thinking about coming out to your children. Protect them by thinking through all of the possibilities.

Chapter **15**

Breaking Up Poly

Breaking up is often more complex in polyamorous social worlds than in monogamous dating and partnership cultures. In monogamous relationships, you're either together and each other's sole partner or the relationship is over and your intimate connection is severed, so that each of you are free to connect with your next, singular forever-partner. In fact, if you don't do this kind of strict split, you're suspect as a candidate for any future partner.

This chapter explores the complexities of polyamorous breakups, which are sometimes like the permanent ruptures that monogamous relationships enact when partnerships end. But often, they're more like an amendment or a transformation than a firewall or total disconnection. Polycules may morph and shift rather than break — not just because breaking up is hard to do, but because poly formations tend to highly value friendships, ex-lovers, and the histories you've created together.

REMEMBER

Even in times of breakups, poly life is more like a crazy quilt of connections and beloveds of all kinds than a shattered path from Relationship A to Partner B.

Deciding When Differences Become Deal-Breakers

While polyamorous relationship endings may not be as rigidly defined as endings in monogamous relationships, that doesn't mean their endings aren't shattering. Change is hard. Disruption is often painful. Given the fluidity of polyamorous arrangements, figuring out when differences have become deal-breakers isn't easy. The following sections help you sift through your relationship values for clues to when you're at an ending point in a poly partnership.

Being worn out and down

Because poly people often feel proud of an ability to discuss issues openly and maintain connection, recognizing when it's time to let go can be tough. Here is a great checklist that works for people in any relationship configuration about how to figure out if you're really at the end of your relationship.

REMEMBER

Hallmarks of a truly terrible partnership — signs that it's time to say enough is enough — include the following:

>> You don't center your own needs in the relationship anymore; you don't even know what they are.

>> You're hooked on your partner's needs, moods, and reactions.

>> You keep having the same fight without any progress or resolution.

>> You're spending more time in conflict than in joy and life-making.

>> You give in and abandon yourself repeatedly because you just want the conflict to be over.

>> Your partner is never wrong or rarely sees their part in any of these problems. You, too, may have become less likely to see your part.

>> Your partner never — or almost never — apologizes.

>> Your partner refuses to get therapy, mediation, or any outside help individually or as partners or members of a polycule.

>> Your partner belittles you, privately or publicly.

>> It feels like you're just trying to survive.

>> Your relationship is impacting your mental and physical health.

- All the work you're putting into this relationship is impacting your work life and job security.

- All the time you're pouring into this relationship is impacting your financial stability.

- All the work you're putting into this relationship is making it hard to stay connected to your friends; you're getting more and more isolated.

- You feel like a failure.

- Sometimes you're afraid of your partner or afraid for your well-being.

If you checked off more than a few of the concerns on this list, then it's time to think about your health and whether you've lost your way in this relationship. Refer to Appendix B for helpful resources.

WARNING

LGBTQ+ women are notoriously bad at breaking up. There's even a name for it — *lesbian torture breakup* — which describes a state of remaining emotionally and sometimes sexually involved while you're also, allegedly, breaking up. Things never end well in this kind of breakup and reconnect, move-out and have-sex-again scenario, so let me save you a lot of trouble.

TIP

Breaking up means creating distance — physical, emotional, social, and sexual — so that you can reset your emotional and intimate life and move into a more detached place of relating to this person. As Dua Lipa notes in her pop epic, *New Rules*: "If you're under him, you ain't getting over him."

Pivoting and grieving

Pivoting involves moving away from the current centering of this relationship in your life; *grieving* means giving yourself the room to feel the loss of it. But, depending on how you're conducting your polyamorous life, relationships can be overlapping, so that one person's deal-breaker doesn't register the same way for another. It's not impossible to be in a situation where you're breaking up with a lover, and your other lover is staying connected to this person.

The question is how to manage such a complex web of associations and intimacies when there's a break. The important thing is simple, but not always achievable, which is to say: "Mind your own business."

As long as you aren't dealing with abuse — and by abuse, I mean someone is attempting to control, coerce, or harm you — what your ex is doing with your other partner isn't yours to decide or comment on.

REMEMBER

Your work is to figure out what you need to do to heal in the aftermath of breaking up and what kind of boundaries you need in terms of interacting with this person so you can restore yourself to relative mental and emotional health.

Here are some basic guidelines for surviving a complex breakup:

>> Mind your business; don't gather info on your ex via friends or other partners.

>> Don't hide in bed or sit at home; see your friends, go to movies, get out there.

>> Do stuff you let go of during the relationship. Remind yourself who you are so you can stop obsessing on what your ex is or isn't doing.

>> Take up active healing practices: therapy, journaling, crying, walking in the woods, traveling, painting, throwing pots, exercising — whatever works for you.

>> If you fall into depression easily, put some structure into your day: Wake up at or near the same time. Shower. Text your best friend in the morning. Make sure you get outside into the sun at some point. Eat something delicious. Don't forget that movement of any kind helps.

>> Make smart choices around how much you see your ex or are exposed to information about them, especially with your other partners.

>> Allow yourself the time and space to grieve the change.

REMEMBER

Pivoting is a poly skill. Grieving is a poly necessity. Don't rush past your grief and don't deny it. Don't pretend you're poly cool so that nobody sees how hard this breakup is on you. It's painful to stop and feel, and so easy to distract yourself with substances, hookups, and trashing your ex as a response to feeling hurt. Addiction and depression flourish in the well of denied grief. Taking care of your grief is a way to take care of yourself, your partners, and your relationships, in whatever new shapes are forming.

TIP

When breakups happen, you can take comfort in physics. *Chaos theory* notes that in the cosmos, chaos indicates that a new order is trying to emerge. Breakup grief is chaos. You're grieving not only the loss of your relationship, but also the loss of a specific future you dreamed about, the loss of what could have been. As your breakup proceeds and your new relationship and life order emerges, embrace your grief, and the emerging form will take care of itself.

OH, YOU KNOW WHAT . . .

When I think about my ex-lover R., she was much more game for poly on a theoretical level. You know: *I want to be open*. But I don't think it always felt so great to her. I think she just felt like — *I'm tired. It's too much*. And she wanted her love relationship to be like an unchanging home.

I think that happens for a lot of people who try poly — energetically or politically, they're interested, and then the demands of more people, more love, more processing, and the amplified sensory demands, the time. It's like, *oh, actually, no, I can't do this*. It turns out, I'm monogamous. **—Amelie**

Holding onto Values and Boundaries During Breakups

In poly relational worlds, you and your partners will find a lot of encouragement to surface differences, because they're less likely to be deal-breakers as they often can be in monogamous partnerships. You don't want to have children? Another partner does. You hate bondage? There's another partner for that. You're a morning sex person? You can find a partner to wake up sexy with. Differences are often incorporated and worked with rather than argued over and worked around.

During breakups, the incredible stretching and bending that poly formations often do has come to a literal breaking point. Something is immovably nonnegotiable, and change has to happen. When you arrive at this point, you can still say to yourself: "Differences are good, and we can often work with them."

REMEMBER

But you must also, ultimately, say to yourself: "I know my values and my limits." And you can proceed through the chaos of a major relationship change with that crucial grounding. In the following sections you can get help thinking through how to honor your bottom lines during a breakup.

Accepting the things you can't change

Like all relationships, polyamorous partnerships are a demanding practice in acceptance. Poly acceptance of change involves more people — so you might get more opportunities to practice accepting changes, but that doesn't mean change isn't hard or that you are more capable of it.

Remember these important points to figure out in times of breakup:

>> **What you need to accept:** What is beyond your control and therefore an exercise in futility to focus on, chase, or attempt to change?

Common things you can't change during a breakup that often take up a lot of mental and emotional space include

- Your ex's story of the relationship, especially around their impressions or evaluation of you.

- Your ex's current dating behavior.

- How your ex is relating to other members of your poly family and friendship circle.

- Your ex's feelings and how they are dealing with them.

>> **What's unacceptable:** What is happening here that pushes against your core values? What do you have to do for yourself to stand with those values and take care of yourself?

Common stands for yourself in a tough breakup period might include

- Removing yourself from certain social or intimate activities to decrease your exposure to your ex and activation that might lead to more engagement and even public fights.

- Taking a break from talking with each other for a time so that you don't get into shouting matches that go over the same old territory and make you break your own rules about yelling.

- Making plans about shared parenting that center drop-off and pick-ups around institutions like school or teams rather than your home to minimize interaction in the short term while emotions are high — this takes care of both you and your kids.

REMEMBER

In poly relational worlds, a breakup often means transformation rather than excision. Your ex may be becoming your *metamour* (your lover's lover), or shifting down from being a primary partner to someone you see once a month, as a romantic friend. As Amelie notes in the nearby sidebar, that doesn't mean you're not grieving, or that you don't need and deserve space to move toward the next place in your relational path. Honor that you are in a strenuous process of change.

I HAVE SOME THINKING TO DO

A beautiful thing that I love to talk about is how you build your own specific clan or team, right? Because, you know — an army of ex-lovers can't fail, right (see Appendix A)? And there's that sensation of, we don't have to have the cutoffs that are scripted in monogamy, because we already know each other's people.

And the challenge is — how the heck do you have maybe temporary boundaries and enough space so that you can grieve? If the ending or change wasn't okay for you, you know? I think my ex wants to jump into more of a friendship than I feel like I'm ready for after leaving our relationship for a monogamous partnership. And now I have some thinking to do about what I want and how I want to be involved. —Amelie

Slowing down

I can't think of a better hot tip in managing breakup grief and taking care of yourself than *taking your time*. Even though things may feel excruciatingly painful, and you're desperate to get to the next, better place — the only way out is through. And letting go of your attachment to someone you loved or cared deeply about, moving toward a less intimate and more distant phase of your relationship, is painful.

You live in a culture that processes everything by not processing it and instead jumping to the next thing. Your attention span has been severely compromised. You're constantly prompted to move onto the next thing — in mere seconds.

That's not how grief works. Respect yourself, your partners, and your process. Give yourself the gift of time for your grief.

All breakups are hard. A possible advantage in poly life is that you may have other partners to comfort and support you during this tender period. You may be someone who centers friendship in your poly life and those relationships might really come to life in your time of need. Lean into your poly skills of surfacing your feelings, sharing honestly, and asking for what you need. You may be surprised by the brilliant support system you have built for yourself in your time of grief.

POLYAMORY STORY

WHEN YOUR FRIENDS ARE BREAKING UP: DON'T JUMP

Go slow. Support folks where you can. How can you listen to people and allow them time and grace? Sometimes there are emotional and even physical safety concerns that are hard to navigate because you know folks are going to be showing up in the same place at some point, right? No matter how much you try for that to not happen.

So, take a deep breath and listen and also check in with your own reactions. Are you throwing your own extra stuff into it? When it has nothing to do with you? Is it triggering something in you? Be open to just sitting with those answers, not that anything has to be done right away. We always think that something has to be done *right now* if we feel crappy, and sometimes there's nothing to be done, we just actually need to be still for a while, instead of trying to find something to do. **—Anna**

IN THIS CHAPTER

» **Dealing with job moves, long distance, and other major shifts**

» **Adapting to changes in libido and your body**

» **Managing aging, illness, and disability**

» **Embracing change; going with the flow**

Chapter 16

Making Life Adjustments

The novelist Octavia Butler notes in her landmark book, *Parable of the Sower*, that "Change is God." She means that the only thing you can be sure of is that change is coming. Change is ever-present. In poly relationships, change really *is* god; this is also true of monogamous relationships, but the poly form is conspicuously fluid, ever-morphing as you navigate the needs of multiple partners.

TIP

When you embrace rather than resist change, you greatly increase your chances of success in your polyamorous life.

In this chapter, you can find discussion of the life changes you might face as you age in polyamory, including a diminishing libido, job and geographic changes, shifts in your gender expression and sexuality, illness, and disability. What's it like to experience and manage these within polyamorous relationships over an extended period of time? Here you can find some thoughts and examples of people making their way as polyamorists over many decades and through all of the many changes that life brings.

Changing Jobs and Making Other Big Moves

When I moved to Michigan in my 50s for a big job, my mover said to me: "Ah, in Russia, we work where we live. In the U.S., you live where you work."

And it made me want to put every stick of furniture back on that truck. I had left D.C., which I'd always imagined as my forever home, for a tantalizing salary and possibly very meaningful work. I had left a number of my most cherished loves behind. It turns out that this mover and I were both quite right — the great job wasn't so great — and I was back three years later.

All of that is to say: You make moves. The structure of life and work can demand changes you may not anticipate or want. Sometimes, you need flexibility, and a move might mean improving your mental health or cost structure so that you can breathe more easily and live better. Sometimes needs in your family of origin call out to you. Sometimes you must move for a partner or for your physical survival.

If you're in a polycule, moves might mean leaving a mix of people who are pivotal to your well-being (see Chapter 4 for an example). In monogamous relationships, such moves often lead to breakups, because of the conflicting needs of the two people involved and the sexually and emotionally exclusive demands of the relationship form. But in poly world, people often just shift, and figure it out.

In the following sections you can find examples of how poly constellations adapt to change and get a sense of the warp and weft of long-term poly life.

Adapting to big moves

ACTIVITY

Is one of your core lovers leaving town for a job or another reason? Here you can figure out what this move might mean to your relationship and what rituals or communication strategies might best support this change. Ask yourself:

>> How might you mark the occasion?

>> What might you commit to so that you can maintain your intimacy?

>> What are your best and most enlivening communication forms?

>> What rituals can you create to solidify your connection?

>> What will this new form of your love look and feel like?

Mark the change by embracing it and your partners. Moving away need not mean losing intimacy and connection.

In my case, I took two of my primary beloveds down to the Lincoln Memorial at midnight the evening before the moving truck to Michigan arrived and had a commitment ceremony with the three of us. I promised to love them forever and asked them to hold me through these big changes. We cried. I still couldn't believe I was going. They promised to be there for me no matter what, and they kept their promises: Each of them visited me through those three years; they each took vacations with me; they celebrated some of the amazing things I got to do on the job; they helped me navigate the crisis that eventually made me decide to come back home. One of them funded the financial demands that unfolded in the chaotic return move.

Even though the broken promises of my employer were the catalyst for my move back to D.C., I remember very clearly realizing that I was in the wrong place when two of my other beloveds became pregnant during my second and third year on this job. I thought: *What am I doing here? Lyndsey and Genevieve are having their babies, and I'm living 600 miles away!* When I thought about my own values and fundamental priorities, I could see that I'd somehow been blown way off course.

People move, pursue their ambitions, chase new love, expand their families — life makes more life. Monogamy may streamline the often-complex decision-making processes that you may face, but it also narrows the field of possibility.

Polyamorous family structures can often flex and adapt to moves and big changes. It's another underappreciated and underreported superpower of the form.

At 56, I'm thinking a lot about my next steps as a chronically-ill and disabled person without wealth or much savings. I want to move out of this expensive and loud city as soon as my kid graduates high school, but my nesting partner has a job here and isn't eager to leave, so this is my first time being in a great relationship that may go through an intentional change like this. —JD

Nesting and empty nesting

Next year, my youngest is going off to college and I'll be sitting in an empty nest for the first time in 26 years — longer really, as I lived with roommates for much of my pre-parental 20s and 30s. Like everyone, polyamorous people face life passages that mean our *nests* — our primary homes, fill and empty as milestones, breakups, and new loves all emerge.

I ask myself what oncoming changes will mean to me. As a solo poly person, I'm excited to continue not living with my lovers, but I don't know what other changes might be afoot.

REMEMBER

How is nesting and empty nesting different when you're polyamorous? It boils down to assumptions about what these changes mean and who is impacted by them. It pertains to whether connections beyond blood family matter and how they matter. Rather than having state-sanctioned and culturally defined roles and regulations around family and children fledging the nest, you get to decide what these relationships mean and how you're going to live in the aftermath of changes.

You get to decide what the polyamorous empty nest experience means to you — and regardless of relationship form, an empty nest always means more social flexibility. Consider the following:

>> If you still have significant parental commitments, like M'Bwende in the nearby sidebar, you may have slightly more room for your solo self, which means more time to travel.

>> If you have long-distance lovers who you've rarely seen, you may get more time together, or even an entirely new chapter of connection and intimacy.

>> If you have a *nesting partner* (a lover you live with), you may have time to dust off your original agreements and see if they still make sense. Chapter 9 discusses poly agreements in greater detail.

TIP

If you've been living a poly life with a full nest for some time, you may feel both disoriented and excited during this fledging era. Breathe and take your time. You and your well-honed poly skills have got this.

POLYAMORY STORY

I'M OPEN TO SURPRISE, AND WE BELONG TO EACH OTHER

My daughter is about to go off to college and my partner's sons are younger and she's like, "You know, you might want to go somewhere. You might want to do *XYZ*." I'm certainly looking forward to seeing my friends more and having space. But these boys — they're attached to me and they're mine. I've heard everything from friends, like — "You could move anywhere" — but it's just not who I am.

At 54, I would like to think I could be surprised by something or someone new, I mean, I don't think I'm shut down about it. But I'm certainly not shopping for it. I'm not going out places thinking I might meet someone — a possibility — or connecting with people in another group that might be interesting. I don't feel that.

My partner on the other hand, I don't know. So, what that means for us, I really can't say, especially once all the children are grown and out of the house. Right now, the bones of life and all the demands . . . I don't have the time or the energy. And I'm a time and energy person. Those are my things. Right? I'm not a buy-me-gifts person. For me, I want your time. And I want your attention. So, when the kids go and demands shift . . . we'll see.

When my daughter goes, I'll take more space but I'm not gonna like go move to another state. I'm gonna have that backpack and an extra pair of shoes probably — a tent rolled up, you know? I'll get some of my nomadic joy on, I definitely want to do that. You know, traveling while Black and all that. I'm going to see things — I need to see things. But they are all here — I'm theirs and I'm here. **—M'Bwende**

Coping with Libido Changes

As you experience the ups and downs of life, so does your libido. Your libido taking a nosedive in the context of having multiple lovers can be difficult. Because time and attention are often a struggle to arrange for and secure in poly relationships, not feeling sexual or being bereft of desire when you finally do meet up with a lover can be frustrating and upsetting.

TIP

The important thing is to own what you're experiencing. Denial or faking it isn't going to help you here. In the next sections you can consider how to manage diminishing libido and body changes in the context of your poly intimacies.

Diminishing libido doesn't have to mean diminishing intimacy

Coping with libido changes means figuring out what you *can* do when your desire has fled, and being open to what might happen, or not happen.

Some years ago, I took one of my lovers to Cape Cod for a spectacular week together. We have lived far apart for the decade of our relationship, seeing each other in 2–3 day slivers a few times a year. This week was a huge extravagance of time and togetherness. We enjoyed each other massively: We saw all the sights, ate all the great food, and didn't have any sex at all.

I SHOULD DO THAT MORE!

I think what my menopausal body needs is the reminder that I still love sex. My libido is no longer questing or yearning for it. It's not driving me anymore, right? So, I need the reminder that sex is actually a really good thing.

One of the yearnings I can still identify is to have that moment again — after everybody's been sexually sated, and you're really comfortable, and you just have naked-body time, and you fall asleep. I would like that. I would like that sense of sexual satisfaction, and then the intimacy that comes with that we have no choice — we're awkwardly naked and we're just going to fall asleep. I would like to have those kinds of moments again, you know? Because it's interesting. Every day, my menopausal body is saying to me — yeah, no, not interested in having an orgasm today. But then when I do, every single time I'm like, *I should do that more!* —**Amelie**

Many changes were happening for both of us at the time — work demands, physical changes, and hormonal shifts. We were wildly romantic all week. We laughed so much. At the end of the week, P. started to apologize for not feeling sexual and I stopped them right there: "Don't you dare apologize," I said. Our week together had been fantastic and our love continues to grow.

During my week with P. we kissed and held each other a lot. I gave them a massage one night. We took romantic strolls on the beach. Sex wasn't on the menu, but intimacy was. Neither of us tried to force anything. We gave up all expectation. And the memories I have of that trip are utterly spectacular.

Undergoing body changes and being post-menopausal

If you're fortunate to have long-term relationships with your partners, you'll observe and experience a lot of body changes over time. As you age, your bodily capacity is in flux. As a result, you'll notice that you have to make adjustments — for example, if you love a sex position that requires a particular kind of body strength like holding yourself or a partner up for an extended period of time, you may have to find a new favorite position. Or one partner might be a dedicated bottom or likes *impact play* (hitting or impacting a partner's body to gratify them), and now you aren't capable of being with them in the ways you were before.

BODY CHANGES ARE REAL

Anna and I are really different than we were 15 years ago. For me, that's about a lot of deformity in my body. I can't be in the same positions or hold the same body posture that I used to. My hands are curved. So, some specific bits of sex aren't as easy for me. I have to think about it, and it becomes like a puzzle, which is sometimes fun and sometimes really frustrating.

I'm also noticing the thing that happens to female bodies when you start pushing 60, and that's a different type of like, moisture, you know? And I want to do all these things before everything dries up and recognizing that I'm almost 10 years older than Anna. So that drive that I'm having to do all these things with all these people, *now*, before I can't — that isn't the same place that my partner is in. And so, I'm trying to figure out how to satisfy the needs I have around this without doing damage to my relationship. Or causing things like jealousy or insecurity or not having enough energy directed at her. This is a real balance, and I don't think I've actually figured it out yet, but I'm aware of it. **—Rox**

If you've been practicing polyamory for the long haul, you've probably become skilled at discussing all kinds of changes around sex and desire. This is yet another strength of polyamorous formations — polyamory practitioners often have experienced a lot of changes over the course of multiple relationships and are adept at welcoming them.

This signature feature of the form is often what attracts people to polyamory in the first place: the idea that relationships change, and you can adapt to your lovers' shifting needs and capacities as they emerge.

Handling Illness, Aging, and Disability

A major selling point for monogamous marriage is the idea that by committing to one person for life as a young person, you'll grow old gracefully with them. Furthermore, the children you have together will take care of your partner and you as you age. The corollary argument against polyamory, then, is that all your connections are impermanent, and you'll end up alone as an elder, with no one to care for you.

Everyone's fears about aging and care are certainly justified. U.S. culture and the structures of care make aging difficult and costly. The dwindling options, a byzantine healthcare system, and mounting financial pressures when figuring out how to take care of yourself and your loved ones as elders all makes growing older more challenging.

TIP

But monogamous mythologies mistake the ever-evolving forms of polyamory as a weakness rather than a strength in this scenario. What if:

» You had a team of people who had an eye on your aging and care?

» Responsibilities could be spread out and strengths maximized?

» All the stress and systems navigation didn't fall on one person, or on a relatively small, nuclear family unit?

Living with a disability and poly life

The United States is a nation of increasingly aged and increasingly disabled people. The Centers for Disease Control note that more than 1 in 4, or 28 percent of the U.S. population is living with some kind of disability. If you're poor, BIPOC, or queer, those numbers are even higher. In the 2023 National LGBTQ+ Women's Community Survey, 50 percent of respondents reported a mentally or physically disabling condition.

POLYAMORY STORY

THE WORST YEAR OF MY LIFE AROUND HEALTH

Last year was the worst health year of my life. It was one thing after another, from stitches to a doctor rupturing a disc in my back, to my first bout of Covid, which was six weeks because I'm immunocompromised, to my son getting diagnosed with a chronic illness, to my mother having a mental health breakdown and interacting with the police, to my knee injury. *All in one year!*

And through all that, I think there was only one time a doctor didn't say it, but she was very close to saying: "Are you having sex? You shouldn't be having sex." I could tell she was going there, like, I could tell it was, like, just on the tip of her tongue. And I just kind of, like, didn't answer the question because I didn't want her to know the answer to that question *because I was having sex.* I was having gentle, calm sex. I wasn't, you know, getting all Olympic about it or anything. But I think that's the closest I've ever come to a medical professional being like, actually, you should wait a minute on this. And . . . I did take care, and sex was meaningful to me in getting through this really tough period. We do what we do. **—Asha**

For a great many people, disability is a fact of life — whether among your family members, friends, or coworkers. And yet systems of care haven't caught up to this reality. The economic support net for people with a disability and their families barely exists; the healthcare system offers only fragmented and expensive care.

That means disability is often a part of any person's intimate and relational life, while structural or institutional supports are low. If you're polyamorous, the likelihood of encountering disability among your partners increases because you're connecting to more people.

In her landmark book, *The Future Is Disabled*, polyamorous poet and disability justice activist Leah Lakshmi Piepzna-Samarasinha urges people to embrace the disabilities on their horizons of intimacy:

> It's radical to imagine that the future is disabled. Not just tentatively allowed to exist, not just *ok I guess there's one white guy with a wheelchair, cool, diversity*. But a deeply disabled future: a future where disabled, Deaf, Mad, neurodivergent body-minds are both accepted without question as part of a vast spectrum of human and animal ways of existing, but where our [disabled] cultures, knowledge and communities shape the world . . . Have we ever imagined this, not just as a cautionary tale or a scary story, but as a dream?

TIP

Here, Piepzna-Samarasinha urges you to throw off ableist fear and embrace changes to your body and your capacities and to draw on the wisdom of your experience of disability and your disabled communities to keep reaching for each other. She expresses faith in everyone experiencing disability to chart new, disabled pathways toward intimacy and community.

POLYAMORY
STORY

My lover, Lindsay is also pretty disabled, and so that's a regular topic on our quarterly check-ins. Like, how are we doing with our disabled bodies, disabled life, and identities? And I just feel like there's so much that polyamorous folks can learn from this disabled political community, because, you know, as disabled people, we have to negotiate the world, and we have to have that conversation verbally and physically in order to get our needs met — whether that's access needs, about physically accessing a space, or, emotional needs, to access community spaces. —**Asha**

TIP

If polyamory means more love and more partners, it often means more disabilities. And, it potentially means more experience with managing disability in your polycule. More resources and expertise. And more support.

POLYAMORY STORY

I think the gift of fully accepting all these changes is having the ability to scan and know my body and know my capacity. And because I have that information, I'm able to communicate it to my co-parent partners, or, my lover who I'm having lots of ambitious sex with, or my team at the sexual liberation collective. For instance, collective members know I have really wicked, terrible seasonal depression and that they're going to see the bulk of my work between April and October every year. And they're going to see a light version of work in the winter months. That's the takeaway — I'm very clear about my capacity and my limits, and I'm able to let people know that without shame, without hesitation. —**Asha**

Dealing with sexuality and gender shifts

Sharing your intimate life with more than one lover often has an impact on your sexual practices and your gender expression. It's possibly one of polyamory's greatest gifts — helping you to see greater depths and breadth in your own self-expression as you relate to wildly different people. These simple observations suggest the positive impact multiple lovers can have in growing different sides of yourself:

>> One lover is shy and reserved? This brings out your talky, protective side.

>> A prospective partner has an inexhaustible libido? Now you're having more sex than you thought was even physically possible.

>> One lover is more lustful when you wear short dresses and combat boots? Here comes your tough femme side.

>> A new partner loves bondage? Now you're taking rope classes.

I used to give a workshop called *Born This Way* to help participants tease out what parts of their sexual practices, gender expressions, and attractions were more fixed and what parts were more fluid or changing over time. I re-create it here:

ACTIVITY

This activity allows you to chart your interests around gender, sex, power, and kink. Put an X in the circle where you land on the chart today. Put an X in different colors where you landed on the chart 5-10-15 years ago. Put an aspirational red X on the chart where you wish to go.

My Gender

Feminine_____Androgynous/Fluid_____Masculine

OOOOOOOOOOOOOOOOOOOOOOOOOOOOOOOOOO

My Partner's Gender

Feminine_____Androgynous/Fluid_____Masculine

OOOOOOOOOOOOOOOOOOOOOOOOOOOOOOOOOO

Power/Agency in Sex

Penetrative_____Versatile or Verse_____Receptive

OOOOOOOOOOOOOOOOOOOOOOOOOOOOOOOOOO

Submissive_____Mutuality/Mirroring_____Dominant

OOOOOOOOOOOOOOOOOOOOOOOOOOOOOOOOOO

High Libido/frequency_____Sex is good sometimes_____No sex

OOOOOOOOOOOOOOOOOOOOOOOOOOOOOOOOOO

Kink Interests

Highly enjoy being hit_____No hitting/impact Play

OOOOOOOOOOOOOOOOOOOOOOOOOOOOOOOOOO

Seek pain with pleasure_____No Pain Play

OOOOOOOOOOOOOOOOOOOOOOOOOOOOOOOOOO

Tie me up/any bondage_____No restraints

OOOOOOOOOOOOOOOOOOOOOOOOOOOOOOOOOO

I like it rough_____I'm the tenderest flower

OOOOOOOOOOOOOOOOOOOOOOOOOOOOOOOOOO

Watch me/you have sex with others_____Sex is just between us

OOOOOOOOOOOOOOOOOOOOOOOOOOOOOOOOOO

Sex in public (safety first!)_____Sex is private

OOOOOOOOOOOOOOOOOOOOOOOOOOOOOOOOOO

Other Interests

Talk to me/tell me what you are doing_____Silence is sexy

OOOOOOOOOOOOOOOOOOOOOOOOOOOOOOOOOO

Major kissing_____Light kissing_____No kissing

OOOOOOOOOOOOOOOOOOOOOOOOOOOOOOOOOO

Body worship/skinship_____Cuddles!_____No cuddling

OOOOOOOOOOOOOOOOOOOOOOOOOOOOOOOOOO

John Wiley & Sons, Inc.

For many years, I used to joke that the only thing that stayed the same on my chart — where all the different color-coded Xs overlapped — was in frequency. Apparently, I was born to have lots and lots of sex. But now, in my 60s, even that X has moved along the spectrum. When I look at my chart I'm struck by the fluidity of my lusts, gender expressions and attractions, and sexual practices and interests. What an amazing journey it has been!

Sharing a chart like this with your partner(s) can be fun under the right circumstances. If you're both or all curious about your sexual histories and where your sexual practices land on your chart, sharing them can create a great story-sharing event full of laughter. It can reveal things you don't yet know about your partner(s) and create intimacy and possibility.

TIP

You know your partner(s). If you're in a space where bringing up past relationships and practices is painful or if talking about aspirational desires is scary, now might not be the moment. Wait for whatever current tenderness or hardship you're experiencing to pass.

WARNING

If you can't share this chart with a partner because you're afraid of the difficulties the conversation will bring, and these issues never improve — you never resolve them and get to a better place of openness — your relationship(s) might be constraining your growth (see sex and relationship jail definitions in Appendix A). If so, talk to your friends about this, and if you need even more support, seek professional help.

Aging means knowing what matters

As you age, you have much more limited patience for things that you perhaps would've given a prospective partner the benefit of the doubt for when you were younger. That isn't a bad thing. By the time you hit 50 or 60, you know yourself and your patterns very well. If you've taken good care of yourself and your healing process, you've likely learned a lot from your mistakes.

Accordingly, people who aren't good matches show themselves fairly early in your dating trajectory. When you're younger, and perhaps highly libido-driven, these yellow flags are less likely to register inside the cloud of excitement and possibility.

As a solo poly person, I've often had to explain my relationship orientation repeatedly to new dates. Especially in the 90s and early 2000s, this kind of relating was relatively rare. In my youth, people laughed and made jokes about it. They assured me that they would change my mind. Or they kept their agendas to themselves, but showed it by pushing to stay over more than I wanted, or to name the relationship in a particular way, or to suggest that one of my lovers didn't really care about me. In my 20s and 30s, this didn't really bother me. I was too interested in *what might be* with these crushes and lust objects.

FEWER FS TO GIVE

I think now, when I meet a person and I can see that they are amazing as a human being — I immediately can see all the other little pieces, you know, the things that are happening in their life — *all the things.*

Maybe it's that I'm more discerning as I get older. I don't know, but if you can't check eight out of my ten boxes, I can't even entertain this idea. When I was younger, I was just like, *Oh, you got three out of ten. Okay, fine, let's go. Let's do it now!* And these days, I'm just like, sorry, six out of ten? Don't even come close to me. **—Rox**

Those days are long gone. And good riddance to them. Self-respect can come slowly, especially around polyamorous identity. I'm relieved to report that in my 60s, mine is hard-earned and unshakeable.

As you move through the decades, the trajectory of your extended relational life comes home to roost. Do you have a lot of estrangements in your relational history? Have you ended relationships in messy or problematic ways and thus created breaches that you regret? As you look at the complex and winding story of your life, is there a need for serious *clean up on aisle 9*? If the answer is yes, you might want to look at some of the exercises in Chapter 15 on breaking up for help with healing and accountability practices.

REMEMBER

Ex-lovers and friends are foundational to polyamorous life. Your ability to continue to grow, adapt, make mistakes, apologize, call in, be accountable, make amends, draw boundaries, and take care of yourself and your loved ones are skills that will not only save your life, but also give you a life worth living. These are skills that enliven and grow relationships, whatever their form and significance.

POLYAMORY
STORY

STAYING FRIENDS

I was recently having a conversation with some young folks — I'd say mid to late 20s — and they were together for some time, and they've just broken up and are on amicable terms. And I just straight out told them both: "I'm going to encourage y'all to stay friends if you can, because you've already loved each other."

The way I see it — if you've already loved each other, then you're likely going to be the people that are there 30 years later. Because that's my ideal around my Army of Lovers

(continued)

(continued)

(see Appendix A) right? I want those long-term relationships, and sometimes those people still drive me freaking nuts, and I still want to figure out a way to be in relationship with them.

Because ultimately, they're the ones who are going to be there unconditionally. And even if we have a rift, we're going to come back to each other. We understand that there's grace for this kind of flowing, and I think that the pieces kind of fly around, but the fragments also ripple out into the health and well-being of the larger community. **—Anna**

5

The Part of Tens

Let go of prejudicial myths about polyamory and start to challenge the idea that it's impossible or will leave you broken and lonely.

Discover crucial relational skills that make being in love with more than one person emotionally manageable.

Get a fast guide to dealing with jealousy and how to escape its damaging clutches so you can have the expansive love you want.

Chapter **17**

Ten Myths Debunked about Polyamory

Many myths function to keep you from pursuing your curiosities. As you mature, you find your way through tall tales that your parents might have perpetuated to protect you (if you cross your eyes, they'll get stuck that way), and those you can see through with your adult perceptiveness. Here are ten myths about polyamory that you can definitely let go of.

Polyamory Doesn't Exist

Polyamory is an ancient practice. Monogamy, marriage, and the nuclear family are much more recent inventions, associated with the rise of the development of agriculture, industrialization, and the ownership and inheritance of land (you can read more on this in Chapter 2). However, recent polls report 50 to 60 percent of Millennials and Gen Zers find open relationships or polyamory preferable to monogamy.

Polyamory Is Unnatural

So many things that were natural a generation or two ago now seem insane — like that hitting children was good for them. Or that women shouldn't hold public office because menstrual hormones would cloud their judgment. The only legitimate way to relate to someone you love is by being fully yourself, whatever that is, and extending yourself to them big-heartedly, honestly, and with tender care.

If You Really Love Someone, Then Jealousy Is Natural

Jealousy is common but not natural. It's driven by a culture steeped in scarcity mythologies — like you better hurry up and find your one true love or you'll miss out and live a lonely, failed life. Or you better lose weight and get to the gym if you want to attract that once-in-a-lifetime love who will be the best sexual partner, roommate, breadwinner, co-parent, caregiver, playmate, and confidante you could ever imagine. Or you better not let your partner pursue their crushes or hookup because they're likely to find someone more attractive and leave you.

REMEMBER

You're conditioned daily to be fearful of competition by better, hotter, richer, and more interesting people, and to control your partner's access to intimacy with anyone else. In the midst of all this, society tells you that jealousy is a sign of your love. But jealousy actually is a sign of your fear inside this scarcity-rigged system.

TIP

Jealousy may be your first reaction, but it doesn't have to be your last. Polyamory rejects the scarcity model and the framework of ownership in a relationship, especially sexual ownership.

Polyamorists Are Really Just Cheaters

Liars and cheaters come in all shapes, sizes, and motivations, and they inhabit all relationship forms. Some people cheat because they're trapped in marriages or monogamous relationships that they can't leave without risking their health and stability. Some cheat because cheating is easier than confronting what's not working in their partnership. Some cheat because they feel superior, entitled to do whatever they want, while requiring monogamy of their partners. Some cheat because their childhood attachment wounds (see Chapter 7) drive them to compulsively repeat destructive behaviors.

REMEMBER

You can cheat in any relationship form you choose, including a polyamorous relationship, but people living in monogamous relationships or marriage tend to have to sacrifice more of their sexual desires within a closed system of two and thus often have a higher level of frustration and motivation to cheat.

Polyamory Is a Cover for Commitment-Phobic People

Not everyone aspires to be in monogamous relationships or marriage. These relationship forms just don't fit for some people. Instead, polyamorous people may make all kinds of commitments that don't read as commitments in a monogamy-centric world, like committing to honesty rather than longevity in relationships or committing to being together as long as all parties are growing and joyful, rather than committing to one person for a lifetime. Commitment-phobes do exist, they just don't live among polyamorous people to any greater degree than they live among monogamous people.

Polyamory Spreads Disease

This myth comes from sexphobia, which associates unrestrained sex with disease. Despite research demonstrating over and over again that limiting sexual partners doesn't necessarily limit the spread of sexually transmitted infections (STIs), this misinformation persists. As a counterpoint, researchers note that consistent use of protection and frequent STI testing, as well as engaging in lower risk sexual practices actually does reduce both pregnancies and STI transmission. The idea that people who have a lot of sex are instigators of disease is a sex-shaming campaign to control your desire, sexual practices, and partnerships.

Polyamory Preys on Vulnerable People

People who lie and seek to control others are predators in social and sexual situations. Monogamy as a system creates a lot of opportunity for predators because it often emphasizes keeping all information private between partners in a couple. It also often suggests that friends are less important than partners, which can also isolate vulnerable people.

REMEMBER

The openness of polyamory, the involvement of more than one partner, and a general emphasis on friendship and community creates opportunity for a person who is vulnerable or in a bad situation to possibly access support or help. But the reality is that predatory and dishonest people can be found in all kinds of relationships, polyamorous and monogamous alike.

Polyamory Is Immoral

You're the only person who can say what's moral for you. Everyone constructs their personal moral code based on a variety of inputs including the values in their families of origin, their religious or spiritual beliefs, their understanding of familial and community history, public conversation on morality, advertising and propaganda, peer influence, governmental structures and constraints, and their own research and experiences among many other things.

REMEMBER

How you construct your intimate, sexual, and familial life matters. It's a foundation for your life. For some, crafting your moral code can be a fraught process that involves reexamining and even rejecting moral and religious practices that were foundational to your upbringing, and that's okay. It's up to you to create the forms that follow your authentic moral compass and help you build the good life you deserve.

Polyamory Never Works

You know what never works? The fantasy of constant wild attraction to one partner who meets all your social, emotional, familial, domestic, and sexual needs for life. Do you know anyone who has this? I'm not sure how the marketing of this impossible mythology has held up for so long.

Polyamory Is a Toxic Way of Life

What is toxic or impossible for one person can be vibrant and freeing for another. Polyamory takes so many hits in everyday discussions that are a mask for the frustrations and fears harbored by the majority as they try to make monogamy work. The one-partner-for-life form was established when humans had far shorter lifespans and a very different set of social, economic, and geographic possibilities.

TIP

Toxic relationships abound in every relationship form. The way to avoid toxicity is to take responsibility for your mental health and healing, grow a set of strong communication skills and deep friendships, discover and articulate your desires, and create a life that makes sense for you. For some, this means living a monogamous life, for others, this means creating a polyamorous constellation that flows, grows, and shifts over your lifetime.

IN THIS CHAPTER

» Assessing your current relational
skill level

» Tracking your feelings and emotional
well-being

» Accepting and appreciating yourself
and where you are right now

Chapter **18**

Ten Ways to Build Your Relational Skills

Asking for what you want — and letting people know what you need — is serious business. I sought help for years as I tried to build the relational skills I needed in order to be honest and intimate with my partners. Many formative experiences in my youth made it hard for me to even identify my feelings in the moment and to articulate what I wanted.

Over time, therapists, friends, and support groups helped me learn to take responsibility for my fears and my confusion and to accept my sometimes overwhelming emotions. I started being able to say what was really happening instead of acting out my feelings all over my partners. As a teenager and young adult, I had no idea what any of that even meant. So don't worry if that's true for you.

TIP

Just because you don't have the relational skills for polyamory *today* doesn't mean you can't build your emotional capacity for any kind of relationship. You can heal. You can grow. This chapter provides ten tips to get you started.

Dream Your Relationship Dreams

Dream up and picture what a great relationship looks and feels like for you. Imagine what you want from everyday intimacies and actions. To support your exploration, read more books about polyamory or take in a great podcast or movie. Check out Appendix B for suggestions.

Create a Feelings Journal

Jot down in a journal how you're feeling at two points during each day. Grow the skill of noticing and identifying your feelings without judgment.

REMEMBER

A feelings journal can be a first step in evaluating your daily emotional landscape, which might give you crucial information about what kind of relational capacities you need to build — like de-escalation from anger or creating more space for joy and lust. You may think you have a good sense of your emotional life and then find surprises when you track it on your journal.

TIP

This exercise gives you a baseline look at your feelings landscape:

>> Color-code what your feelings are at two designated points every day for a month.

- **Red:** For angry or hurt feelings activated by someone else's behavior
- **Yellow:** For sunny, bright, or happy feelings
- **Green:** For lusty, sexy, or relational feelings
- **Blue:** For chill or at peace or calm feelings

>> Write captions for the feelings: What's happening at these times?

>> At the end of the month, take stock. Evaluate the state of your emotional life. Are you very often angry? Mostly happy? Is there space for your sensual or sexual feelings?

Consider Getting a Therapist

Start to identify the strengths and burdens in your childhood story around attachment and trust. A therapist can help you sort through the ways formative experiences impact your present. They can also help you identify your strengths as a communicator in relationships and suggest avenues for you to pursue to build your relational skills. (Chapter 7 provides more insight on attachment theory and help for you in hiring a professional.)

Do Some Research

Ask a friend for a referral or look up therapists online (*Psychology Today* provides regional lists; there are also BIPOC and queer and trans therapist networks). Seek out practitioners who are polyamory-positive; doing so can be challenging, so look for therapists who mention treating polyamorous clients on their websites or in their practitioner biographies.

Look for a Bodyworker

Find a massage therapist or bodyworker who specializes in trauma and the body. Get help identifying when and where in your body that trauma gets reactivated when you're fearful about abandonment or feeling jealous. If you discover that you have a lot of trauma burdens trapped in your body, commit to seeing a bodyworker who can help you pursue long-term health strategies. See Chapter 8 for more about trauma survivors and polyamory.

Find Free Resources and Trainings

Get some free help or coaching on communication skills. Begin to identify your strengths and weaknesses as a communicator in intimate relationships. Go to a conference or a workshop on building relationships. Find like-minded people who are also trying to develop these skills. Consult Appendix B for ideas about where you can begin.

Attend a Free Support Group

You can go to a free support group to address underlying trauma or addiction issues that make it hard for you to trust and make healthy attachments. The best part about free support groups — aside from the free part — is that most of them don't require you to speak. You can just relax and listen. You can hear stories from other people trying to grow in similar ways that you are. You can identify possible friends and supporters.

Set Boundaries around Conflict

Stop acting from a place of anger in your existing relationships, whether with friends, family members, or lovers. Start to develop skills for dealing with anger and fear — especially of abandonment — in healthier ways by setting clear boundaries and keeping them. Chapter 6 gives you a lot of information and tips on setting boundaries.

REMEMBER

Setting and keeping boundaries in low-stakes environments can be a great training ground for learning how to sustain them in your polycule. Have a draining work colleague who is always asking you to come to happy hour, or sitting next to you during staff meetings and trying to start side conversations that you don't want? Try out boundary-setting with them:

>> Thanks, but I prefer to keep my work life and my social life separate.

>> I can talk on work breaks but not during meetings.

These are great skills-building opportunities for when you'll need to speak up in your romantic relationships:

>> I really like your new girlfriend, and I also need to us have at least three nights a week alone together right now.

>> I appreciate that you need things to slow down right now. I'd still like to keep seeing M. on Tuesday nights.

Show Appreciation to Friends and Lovers

Recognize and affirm the friends and partners in your life who support and care for you every day. Start growing a practice of expressing gratitude and nurturing connection. Building your friendship network can be a great fortifying practice in supporting your polyamorous life (see Chapter 11 for more).

Love Yourself, Just as You Are

Appreciate how perfectly imperfect you are. By caring for yourself extravagantly, you'll expand your capacity to care for your partners. Check out Chapter 3 as you figure out your polyamorous desires and Chapters 7 and 8 for more on attachment and trauma.

Chapter 19

Ten (or So) Ways to Avoid or Address Jealousy

Monogamy thrives on the myth of scarcity: Only a few truly amazing people are in the world, and your one true love is out there, so don't delay, or you'll miss your only chance. Entire industries have grown up around the monumental task of finding, attracting, and snagging this one and only person. Just a few worthy people accomplish it. You're known as one of these people by the staggering size of your wedding reception or through the constantly shared bliss on your social media.

Enter stage right: jealousy. Monogamy's myth of scarcity drives jealousy. You're one of the lucky ones who found your person amidst the churning masses. And now, your only job is to stand guard against anyone else who dares ever to look their way.

Every romance novel and romcom hinges on jealousy at some point. Jealousy fires so much of the plot. It's natural. Essential. Funny in a lot of movies, until — as you likely know from experiencing it in real life — it really isn't.

The reality is that jealousy is very often a part of the polyamory dating and romantic journey. Here are ten (or so) great ideas about how to support yourself when you feel jealous. Chapter 12 discusses jealousy at length.

Own That You're Jealous

When addressing your jealousy, rather than taking your fears out on your partners, own it. Stop deflecting or denying that you're jealous so that you can appear to be a cool polyamorous person. Stop stonewalling dialogue with your partner(s) by pretending that you're okay and then growing resentful.

REMEMBER

Owning your jealousy means you always start with the focus on you. It's an "I" situation rather than a you or they situation. Accordingly, it may start by looking at yourself in the mirror and saying something like: "I'm jealous when Katrina cuddles with Bill."

This might be what you've arrived at after sitting in bed half the night thinking: *Katrina ignored me at the party and was all over Bill. She's going to leave me. Bill is much hotter than me. I hate Bill. Katrina pushed me into this open relationship because he's so much more interesting than me.*

Addressing your jealousy starts with your in-the-mirror jealousy confession and then possibly moves into your morning with Katrina. When she asks how you enjoyed the party, you could say: "Not so much. I got so jealous when you were cuddling with Bill last night. And now I just feel like I'm failing at this."

Write an Angry Letter

As you put pen to paper, let your partner know how jealous you feel, lean into your jealousy, and let it all out. You're not going to send this letter. Allow yourself to feel all the really unacceptable, small-minded, distrusting parts of yourself. Take your suspicious, negative, doomsday thinker out for a long drive. Let it all flow onto the page. Writing about your jealousy can be a great step toward identifying your deeper truths around love and scarcity.

After you finish it, read it again to yourself. What's underneath the hurt? What's the feeling behind the jealousy? Get to the root.

Chapter 7 discusses attachment theory and how your childhood attachments and familial wounds can drive your inner dialogue around scarcity. Writing a full-on furious letter to your partner about your jealous feelings can help reveal parts of your attachment story that you may be unaware of.

TIP

Keep this letter as part of your self-discovery journey. As you heal some of these wounds and let go of jealous behaviors, you can have a letter-burning party, solo or with your partner(s).

Listen to What It's Telling You

What's working or not working between you and your partner(s) right now that has left you feeling so let down or dismissed? Ask yourself these questions to figure out what your jealousy is trying to say:

» Are you feeling disconnected from your partner lately?

» Is your nesting partner doing life and logistics with you and sex and dates with their new crushes — and is this feeling more and more like taking you for granted?

» Are you responding to your partner keeping all the fun to themselves while you manage the household, the kids, or some other responsibility?

» Are there external stressors that are making you feel less-than with this partner?

» Is there a terrible situation at work that is just cutting you down and leaving you extra vulnerable?

Many people explore polyamory because their values around possession and ownership in relationships make them want to strike out and try something more expansive, only to find that their conditioning around monogamy and possession is much stronger than these new ideas or aspirations.

Walk in Your Partner(s)' Shoes

A good strategy when feelings of abandonment or jealousy are heightened is to decenter yourself as you examine this situation. Broaden your perspective.

Think about possibly hidden unmet needs that your partner is carrying. Breathe. Assess what's going on with your partner: Are they struggling at work? Are they exhausted by a recent grief? Are they in an exciting period of self-exploration around their sexuality? What need might they be looking to soothe or satisfy right now?

Remember the love that brought you here. Don't be hard on yourself and don't put down your partner. Breathe some more. Determine what step you can take to affirm your partner, and yourself, and to learn more.

Ask for Help from Poly Friends

Reach out to your poly friends who have handled jealousy or other difficult issues, selecting people whose relationships you admire and who have more experience than you with adjusting to relationship changes. Ask them to tell you stories about their jealousy, so you don't feel so pitiable and alone.

TIP

Share honestly and share what feels right. Be sure to keep your partners' confidences while you discuss what you're feeling and working through. Take care to avoid people who are critical of polyamory and might be likely to judge your partner harshly. You're vulnerable, so treat yourself with tenderness and care by finding people who will do the same.

Get Out of Your Head

One of the best ways to manage your jealousy is to focus on something else. Here are some suggestions to distract yourself.

Do:

>> Something fun and enlivening with your friends or another partner.

>> Something joy-generating to pull you out of your doomsday thinking.

>> Something physical, something that helps you work up a sweat and dislodges the frozen or negative energy in your head.

You're alive! You have a wonderful partner. You can survive these difficult emotions and figure out your next best move.

Don't:

>> Do something spiteful.

>> Start pointless fights to cover your jealous feelings.

Go Out of Town

Take a mini trip. Hike up a mountain. Dip your toes in a stream or the ocean. Engage with the larger world in ways that remind you of how big the possibilities are. Do what you need to do to physically remove yourself from the situation.

Possessiveness and ownership shrink everything down to two people, fighting against all odds, against the world. Being in nature or walking through main street in a new town where nobody knows you exposes the lie that your world is limited to what's happening between you and your partner, and that this is the only thing that matters. You're a part of that sprawling diversity of people, places, and things. Like everything around you, you can grow and change and adapt.

Take in Some Good Resources

To deal with the jealousy, look at the wide array of resources available, such as:

>> Read books on jealousy in polyamorous literature.

>> Listen to an excellent polyamory podcast on jealousy (see Appendix B for suggestions).

>> Find funny episodes on typical mistakes that people make in poly relationships.

>> Discover a new writer or podcaster whose voice you love and whose wisdom is comforting.

>> Read about polyamorous relationships that have lasted for decades and soak up the secrets to their success.

REMEMBER

You don't have to go through this situation alone. Every polyamorous family has had to manage jealousy. Change is easier when you can locate sympathetic and like-minded travelers on this journey.

Go to a Support Group

Find any kind of group that helps identify and support complex emotional processes — such as a 12-Step meeting, a grief group, a cognitive behavioral therapy group — anything that connects you to others who you can share with, listen to, and learn from.

A lot of these groups are free and can provide an ongoing touchstone if you need consistent help. There's nothing wrong with needing help with jealousy. Let me say it again: Monogamy, and the idea that the only way to love someone is to be sexually possessive of them, is a truly foundational idea in society. No matter how open you are to the idea of polyamory, your feelings may be wrapped around practices of sexual exclusivity with your partners.

You might need professional help if your jealousy is persistent and disruptive. Breathe. Let yourself know what you need and go find the help you deserve. With the right support, you and your partners can accommodate and address your jealousy together.

Appendix A

Glossary

activation: The state of being launched into a fight, flight, freeze, or fawn response. See *trigger*.

anchor partner: Your rock, the person you rely on emotionally to see you through rough seas. This person may or may not be a *primary* or *nesting partner*.

army of lovers/ex-lovers: In the '70s, writer Rita Mae Brown referenced the significance of lesbians and their relationships in the fight for women's liberation in her poem, *Sappho's Reply* with the line: an army of lovers cannot fail. Later, the writer Amy Hoffman titled her memoir of life at Boston's Gay Community News in the '70s: *An Army of Ex-Lovers*.

BIPOC: An acronym meant to emphasize the genocide of Indigenous people and enslavement of Black people as foundational to the formation of the country, alongside all people of color who experience racism in the United States.

birthday polyamory: Also referred to as *garden party polyamory*, it describes relationships with your partner's partners wherein you aren't close friends but show up for each other at milestone events or parties.

butch: A masculine gender identity or expression often but not exclusively associated with lesbians or nonbinary people assigned female at birth.

calendaring: Polyamorous families struggle and thrive through calendars and calendaring practices because polycules may have infinite capacity for love, but time is short.

cancel culture and carceral responses: Cancel culture in the United States is part of the binary culture of policing — people are good and bad, and bad people deserve punishment and exclusion from society. Transformative justice is the opposite and rests on the idea that all people can recover and do better; all people deserve the opportunity to heal and stay connected.

cheating/cheaters: Descriptor of a person who commits to any relationship configuration (monogamous, monogamish, polyamorous, and so on) and then breaks the covenant through lies (of omission or commission) and deceit.

cisgender: Also referred to as *cis,* this term describes someone whose gender identity and presentation matches the sex they were assigned at birth.

compersion: The feeling of expansive love and enjoyment one experiences while observing your partner being loved or sexually attended to by another lover.

compulsory monogamy: A dominant social organizing framework that promotes and enforces monogamy as the only true, legitimate, or functional relationship form

de-escalation: A practice encouraged by therapists, body workers, and somatic practitioners so that clients can come out of a state of *activation* and return to the present moment.

desire: A yearning, centered in the body, mind, heart, and/or spirit to connect with or enter the body, mind, heart, and/or spirit of another or the self. Often experienced as a surprise, a shock to the system, a loss of control, heat, chill, stammer, a roil of embarrassment, or an ecstatic revelation.

desire mapping: A process of individual or collective inquiry that uncovers a person's sex and desire stories for the purpose of claiming and pursuing one's authentic desires.

dominant: A kink identity or role that derives pleasure from controlling the sexual action. Dominant/submissive dynamics can be limited to a highly choreographed scene, or become a part of a daily life, depending on the consensual structure partners have co-created. See *kink*.

don't-ask, don't-tell (DADT): Some polyamorous partners thrive on knowing little or nothing about what their lover is doing with their other lovers. If all partners don't agree to the arrangement, then it's cheating.

ethical non-monogamy (ENM): Sometimes referred to as *consensual non-monogamy (CNM)*, ENM describes any non-monogamous relationship wherein all partners are fully informed about any other partners or lovers in the poly constellation.

friend-zoning: When a crush or potential lover considers you as a friend, only.

gay: The sexual orientation of men seeking male sex partners. Gay is often used casually as an umbrella term for the LGBTQ community. Some women use gay to describe their same gender loving orientation, as in *gay woman.*

gender: A spectrum of characteristics pertaining to masculinity and femininity. In mainstream U.S. culture, gender is posited as a binary of male and female.

gender expression: How a person presents or expresses their gender to others, often through manner, clothing, hairstyle, voice, body art, and/or body modification.

genderfluid: A person whose gender moves along a spectrum of possibility throughout their lives. Some genderfluid people may identify as more masculine or more feminine along the spectrum, but the key characteristic is the mobility of their gender expressions.

gender identity: A person's internal sense of gender. Because gender identity is internal, one's authentic gender identity may not match the gender assigned on a birth certificate, or be visible to or easily perceived by others.

gender nonconforming: Individuals whose gender expression is different from societal expectations around gender binaries and/or expressions assigned to a particular gender. See *genderqueer.*

genderqueer: A person of any gender or sexual orientation who rejects the prevailing binary system of gender that recognizes only two genders, male and female. The 6,500 respondents in the National Transgender Discrimination Survey (Grant, 2011) reported or described more than 500 distinct genders.

heteroflexible: A sexual orientation wherein the person generally identifies as hetero-sexual but under specific circumstances, often within a polyamorous or kink context, they're open to partners of a wider range of genders.

heteronormative: Also referred to as *heterocentric,* this term describes a system that holds heterosexuality as a primary, central, or best sexuality and all other sexualities as secondary, outsider, or deviant.

hinge: The person in a V-shaped threesome (see *vee*) who is connected to both partners intimately and/or sexually.

ho'tation: Also referred to as *hotation,* a rotating band of recurring hookups. A loving contraction of ho (for whore) and rotation.

impact play: Consensual erotic activity wherein one partner hits or otherwise creates impact on the body of their partner to gratify them.

inappropriate attachment: An attachment that endangers or controls a partner due to their vulnerable status. This vulnerability may be based in age, immigrant or citizenship status, gender, partnership commitments, language, employment status, housing situation, mobility, sexual orientation, or economic circumstance. Or it may be based in something not listed here.

intergenerational sex: Sex between consenting partners of legal age whose ages span at least one generation (commonly defined as at least an 18-year age difference). Sex with a person who isn't of legal age is statutory rape, not intergenerational sex.

kink or kinky: Activities that lie outside of traditional sexual practices (sometimes called *vanilla sexuality*) form a loose category of kinky sexual expressions. Kink activities may involve domination, role-playing, sensory deprivation, piercing, playing with bodily fluids such as urine or blood, multiple partner scenarios, binding, or spanking and/or other physically impactful acts such as punching or caning.

kitchen table polyamory: A polyamorous configuration wherein partners are all familiar with each other and can hang out informally, perhaps in each other's homes, and presumably at the kitchen table.

LGBT, LGBTQ, or LGBTQ+: Short for Lesbian, Gay, Bisexual, Transgender and Queer.

libido: One's desire for intimate or sexual connection, commonly discussed as *sex drive,* but many people who don't pursue sex with others have robust libidos. Libido fluctuates wildly among people and across the lifespan.

masculine spectrum: People who express their gender on the masculine spectrum often pursue clothing, mannerisms, and actions typically assigned to the male gender category within a traditional, binary system.

metamour: Your partner's or partners' lover(s).

monogamish: A relationship configuration wherein partners agree that one may have sexual contact outside the primary relationship or recruit playmates for shared activities but emotional attachments or significant, ongoing relationships are prohibited.

monogamy: A relationship configuration wherein partners agree that all sexual and romantic activity resides exclusively within the relationship between the two partners.

nesting partner: A polyamorous partner or lover you live with who is often, but not always, your primary partner.

new relationship energy (NRE): The obsessive, all-consuming feeling that often accompanies the beginning of a new relationship.

nibbling: A gender-neutral term for niece or nephew.

nonhierarchal polyamory: A polycule wherein all partners have equal significance in each member's life. There are no primary or secondary partners.

open marriage: A broad umbrella term for a marriage that welcomes additional sexual connections and partners.

open relationships: A relationship configuration wherein partners create guidelines for engaging in fleeting sexual activities, ongoing sexual relationships, or significant additional partnerships, depending on the needs and values of the partners.

OPP — one penis policy: A polyamorous situation wherein one lover is invested in being the only person with a penis in the couple or group. Accordingly, partners are free to seek other lovers, but none with a penis.

OVP — one vagina policy: A polyamorous situation wherein one lover is invested in being the only person with a vagina in the couple or group. Accordingly, partners are free to seek other lovers, but none with a vagina.

parallel polyamory: You and your lovers have separate relationships that don't overlap — no relation between sets of lovers, no intersection.

paramour: Your lover.

pegging: Sexual activity wherein one person straps on a dildo and anally penetrates another. Pegging is a practice most often associated with heterosexual, bi, and pansexual women as initiators with their male partners.

polyamory: Modern polyamory describes a relationship of more than two partners built upon consent among relative equals, full disclosure among all partners, and mutual respect, even if each partner has a different role, significance, or meaning in one's life.

polyandry: A relationship configuration in which a woman or femme has more than one male or masculine partner.

poly constellation: The group of lovers, partners, and/or polyamorous family members in your orbit.

polycule: A polyamorous family unit consisting of more than two lovers or partners; the word itself is a contraction of polyamorous and molecule.

polyfidelity: Loving more than one person and coming through on one's commitments to those people.

polygamy: A polyamorous relationship driven by a heterosexual man, who chooses as many lovers or wives as is his prerogative.

polygyny: Another term for *polygamy,* thought to more accurately describe the collection of women as lovers or wives per the desires and purportedly sanctified demands of a heterosexual man.

polysaturated: When a polyamorous person has reached their limit of partners that they can reasonably care for and attend to.

power play: Sexual activities wherein one participant consensually relinquishes power to another, and one partner assumes control, or dominates a sexual situation or relationship to the delight of all. Power play is common in *kink play.*

Primacy of Nice: An imperative foisted in women and femmes (especially) to take care of everyone else's needs but your own, and to do so with a smile on your face. People-pleasers live in the Primacy of Nice.

primary partner: Some polyamorists choose a core partner whose desires and limits are prioritized in the creation of a polycule or poly family.

processing: Deliberative discussion to grow consensus or solve problems among poly partners and lovers. Often extensive, processing is a hallmark of polyamory to the point of it being the punchline of many jokes.

quad: In a polyamorous quad, all four people are primary partners, and they may have similar or quite varied levels of intimacy with each other.

queer: An umbrella identifier that lesbian, gay, bisexual, and/or transgender people use to describe the LGBTQ+ community. For some, the term is a political assertion of resistance to heteronormative culture and society and describes identity and community across sexual orientations and gender identities.

relationship anarchy (RA): A theory of value in relationships that champions autonomy, applying anarchist principles to intimate relating. RA rejects the prioritization of one intimate partner over another, lovers over friendships, blood family over chosen kin. Relationship anarchists are often but not always non-monogamous, solo poly, or single.

relationship escalator: A typical relationship escalator looks something like this: crushing > dating > kissing and making out > having sex > becoming sexually exclusive > dating over time > moving in together > becoming engaged > getting married. The classic relationship escalator creates a direct link between escalating, exclusive emotional and sexual involvement, and monogamous, lifelong commitment.

relationship jail: An eventually stifling enclosure that is often mutually constructed when two or more people first fall in lust or love to the exclusion of all others, especially close friends. Alternately, relationship jail may develop later in a relationship if commonplace jealousies and insecurities aren't addressed and partners become controlling.

safer sex: When all of the related risks of sex — emotional, social, and physical — are put on the table for you to consider in deciding what actions or intimacies meet your needs and also take the best care of you. Safer sex often involves the use of barriers such as condoms or gloves, for example, to prevent pregnancy or the spread of STIs.

safety: While co-creating poly agreements, talk often centers around safety, both physical and emotional. But physical and emotional safety are embedded in superstructures of violence and control, so that people in the polycule may possess very different *foundations* of safety based on race, gender, ability, citizenship, age, and so on. Poly agreements can't guarantee emotional or physical safety, but they can account for and address inequities while attempting to create a container for emotional and sexual experimentation and love.

satellite partner: A polyamorous partner you don't live with; someone who lives outside of the nest — see also *nesting partner*.

sexile: To exile a roommate or polyamorous partner to seek alternative accommodations for the night so that you may have sex with another partner.

sex jail: A stifling enclosure that is constructed when one partner non-consensually imposes the terms of appropriate or acceptable desires or sexual activities in a fleeting or ongoing sexual partnership. In this case, one person's desires rule and the other is jailed.

sexual orientation: Describing a person's sexual attractions, behaviors, or identities, usually as it relates to the gender of their partners. Common sexual orientations pertaining to gender include lesbian, gay, bisexual, or heterosexual and can also include queer, pansexual, demisexual, and asexual, among others. However, more and more, some are foregrounding sexual activity or relationship configurations in their sexual orientation, so that *Kinkster*, for example, or *Polyamorist* might be one's primary sexual orientation, with gender playing a less relevant or defining role.

solo poly: You're the hub of your poly life. Your hub may have zero or many relationship spokes on its wheel. Often, solo poly people have no *escalator* in their relationships. Often they don't have *nesting partners*.

somatic: A framework for healing practices that emphasizes full embodiment. Somatic practitioners often work with trauma survivors to identify how trauma lives in the body and to establish everyday practices to address and heal traumatic wounds.

straight: The sexual orientation of men and women seeking opposite-gender sex partners. Straight may also be used to describe someone who eschews kink or other outsider forms of sexuality.

submissive: A kink identity or role wherein the person finds turning over control to a partner enormously pleasurable. See *kink*.

swinging: Also known as *partner* or *wife swapping*, swinging takes many forms: from one-time sexual encounters with other couples to periodic connections over decades, to next-door-neighbor relationships for life.

switch: Describes someone whose interest in topping or bottoming, as in being in a dominant or penetrative versus a submissive or receptive position sexually — is versatile. This person is happy to switch positions.

throuple: A threesome, usually referencing one in which all parties are intimate and sexual with each other.

tolyamory: Coined by advice columnist Dan Savage, tolyamory refers to the silent agreement by married monogamous couples to tolerate and not notice or discuss hidden romantic or sexual affairs that break their marital vows.

toxic masculinity: Toxic masculinity's relationship to polyamory is: real men partner with monogamous women (while they do whatever they want); women who have multiple lovers or relationships are objects of disgust. Sexism, colonialism, and white supremacy have combined over centuries to create toxic masculinity.

traditional sexuality: Also referred to as *vanilla sexuality,* it has been constructed on a foundational view of a male dominant partner penetrating a female partner in the missionary or bottom position.

transgender: An umbrella identifier for people whose gender identity or expression is different from that commonly associated with the sex assigned on their birth certificates. This includes trans men and trans women, as well as nonbinary and androgynous people or genderqueers.

transparency: In polyamorous communities and families, every partner in the polycule is fully informed about all the relationships in the constellation and about all the crucial needs, limits, and commitments in the group.

trauma-informed practitioner: A therapist, teacher, or bodyworker who is trauma informed has specialized training in addressing fight, flight, freeze, or fawn responses that trauma survivors develop as a coping mechanism in processing and living with their experiences.

triad: All three people are primary partners with each other, and yet they may have varying levels of closeness.

trigger: A word, action, gesture, sight, sound, or smell that moves you from the present moment to a previous moment that involved abuse or violation.

truth: A belief or report reflecting your authentic experience, understanding or observation; in terms of sexuality, truth is often a deeper knowing that hides or rests beneath a carefully constructed presentation.

unicorn: A fantastical being that doesn't actually exist, hence this term for bisexual or pansexual woman who will join an existing heterosexual couple and fulfill all their fantasies without having any actual needs herself. Today, many claim the identity or term unicorn playfully and with good intent.

vee: In a polyamorous vee, the person at the bottom of the vee has two primary partners that aren't partners with each other. These top-of-the-vee partners may be close, but they make no partnership commitments to each other. In some vees, the two partners at the top of the vee never meet.

verse or versatile: Describes being interested in topping and bottoming, as in penetrating one's partner anally or vaginally, or being receptive to penetration, depending on a partner's interests.

veto power: A power that poly constellations can agree to confer a member, wherein they can veto or bar another partner from engaging romantically or sexually with someone they're interested in if the existing partner has concerns or fears about that person.

women and femmes: An expansive descriptor of women that encompasses all people who identify on the feminine spectrum, regardless of their sex assigned at birth.

Appendix B

Resources

This appendix is chock-full of helpful resources that you can refer to and enjoy as you move along your polyamory journey.

Books

Here's a great mix of poly-affirming how-to books and novels:

>> *All About Love*, and *Communion* by bell hooks

>> *All Fours* by Miranda July

>> *An Intersectional Approach to Sex Therapy: Centering the Lives of Indigenous, Racialized, and People of Color*, Reece M. Malone, et al, editors

>> *Great Sex: Mapping Your Desire* by Jaime M. Grant with Amelie Zurn

>> *Intermezzo* by Sally Rooney

>> *Love in a F'ed-Up World: How to Build Relationships, Hook Up, and Raise Hell, Together* by Dean Spade

>> "Love Is Not a Pie" by Amy Bloom (short story) in *Come to Me*

>> *Opening Up: Creating and Sustaining Open Relationships* by Tristan Taormino

>> *Pleasure Activism: The Politics of Feeling Good* by adrienne maree brown

>> *Polysecure: Attachment Trauma and Consensual Nonmonogamy* by Jessica Fern

>> *Refusing Compulsory Sexuality: A Black Asexual Lens on Our Sex-Obsessed Culture* by Sherronda J. Brown

>> *Stepping off the Relationship Escalator: Uncommon Love and Life* by Amy Gahran

>> *The Color Purple* by Alice Walker (novel, two movies, Broadway musical)

>> *The Future Is Disabled: Prophesies, Love Notes and Mourning* by Leah Lakshmi Piepzna-Samarasinha

>> *The Ethical Slut* by Janet Hardy and Dossie Easton

>> *Uses of the Erotic: The Erotic as Power* by Audre Lorde

Podcasts

For the audio learners and enthusiasts:

» *Basically . . .Life* with Tiffany Mugo, several poly-specific episodes

» *Curious Fox* with Effy Blue and Jacqueline Misla

» *Just Sex: Mapping Your Desire* with Dr. Jaime M. Grant

» *Making Polyamory Work* with Libby Sinback

» *Modern Anarchy* with Nicole Thompson

» *Multiamory: Rethinking Modern Relationships* with Emily, D., and J.

» *Remodeled Love Podcast* with Ash, Joseph, Jessica, and Dr. M.

» *That Black Couple Podcast* with Jenn and Daren, especially episode 27

Organizations and Websites

These organizations are poly-positive and healing-centric:

» Afrosexology with Dalychia Saah and Rafella; https://afrosexology.com

» Building Accountable Communities Consortium with Shannon Perez-Darby; https://accountablecommunities.com

» Find a free AA, NA or other meeting near you; www.aa.org/find-aa; 1-800-662-HELP (4357); www.nami.org/Support-Education/ Support-Groups/

» Sex Down South: A Southern, BIPOC, women-led sex and sexuality experience; www.sexdownsouth.com/

» National Queer and Trans Therapists of Color Network; https:// nqttcn.com/en/fr

» The Chosen Families Law Center; https://chosenfamilylawcenter.org

» The Heal Project with Ignacio Rivera and Aredvi Azad; https://heal2end. org/links/

» The Polyamory Legal Advocacy Coalition; https://polyamorylegal.org

Help Surviving Violence or Abuse

If you're being belittled, controlled, or abused by a partner, check out:

» **The Network La Red:** Survivor-led organizing to end partner abuse; 800-832-1901. The Network's 24-hour hotline provides confidential emotional support, information, referrals, safety planning, and crisis intervention for polyamorous people who are being abused. You don't have to leave or want to leave your relationship to get support, and it's free.

» **If you need confidential help due to sexual assault:** Check out https://rainn.org/about-national-sexual-assault-telephone-hotline or call 800-656-4673.

These may also support your healing from interpersonal violence:

» *Beyond Survival,* Ejeris Dixon and Leah Lakshmi Piepzna-Samarasinha, eds.

» *The Revolution Starts at Home,* Ching-In Chen, Jai Dulani, Leah Lakshmi Piepzna-Samarasinha, eds.

» *What it Takes to Heal* by Prentis Hemphill

» Barnard Center for Research on Women's Accountable Communities series: https://bcrw.barnard.edu/building-accountable-communities/

Poly Movies and TV Series

A mix of classic and new, fun and train-wreck representations:

» *Black Mirror's* incredible episode: "Striking Vipers" (2019)

» *Couple to Throuple* (series, 2024, largely examples of what-not-to-do)

» *Dirty Computer,* Janelle Monae short (2018)

» *Frida* (2002)

» *Jules and Jim* (1962)

» *Professor Marston and the Wonder Woman* (2017)

» *Scenes from a Marriage* — Nicole Beharie's amazing dinner scene (2021)

» *Sense8* (2015–2018)

>> *She's Gotta Have It* (Original movie (1986) and the series (2017–2019)

>> *You Me Her* (comedy series 2016–2020)

Poly Playlist

Music for the poly journey:

>> "Around the World in a Day" by RM (feat. Moses Sumney)

>> "Back Burner" by Jamila Woods

>> "Can't Help but Fly" by Climbing Poetree (feat. Be Steady)

>> "Love the One You're With" by Crosby, Stills, and Nash

>> "Make Me Feel" by Janelle Monae

>> "Mambo Number Five" by Lou Bega

>> "My Girlfriend's Girlfriend" by Type O Negative

>> "Polly" by Moses Sumney

Poly Videogames

The Sims 4 Lovestruck Expansion Pack: Critiqued for its centering of jealousy in its "romantic boundaries" section, while appreciated for its offering off all kinds of ways to pursue pleasure with partners in its turn-ons and turn-offs feature.

Best Poly Dating Apps

Feeld, Open, and Plura and there are many people identifying as polyamorous on all of the apps these days.

Index

A

men, heterosexual, 48

menopause, 280–281

mental health challenges, 88–89

metamour, 272, 311

milestone events, 309

millennials, 31

mindfulness apps, 131

Mingus, Mia (activist and writer), 111, 151–152, 206, 247

minimization, 109

mirroring, 285

Misla, Jacqueline (podcaster)
Curious Fox, 318

mission statement, 157–162

Mississippi River, 67

Modern Anarchy (Thompson), 318

Monae, Janelle (musician)
Dirty Computer, 319
"Make Me Feel," 320

monogamish, 311

monogamy
challenges of, 31–33, 67, 294
culture, 217–219, 226
definition of, 1, 312
history of, 16
sexual beliefs in, 47
supremacism, 53
transitioning from, 12, 37, 73–75, 177–196

monogamy-only messages, 183

moral code, 294

Mormons, 165

Morning Glory Zell-Ravenheart (author), 17

mother-child relationship, 114

motivations for polyamory, 9

movies, 319

moving, 276–279

mudita, 233

Mugo, Tiffany (podcaster)
Basically. . . Life, 318

Multiamory: Rethinking Modern Relationships, 318

multi-lover relationships. See polyamory

multiple partner scenarios, 311

mutual respect, 17, 23–25

mutuality, 285

"My Girlfriend's Girlfriend" (Type O Negative), 320

Myers, Isabel (writer)
Myers-Briggs Type Indicator, 81–83, 89–90

Myers-Briggs Type Indicator (MBTI), 81–83, 89–90

myths, polyamory, 291–295

N

Nairobi, 31

naked-body time, 280

name tag exercise, 40–42

narcissistic personality, 88–89

Narcotics Anonymous, 318

National Alliance of Mental Illness (NAMI), 88–89

National LGBTQ+ Women's Community Survey, 181, 200–201, 282

National Queer and Trans Therapists of Color Network, 318

National Transgender Discrimination Survey, 310

naysayers, 45–46

needs, 68–69

nephew, 312

nervous system, 131

nesting, 277–279

nesting partner, 60–61, 277–279, 312

The Network La Red, 319

neurodivergence, 82–85

neurotypicality, 82–85

New Orleans, 67

new relationship energy (NRE), 26, 312

New World, 16–17

New York Times, 31

nibbling, 312

Nicosia, 31

niece, 312

no escalator, 64

nonbinary, 158

nondiscrimination legislation, 165

nonhierarchical polyamorists, 62–63, 169, 312

non-monogamous experimentation, 30

non-monogamy, 17

non-parental events (NPE), 33

nonviolent resolution, 158

novelty, 26

NPE (non-parental events), 33

NRE (new relationship energy), 26, 312

nuclear family, 291

nutrition, 137

Q

quad, 313

queer, 313. *See also* LGBTQ+

queer relationships, 16

questions

  about dishonesty, 242

  about full disclosure, 21–22

  about handling conflict, 87–88, 111

  about intimacy, 149

  about jealousy, 216, 221

  about respect, 24

  about wants and needs, 68–69

  adverse childhood experiences (ACE), 137–138

  de-escalation, 142

  exploring polyamory, 39, 71, 179, 208

  family story, 220

  functionality, 172

  parenting, 254, 265

  pod mapping, 206

  self discovery, 40

R

RA (relationship anarchy), 62–63, 313

racism, 19–20, 49, 98, 139, 309

rape, 136, 311

reactivity, 109

READ (reassure, embrace, affirm and de-escalate), 229

readiness inventory, 180–181

reassure, embrace, affirm and de-escalate (READ), 229

reconciliation, 248–250

recovery, 239–241, 247–251

re-creation, 148–149

Refusing Compulsory Sexuality (Brown), 317

relational maps. *See* polycule

relational skills, 297–301

relationship agreement, 160–162

relationship anarchy (RA), 62–63, 313

relationship changes, 26–27

relationship escalator, 64, 313

relationship jail, 313

relationship-light, 143

religious community, 204

Remodeled Love Podcast, 318

reorientation, 147

resources

  Afrosexology, 318

  Alcoholics Anonymous, 318

  All About Love (Hooks), 317

  All Fours (July), 317

  ancestry.com, 33

  An Army of Ex-Lovers, 309

  "Around the World in a Day," 320

  The Bachelor, 25

  "Back Burner" (Woods), 320

  Barnard Center for Research on Women's Accountable Communities, 319

  Basically. . . Life (Mugo), 318

  Beyond Survival (Dixon and Piepzna-Samarasihna), 319

  Black Mirror, 319

  Building Accountable Communities Consortium, 318

  "Can't Help but Fly" (Climbing Poetree), 320

  The Chosen Families Law Center, 318

  Co-dependent No More (Beattie), 102

  The Color Purple (Walker), 317

  Come to Me, 317

  communication, 299

  Couple to Throuple, 319

  Curious Fox (Blue and Misla), 318

  Dirty Computer (Monae), 319

  The Ethical Slut (Easton and Hardy), 19–20, 227, 317

  The Future is Disabled: Prophesies, Love Notes and Mourning (Piepzna-Samarasinha), 283, 317

  Great Sex: Mapping Your Desire (Grant), 73, 208, 317–318

  The Great Gatsby, 17

  The Heal Project, 318

  Intermezzo (Rooney), 317

  An Intersectional Approach to Sex Therapy (Malone), 317

  jealousy, 307

  Jules and Jim, 319

  Just Sex: Mapping Your Desire (Grant), 318

  Lessons from a 20-Person Polycule (New York Times), 31

  Love in a F'ed-Up World (Spade), 317

  Love is Blind, 25

  "Love Is Not a Pie" (Bloom), 317

  "Love the One You're With" (Crosby, Stills, Nash), 320

  "Make Me Feel" (Monae), 320

  Making Polyamory Work (Sinback), 318

  "Mambo Number Five" (Bega), 320

  management of, 104

  Modern Anarchy (Thompson), 318

V

Vaid-Menon, Alok (comic), 60
values, parenting, 258–259
values in breakups, 271–274
vanilla sexuality, 311
vee, 56, 315
versatile, 285, 315
verse, 285, 315
veto power, 167, 316
Victoria Woodhull (activist), 17
video communication, 92, 209
videogames, 320
Vietnam, 31
village, 257
violence
  impact on mental health, 88–89
  intimate partner, 20, 181
  introduction to, 11
  systemic, 30, 122–123, 138
  victims of, 23
virginity, 48
visibility, 30
vision statement, 208
volatility, 124
vulnerability, 293–294

W

Walker, Alice (author)
  The Color Purple, 317
walking, 143
wants, 68–69
websites
  Afrosexology, 318
  Alcoholics Anonymous, 318
  ancestry.com, 33
  Barnard Center for Research on Women's Accountable
    Communities, 319
  Building Accountable Communities Consortium, 318
  The Chosen Families Law Center, 318

The Heal Project, 318
Narcotics Anonymous, 318
National Queer and Trans Therapists of Color
  Network, 318
The Polyamory Legal Advocacy Coalition, 318
Sex Down South, 318
sexual assault hotline, 319
23andme.com, 33
weight loss, 137
West Coast Kerista commune, 16
What it Takes to Heal (Hemphill), 319
white supremacy, 222, 315
wife swapping, 314
women
  barriers for, 48–49, 98
  bodily changes, 280–281
  defined, 316
  heterosexual, 48
  social movement, 16–17
women's rights movement, 16–17
women's studies, 127
Woodhull, Victoria (activist), 317
Woods, Jamalia (musician)
  "Back Burner," 320
workplace discrimination, 30
World War II, 18, 81
writing letters, 304–305

Y

Yang, Shen (comic), 49
yearly free pass, 28
You Me Her, 318
you-statement, 238–239

Z

Zoom, 209
Zurn, Amelie (author)
  Great Sex: Mapping Your Desire, 317

About the Author

Jaime M. Grant, PhD, author of *Great Sex: Mapping Your Desire*, is an Irish-American sexpert, grassroots researcher, and activist who has been engaged in LGBTQ+, women's, and racial justice movements since the late '80s. Having survived sexist violence and anti-lesbian disownment as a youth, she became a go-to resource on gender and sex among her peers as a matter of survival.

This led to doctoral study in gender and sexuality and the creation of the Desire Mapping process, which she has offered for 20 years via individual coaching as well as in workshops at community centers and universities throughout the United States and human rights convenings around the globe — Russia, China, South Korea, Vietnam, the Philippines, Cyprus, Kenya, South Africa, New Zealand, and Mauritius.

In the '10s, she served as principal investigator for the National LGBTQ Task Force's groundbreaking reports on aging, *Outing Age* (2010) and anti-transgender discrimination, *Injustice at Every Turn: A Report of the National Transgender Discrimination Survey* (2011). In 2017, she co-edited a global anthology on friendship as fuel for movement-building entitled *Friendship as Social Justice Activism*. Most recently, she co-authored the report of the nation's largest grassroots survey of LGBTQ+ women who partner with women, "We Never Give up the Fight": A Report of the National LGBTQ+ Women's Community Survey (2023).

Dedication

To the lesbian revolutionaries whose love and genius gave me my world and my assignment — Barbara Smith, Minnie Bruce Pratt, Amber Hollibaugh, Joan E. Biren, and Urvashi Vaid.

Acknowledgments

I'm so lucky to have been raised in the '70s, when women's activism, LGBTQ+ liberation, and movements for racial justice were ascendant. Some 50 years later, my polycule is an intrepid raft of beloveds that came together via the explosive promises of that era. Darlene Nipper, Amelie Zurn, Jack Harrison-Quintana, Ignacio G. Rivera, Andrea Jenkins, Lyndsey Miller-Vierra, and Genevieve Villamora — thanks for loving me so well, bailing me out over and over again, nurturing and protecting my children, bringing me constant joy and laughter, and for never letting me go.

Thanks to the National LGBTQ+ Task Force and especially Sue Hyde for supporting a vibrant sexual liberation track at its annual conference of organizers, Creating Change. So much of the work here has been developed and workshopped there over the past 35 years.

Thanks to my kids for cementing my commitment to fight for a world worthy of them and to my lifelong champion, my sister Stephanie Grant who instilled in me the courage to take on . . . everything. I'm so grateful to David Stewart for the spiritual and medical choreography that brought my children into the world, and for my parenting partner of two decades, co-survivor of a jillion chaotic forks in the road, M'Bwende Anderson.

Thanks to the members of my Monday night meeting, *Loving Ourselves to Freedom*. You know who you are, and you know I could never have done this without you. Thanks to my body alchemist and vitality coach, Elizabeth Goldberg, whose magic hands and big heart have transformed my life.

Thanks to the handful of visionary funders who have kept me afloat over many decades and made my sexual liberation work possible, especially Weston Milliken at the Freeman Foundation and his teammates, Tim Sweeney and Ben Francisco Maulbeck; also to Elizabeth Scott; Cindy Rizzo; Ana Oliveira; Hez Norton; and my beloved, indomitable anonymous donor (winky emoji).

Thanks to my dear loves who gave me two Cape Cod residencies to write while doting on my every need: Christoper Shaw and his husband Tim Johnson and Ellen Glazerman and her husband Harvey Kaufman.

Thanks to BTS, the best fantasy poly boyfriends a pop music lover could ever hope for, and the generators of endless joy in my life. And to my BTS comrade in fandom, Ace, whose faith in me birthed this book.

Massive thanks to my agent, Kara Rota who brought me this project via the wonderful Alicia Sparrow at Wiley. And to Chad Sievers for showing me the *Dummies* world and never complaining that I don't read the directions. My partner in sex lib Jack Harrison-Quintana did a very heavy lift organizing many different pieces of the book while cheering me on every step of the way.

Finally, emphatic thanks to my Desire Mapping collaborators — my team of sexy resistors. Their stories light up this book at every turn of the page: Amelie, Anna, Aredvi, Asha, A., Bishop, Cavanaugh, C., Dean, Elizabeth, E.T., Ignacio, Jack, JD, Kamilah, LP, M'Bwende, Mija, Rob, Robin, Romeo, Rox, and Shannon. Let's keep on keeping on together.

Here's a bit about these amazing contributors:

- » A. and C.'s contribution to the book is anonymous to preserve their safety.

- » Amelie Zurn-Galinsky (she series) is a queer polyamorous dyke comrade organizer, healer, and mother creating justice in our world for all human bodies, sexualities, and genders. Email: azurn2@icloud.com.

- » Anna Meyer is a mixed-race queer organizer, healing practitioner, and consultant working for social justice and liberation. www.formationhealingarts.com

- » Mx. Aredvi Azad is a speaker and trainer on sexual healing and liberation, and a practitioner of transformative relationships. They are an Irani-American immigrant living in rural Massachusetts. https://aredviazad.com.

- » Asha Leong is a life coach, sexual liberator, and writer living in Atlanta. www.dreamingdesires.com.

- » Bishop Howard LCSW (they/them) is a Black, queer, nonbinary therapist, and sexual liberation activist. www.psychologytoday.com/profile/932330.

- » Cavanaugh Quick is a Black femme, among other things. They're a social worker by nature and by nurture. www.cavanaughquick.com

- » Dean Spade is an organizer/writer focused on queer and trans liberation and ending cops, borders, prisons, and U.S. militarism. He is the author of *Love in a Fed Up World: How to Build Relationships, Hook Up and Raise Hell, Together*. www.deanspade.net.

- » Elizabeth Scott is a queer, poly dyke living and loving in Minneapolis. @elizscottmpls on Instagram.

- » E.T. is a genderqueer bi+ switch, tree-kisser, writer, audio artist, and therapist. www.psychologytoday.com/us/therapists/et-townsend-grand-rapids-mi/890532

- » Ignacio Rivera, is a queer, genderfluid, independent-polyamorist, healer, activist, and writer. https://beacons.ai/igrivera.

- » Jack Harrison-Quintana is a queer Latino activist, author, and researcher. https://linktr.ee/jchq.

- » JD Davids is a queer, trans, chronically-ill, disabled strategist and writer: The Cranky Queer Guide to Chronic Illness: https://thecrankyqueer.substack.com

- » Kamilah Glover is an oral femme, domme, poly, vampire, healer, and teacher. https://afam.vcu.edu/directory/faculty-affiliates/glover.html

- » LP is a writer and activist living in the Midwest.

» M'Bwende Anderson is a nature-loving, enigmatic nonbinary Black queer nomad. https://taplink.cc/mbwende.anderson

» Mija (they/two spirit) is an Indigiqueer educator and organizer.

» Rob Reichhelm, LCSW-C, is a poly, cisgender therapist, songwriter, musician, dad, and partner near Baltimore. Instagram: @the.polytherapist. Website: https://animalsawake.bandcamp.com.

» Romeo Jackson is a Black queer femme scholar-healer-organizer. https://www.linkedin.com/in/romeojackson/

» Rox Anderson is a Black, queer, gender nonconforming, multiracial, artivist, kinky, leather top daddy. www.linkedin.com/in/roxanneanderson1/

» Shannon Perez-Darby is a queer, mixed-race Latina creating the conditions to support loving, equitable communities. www.accountablecommunities.com

» Sonja is a pseudonym used in the book when one of the listed contributors prefers this particular story to be anonymous.

Publisher's Acknowledgments

Acquisition Editor: Alicia Sparrow

Project Manager and Copy Editor: Chad R. Sievers

Technical Editor: Jack Harrison–Quintana

Production Editor: Tamilmani Varadharaj

Cover Image: © MicroStockHub/Getty Images